CHICAGO, MILWAUKEE, ST. PAUL AND PACIFIC 4-6-4 Class F-7,
crossing Mississippi River Bridge with the Hiawatha.

Courtesy of the Milwaukee Road.

RAILROADING FROM THE HEAD END

BOOKS BY

S. Kip Farrington, Jr.

Railroading from the Head End

Atlantic Game Fishing

Bill, the Broadbill Swordfish

Pacific Game Fishing

Photo by W. H. Thrall, Jr.

THE SANTA FE CHIEF NO. 20, eastbound near Pine Lodge, California, climbing Cajon Pass, California, on the Santa Fe's Los Angeles Division, with the great 3765 class, 4-8-4 type locomotive built by the Baldwin Locomotive Works.

Railroading FROM THE HEAD END

S. KIP FARRINGTON, JR.

1943
DOUBLEDAY, DORAN & CO., INC. Garden City, N. Y.

PRINTED AT THE *Country Life Press,* GARDEN CITY, N. Y., U. S. A.

CL

FIRST EDITION

This book is gratefully dedicated
to the railroad men of the United States and Canada,
all of whom have my greatest admiration.

Foreword

For the last twenty years it has been my good fortune to have excellent opportunity to view the great strides America's railroads have made in improving and speeding up their passenger and freight service, as well as their motive power, yard facilities, signals, train dispatching, maintenance of way, and all-around operation. The foresight of the officials in putting the various roads in the high state of efficiency that they are in today has shown up very clearly since the United States entered the war, and the railroads have been carrying the heaviest amount of freight and passenger traffic that they have ever been called upon to carry and are successfully accomplishing the greatest task in the history of transportation.

I am particularly indebted to and wish to thank not only the railroad companies that are mentioned in this book but all others who have been kind enough to give me permission to ride their locomotives and freight trains and view their operations at first hand. I appreciate also the many courtesies the American Locomotive Company, the Baldwin Locomotive Works, the *Railway Age* magazine, Paul W. Kiefer, chief engineer of motive power of the New York Central, and J. E. Bjorkholm, superintendent of motive power of the Chicago, Milwaukee, St. Paul and Pacific Railroad, have shown me while gathering data for this book. W. H. Thrall, Jr., R. H. Kindig, and H. W. Pontin have been most kind in allowing me to use their very excellent photographs. My thanks are also due to Charles Tyler, Olive B. Flannery, and Herbert Worthington for their work on the manuscript and to Colonel John A. Appleton for his kindness in contributing the introduction to this volume.

S. Kip Farrington, Jr.

East Hampton, New York
September 15, 1942

Contents

Illustrations

Introduction

Since the operation of a war is perhaps the most complex of all the businesses that man has fashioned, it is understandable that to the average layman, and, for that matter, to the average participant, many of its elements are a complete mystery.

Most of us think of war in terms of dive bombers, mine fields, submarines, battleships, trench mortars, tanks, cold steel, and hot lead. But the military strategist—the student of war in all its possible phases—goes a great deal farther in his thinking; he thinks first, last, and always in terms of Transportation. He knows that men, arms, bombs, mines, tanks, and bullets are of no earthly value unless they can be transported promptly, swiftly, and safely to wherever the need for them is urgent and imperative.

Because of their importance to victory, the majority of the operations of our transportation services must be veiled in secrecy. But when the victory is won, and the history of the war is written, one of the most significant chapters will concern transportation. It will be a chapter showing the accomplishment of the "impossible" and the overriding of the "insuperable" by transportation men—labor and management alike.

Transportation embraces movement by water, by highway, by air, and by rail. For the present, it is unnecessary to say more than that each of these agencies has performed and is performing with distinction. Since this splendid book has to do only with railroads, it is fitting that the remainder of these introductory remarks be confined to their part in our transportation system.

The railroads of North America have done and are doing a magnificent job. Perhaps no industry, no agency, was as well prepared for war on December 7, 1941, as the railroads. They had been building up a "head of steam" almost since the Day of Armistice in 1918. They were set and ready to roll at full speed the minute the signal was given.

Little can be said now about the wartime operation of our railroads without revealing "military secrets." But if you, Mr. American Citizen, find your patience tried by train schedules somewhat awry, if you are irked because you can't take a pleasure trip, if you are annoyed because you can't get a "lower," or even an "upper," just stop and think: Those schedules are slightly awry at times, your pleasure trip has been banned, in order that fighting men and their equipment can be moved into battle.

Winning the war is America's one really important job,

and the railroads are doing their gigantic part of the job in great style—and with astonishingly little inconvenience to the general public of a nation at war.

J. A. Appleton
Colonel, Transportation Corps, U. S. A.
Chief, Rail Division

"NEITHER SNOW, NOR RAIN, NOR HEAT, NOR GLOOM OF NIGHT STAYS THESE COURIERS FROM THE SWIFT COMPLETION OF THEIR APPOINTED ROUNDS"

The inscription from Herodotus on the frieze of the New York Post Office Building, which spans the tracks of the Pennsylvania Railroad, as they enter the Pennsylvania Station from the Hudson River Tunnels.

RAILROADING FROM THE HEAD END

CHAPTER I

Fast Freight

FAST FREIGHT is the king of America's railroads. The limiteds, the streamliners–passenger, first-class–superb trains, rocketing to new streamlined heights in swift, luxurious travel, occupy a high place in American railroading, but freight is the gravy train. It is freight that pays off.

Freight is the hot and pulsing blood stream of these United States. Passenger is the nervous system, sensitive, sharp as a honed blade, keyed always to high pitch; serving, and serving well. But these past few years there have been many changes and the entry of new agencies in the field of transportation.

As a result, the once-lowly Ishmael of the rails, the slogging freight, burdened with general merchandise, has come into its own.

Few of us have, perhaps, paused to realize that a large percentage of the things that go to make up our daily lives has reached us through the medium of the boxcar: the material of which our houses and apartments are fabricated, our furniture, the car we drive, the gasoline that propels it; the tools of trade and profession; luxury and necessity—almost every commodity under the sun.

Trucks and a growing competition between rival railroads put the pressure on. The officials soon went into a huddle, and as a result the boxcar wheels rolled faster and faster, until that once-crawling freight has become the overlord of the rails. Freight, roaring down the smoky road in a way that threatens to pin back the ears of the fast passenger jobs.

Not long ago a disconsolate vagabond sat complaining by a water tank, as he watched a merchandise train screaming past. "To think," he said, "that I'd live to see the day freight trains traveled so fast a bum is afraid to ride 'em."

That we may have a better, more intimate understanding of what has been accomplished in the matter of high-speed freight service, we are going to ride one of these thunderbolts on wheels.

This is the Merchant Prince, the last word in l.c.l. (less-than-carload) freight trains. The Merchant Prince, covering a distance of some 430 miles between two metropolitan areas, has its counterpart on every railroad system worthy of the name in America.

The Southern Pacific has its overnight freight, running between Los Angeles and San Francisco, and operating on a schedule comparable to that of its crack Daylights, of passenger service. There are the fruit blocks of the Union Pacific, the Rock Island, the S.P. and the Santa Fe; No. 39, time freight, between Chicago and Kansas City; No. 263 on the Chicago, Milwaukee, St. Paul & Pacific; the Speedwitch, of the New Haven and Pennsy; the Silver Bullet, of the Louisville & Nashville; the Atlantic Coast Line's northbound perishable.

There is the Merchandiser, of the New York Central, symbol No. NB-1, running both ways nightly between New York and Buffalo, with an authorized speed of 65 miles an hour, 40 cars or less, and covering the 429 miles in the remarkable time of 10 hours and 50 minutes.

Time was when only the limiteds boasted high-sounding names. That day is gone. The roster of fast freights on the Pennsylvania, for instance, reads like the description of an explosion on Mars. Listen to this: the Rocket; the Big Smoke; the Purple Emperor; the Meteor; the Comet; the North Star; the Flying Cloud; the Mercury, and others.

Thunderbolts of steam and steel, walking down the railroad. Stalwarts of the iron trail, whipping time and distance the clock around.

Let's see what it is like to have an orchestra seat for the show, right up front in the cab of a great locomotive hauling a red-ball manifest.

Night is drawing the shades; a mist is falling, and we gingerly pick our way across a maze of tracks toward the roundhouse. Everything seems in a state of organized confusion, a kind of ordered bedlam. There is neither beginning nor end to it all.

There is the gloomy bulk of the coal sheds, of power plant, of shops. There is the semicircular shape of the engine house, with stub tracks stopping at the rim of the turntable pit.

From its dingy depths come the deafening howl of escaping steam, the hollow blast of blowers. Men are moving there. Beside the drivers of a giant locomotive, a yellow-flaring torch gives grotesque outline to other figures.

There are steamy washing and cleaning pits, with smudge-faced men in greasy overalls busy beside hissing engines. A passenger engine has just backed down from the station, and figures are swarming over and around and under her, like the servants of some pampered dowager, attentive to the lady's every want and whim.

We pass the office of the crew dispatcher, with its roster of names chalked on the "board." There are the sand shed and stock room and crews' locker rooms.

A hostler bobs his head, and, in answer to our inquiry, directs us to a big locomotive that has just nosed up to the engine house lead to take a long drink at a water crane.

This is the motive power of the Merchant Prince, receiving her last touches before backing onto the waiting train in the yards beyond. We observe that this is a 4-8-2 or Mountain type.

We climb aboard, and stand on the threshold of a new and awesome world. There are gleaming gauge faces, and levers, and gadgets, crowded over every inch of the great back head. We recognize the slender throttle lever, the lever of the power reverse, the shiny brass handles of the air-brake equipment, the valve pilot, sanders, bell ringer, cylinder cocks, lever, feed-water pump valve, injector and stoker valves, blower, air whistle, and others.

The engineer and fireman have just climbed aboard, and we show our credentials. They do not seem particularly impressed, and we gather that they feel they could manage quite all right without us. These men are quiet-spoken veterans, with a look of absolute competence. Their growled complaints at the moment have nothing to do with railroading, but rather with the misbegotten fate of the Dodgers and that dropped third strike. They go about checking the various appliances, leaving no small detail overlooked. With them, this is more than routine: it is essential, vital.

The fireman starts work on his fire, smoothing its surface, building up its body to meet the tearing forces of the roaring exhaust that will soon attack it. The engineman gets down for a look around and invites us to go along, and we learn something of this big freight locomotive.

It was designed not only for fast freight service, but for fast and heavy passenger service, as well. The drivers are 72 inches in diameter, with a tractive force of 62,000 pounds. The boiler pressure is 250 pounds. This locomotive was designed to operate at 80 miles an hour. At 50 miles an hour the engine develops a cylinder horsepower of close to 4,400. Drivers, engine trailer, and tender trucks are roller-bearing equipped. The tender capacity is 30 tons of coal and 22,000 gallons of water.

Locomotive and tender weigh 375 tons, and that, we marvel, is a lot of motive power. It's more: it's dynamite. It looks big, and it is big, and yet no railroad man's watch was ever built with finer care and precision.

All cars on the Merchant Prince, we are told, are specially equipped with high-speed passenger trucks, while tacked on behind in place of "the old red hack" is a "crew coach," which is heavier than the lighter-weight freight-train caboose.

Thus, we gather that we are going for a ride.

One thing in particular that impresses us is the unhurried preparation, and yet there is not a particle of lost motion, no moment wasted. There is, it seems, exactly time for every detail to be attended to; no more.

The head brakeman climbs aboard, a jaunty individual, with hatbrim turned up, wide-awake fashion. In old-time railroad lingo, he has been termed a "shack," as long ago a fireman gained the name of "tallowpot," and the engineer a "hoghead." Our head-end man is the sort who seems to know all the answers.

Things begin to move now with a clocklike precision that makes a deep impression. The engineer looks at his watch, glances at the steam gauge, the water glass, and settles to his seat. He tries all the gauge cocks.

Out ahead a switch lamp, one of a myriad of lights, winks from red to green, and a lantern lifts and lowers in a "come ahead" signal. The engine brakes go off, the bell clangs, there is a hiss of steam and a soft mutter in the squat stack.

We drift forward, switches and frogs racket under our drivers. We trundle across other switches and then are backing down a long lead to a place where figures with lanterns are waiting at a car end. We ease up, as daintily as a curtsying maiden, and there is a gentle bump and the sound of giant knuckles closing. We are shaking hands with our train.

The air hose is hooked up. Figures appear under the cab. The air pumps go to work briskly, building up pressure in the train line. When the needles of the air gauges on the back head are at their proper position, the pumps taper off to an occasional, spasmodic throb.

Then the car inspectors move back along the cars, checking the brake equipment. The conductor appears. He has train-order tissues and a clearance. The engineer reads them, repeating these orders from the dispatcher aloud. The fireman listens attentively, then reads them carefully himself.

The mist has become a light rain, making for a bad rail. Someone says, "A little wet." And the fireman says, "A good night for ducks."

The train line is holding its pressure; there are no leaks. The conductor starts back. We see the head brakeman's lantern out on top. There is a low drumming at the steam dome. The needle of the steam gauge is "on the pin," standing at exactly 250 pounds. A pop opens, and a white plume waves in the soggy gloom. The head brakeman comes over the tank and gives us our tonnage: 2,820.

And then, in that same well-ordered sequence of things, a light on a signal bridge casts its emerald eye down the way. A high-waved lantern swings its "highball"—the final word. The Merchant Prince is getting out of town.

The brakes go off. There are two curt blasts of the whistle. The engineer drops the reverse lever into the full forward motion, the working corner of the quadrant, the throttle comes back, steam rushes into those powerful 25 × 30 inch cylinders, and the drivers take their first bite at the sanded rail.

There is a heavy concussion in the squat stack, and we ease slowly forward. The exhaust thunders again. The slack runs out; the engine begins a slow-measured chant, and our train of 50 cars is moving with almost passenger-train smoothness and dispatch.

The locomotive noses out onto the main track, with its trailing cars snaking behind like the pliant body of a hot-mouthed dragon. The pulse of our going quickens. The yards are slipping behind us, and we are looking at a wall of night into which reach rails, silvered by our headlight.

The engineer latches back the reverse lever, which shortens the valve play, quickens the stroke. "Hooking her up," they call it.

Crossing gates are down, motorcar lights have bunched up on a busy thoroughfare. We look at them pityingly, scornful of earthly mortals shackled to so ordinary a thing as an automobile. We crash past a suburban station, glimpsing figures and pale faces turned toward us.

We are beginning to step, but with a kind of guarded reserve. The whistle screams frequently for crossings. Once a car beats us to it by an eyelash, and the engineer curses softly. More a prayer, it is, that this and other fools will fry in a hot hereafter, but wishful that he will have nothing to do with sending them there on the pilot of his engine.

Our speed indicator is climbing, as we enter a sweep of open country. Our forty miles an hour raises to fifty. Fifty-five! We are doing it with deceptive ease. There is only the rippling roar of the exhaust and the crashing whip of drivers and side rods to press home the realization that we are really giving some 2,800 tons of general merchandise a ride.

Signal lights rush to meet us. Green lights beckoning. A clear track for the Merchant Prince.

The fireman watches the gauges, keeps a close check on his fire, fed by a mechanical stoker. He hand-fires the back corners, filling them with green coal to check the rush of cold air being sucked through the grates.

The engine heels off a tangent, begins the sweep of a left-hand curve, and far across it a pin point of color glimmers through the sodden blackness. Eyes are watching for it on the fireman's side of the cab.

Now we can identify it, and a prompt, half-exultant call goes across to the engineman. "Green on the block! All green!" And the echo comes back from the engineer, "Green eye!"

There is a smudge of shapes and the warm glow from the windows of a farmhouse. A river is winding there, and now our headlight snatches at the skeleton superstructure of a steel bridge. The song of steel takes a new note, a brief, vibrant strumming thrown off by truss and girder.

Other lights are twinkling now, as we rush headlong at a town. A checkerboard pattern of lights marks a factory, working a night shift. Main Street glimmers briefly. We have passed a distant signal, standing remote but stiffly on guard. Our headlong rush eases a little; the whistle screams, its high clarion note losing a little of its edge in the wetness.

There is the sharp clatter of switches under our trucks.

The home signal is green, as is the light of the order board, high above the bay of the telegraph office. A green-shaded figure in shirt sleeves within waves us on with a flip of his hand.

The exhaust is roaring full again. Its tempo increases as we tip over the lip of a sag. Sixty! says our speed recorder. The rain hasn't slowed us. Visibility is fair. Sixty-five now, a breath-taking sixty-five, like dropping to the bottom of the world in an express elevator.

The Merchant Prince has a lot of tough miles to go, and there is no time for dallying. We come out of the sag, running like a bat from perdition. Now we become aware of the drag of a grade. The engineman drops the reverse lever forward for a bigger bite.

The tone of the exhaust changes to a deep-throated roar. Our speed drops to forty. Switch lamps and a long siding; a freight is waiting in the clear. Comes the impact of our passing. Then we are over the hump and gone.

One thing we miss, and that is watching the artistry of a locomotive fireman down on the deck, swinging back and forth between coal gates and fire door. That is something to see—the timed swing of that No. 2 scoop, heaping with black diamonds, the quick opening of the air-operated doors, as his toe hits the pedal, the deft twist of his wrist as the scoop clatters on the door ring, spraying the fuel neatly at exactly the right place in that roaring, white-hot inferno.

We speak of it to the fireman, and he nods. "I fired plenty of those old 'muzzle-loaders,' " he tells us, referring to hand-fired engines, "but the locomotives got too big for it. The mechanical stoker does a better job anyway. The jets spread the coal more uniformly, making for better combustion, which means more economy, better steaming."

A descending grade lends to our momentum; the rails reach away, straight as the path of a bullet. The exhaust is close to a solid roar. The iron thunder of the Merchant Prince rips the night apart. There is a building crescendo; the engine sways; there are breath-taking little side pitches.

We are hitting sixty-five again, and liking it. The sound of the whistle for a crossing is partly smothered by our tornado-like rush. The smoke flattens tight over those trailing car roofs. "Her tail is over her back!"

The head brakeman yells that we are making the same time as the fastest passenger job on the road before they streamlined the limiteds.

We can understand how shippers welcomed the coming of the fast freight and this overnight service. Goods that today were in the wholesalers' warehouses in the city we have left will be on the retailers' shelves, 429 miles distant, and ready for the customers when the doors are opened tomorrow morning.

The rain eases, stops. Now and then a star winks through a break in the low scud. The towns now are less brightly lighted. Farmhouses mostly are dark. We streak through a corridor of woods, skirt the smooth, dark waters of a lake. We look across at the engineer, crouched over his arm rest, watching past the glass windshield wing. Now his glance sweeps those silver-faced gauges on the boiler head; now his alert eye is again down the rails, streaming under our snub-nosed pilot.

We are reminded of the awe we had as youngsters for the locomotive engineer; we still feel the same. This man stands for tops in the boiling rush of American railroading. Lives and property are in his keeping, and they are in safe hands.

We come off a curve with a staggering lurch, and for the first time there is a discordant note. Far ahead a jaundiced eye is looking us in the face. A yellow block. Caution.

The cry goes across the cab: "Yellow on the semaphore! Yellow block!" The exhaust trails away. The engineman makes a precautionary air reduction, or brake application, and later a second, for before entering this cautionary block ahead he must have his train under absolute control.

We are drifting now, watching, hoping that the next block will be green, but it is not. "Red eye!" growls the engineer. And the fireman barks back, "Red eye!"

Sullenly smoldering, this red signal, but imperative in its demands. We come to a dead stop; then crawl ahead to pick up a flagman of an extra. He climbs into the cab with his red and white lanterns and sticks of fuses, and is received like a man with a plague.

"Hot box," he says apologetically.

We ease along toward those red marker lights ahead and stop. A lantern is already bobbing on the footboards of the car roofs behind us. It is the conductor of the Merchant Prince, and we can hear his loud lament before he ever comes over the tender. If he had been stabbed in the back, his plaint could have been no more acrimonious. No language in the world can reach the satisfying peaks of profanity attained by a railroad man in times of duress.

There are five distant whistle blasts from the engine of the train ahead—calling in the flag. The lantern of the extra's rear-end man jerks from the top of the buggy, or caboose. Our engine barks two impatient blasts, saying in effect, "Get going! And God have mercy on your soul!"

By the time the extra has reached the next siding and wormed into the clear, we have lost better than ten precious minutes. Those miles now to our first division point are the scene of a grim, relentless battle to make up time.

Ten minutes, an eternity when the schedule already demands peak performance all the way. The engineer calls on this battling giant for every last ounce of power on the hard drags, nurses her on the curves and through yards with beautiful running, lets her out on the straightaways in a manner that whips up your blood stream as nothing ever has before.

This is railroading, and we are wheeling. Parts for an airplane factory, machinery for an arsenal, material for a construction job, hurrying to completion; an apple for teacher, a bib for Junior; wares for a merchant, sugar for the grocer, tools for the mechanic, seed for the farmer—this, and more, riding in the cars of the Merchant Prince.

We gnaw hard at the black miles, the silver beam of our headlight boring into the night. The world is reeling past in blurred silhouette—town and countryside linked close. Lights leap at us; under our wheels the cacophony of switches and cross-overs; the scream of flanges knifing against curving rails. And, topping it all, the breathless roar from that squat stack and the answering song of steel on steel.

We are nearing the end of the division. There is at last a shrill, triumphant wail, announcing our coming. The exhaust is cut; there is the backward surge, as brake shoes clamp against flying wheels, and we come to a grinding stop.

Lanterns are there, winking like fireflies. There is neither haste nor dawdling, but, rather, that same clocklike precision that marked the beginning of our run.

The engineer holds his watch under a gauge light and gives a lean-jawed nod. We are on time. The Merchant Prince has maintained her tradition, and we take our first really deep breath.

A new engine crew takes over now, and the second division of this night run is accomplished in much the same manner as that of the first.

The third division is whipped by the same headlong flight. Dawn cracks, and a fresh, green world unfolds; daylight, sharpening the focus. In the brief span of one night the Merchant Prince has welded two great centers of population close in this booming era of modern high-speed freight transportation.

Our l.c.l. has made four stops to pick up and drop cars en route. It has averaged better than 39 miles an hour, including all stops, slow downs, and delays. Without stop, the Merchant Prince has maintained the high average of a fraction better than 45 miles an hour, and does it night in and night out, all around the calendar, holding to her bruising schedule 97 per cent of the time.

The veteran crews who have handled this train are typical of the high standards of personnel of American railroads.

The same locomotive has made the complete run and comes rolling down the main iron of this distant terminal with a jaunty white feather fluttering at her dome—on time.

CHAPTER II

Development of Freight Motive Power

THE FORWARD MARCH of America has been paced always by the railroads of the country, and the locomotive builders have kept in step with the development of our vast transportation systems.

Out of the world's oldest locomotive works, Robert Stephenson & Company brought the Rocket, with its high, crown-pronged stack; the North Star; the Dorchester. Matthias W. Baldwin's first locomotive appeared, making its historical trip on the Philadelphia, Germantown & Norristown Railroad in November of 1832.

The years fled, and the railhead stood at the bank of the Big Muddy. Then Stanford and Huntington and Holliday and Dodge began throwing steel at the prairie, the Rockies, the High Sierras.

Casement and his fighting Irish tracklayers; Charles Crocker and his Chinese coolies. Screaming Sioux warriors;

Courtesy of New York Central System.

NEW YORK CENTRAL'S XN-2, eastbound, hauled by Engine 3006, Class L-4, 4-8-2 type, passing East Rochester, New York, on the Buffalo Division. Note the 43-ton tank.

Photo by George Williams.

SOUTHERN CALIFORNIA FAST FREIGHT pulling into Vaughn, New Mexico, with Engine 5005. The locomotive has come all the way through from Barstow, California and will be cut off at Clovis, New Mexico, eastern terminus of the Pecos Division of the Santa Fe.

Courtesy of Baldwin Locomotive Works.

LEFT SIDE OF CAB OF OIL-BURNING SANTA FE 5005, 2-10-4 type, pictured above.

moving towns, "Hell on Wheels"; blizzards, floods, death; but the empire builders went on.

In one day the sweating gangs of the Central Pacific laid 10 miles and 1,800 feet of steel—144 feet a minute—between sun and sun, a record never since equaled.

And then, on May 10, 1869, the meeting of the rails at Promontory, Utah, writing there a flaming page of conquest. Two eight-wheelers stood pilot to pilot—the funnel-shaped Jupiter-60, of the Central Pacific, and the straight-stacked Rogers-119, of the Union Pacific.

W. N. Shilling, of the Western Union, crouched in the sage beside the rails, watched the driving of the golden spike, and flashed to the world the news. The far distances between the Atlantic and Pacific had been banded by steel, never to be broken.

Now, however, new problems presented themselves, and these were problems of motive power. Engines had to be designed that could whip the Sierra grades. Here were bruising ramparts; high passes of better than seven thousand feet above sea level. This was mountain iron with a vengeance, and there was freight to be moved.

Here was a demand for Yankee ingenuity, inventiveness, Yankee brains, and Yankee brawn. In 1882 the Central Pacific built at last in its Sacramento shops a twelve-wheeled locomotive, a 4-8-0 type, which means there were four engine-truck wheels and eight drivers. It was designed by A. J. Stevens, general master mechanic of the road, and was at that time the largest and heaviest engine in the United States.

This locomotive was called the Mastodon, with an arrangement of valves and valve gear, also designed by Mr. Stevens, which incorporated separate cut-off valves riding on top of the main valves. There were two main valves to each cylinder, one controlling the front port and the other the rear port. These were operated by the usual arrangement of Stephenson link motion. A power reverse was operated by water taken from the boiler.

The boiler of the Mastodon had a long firebox which was placed above the rear driving axle, and a combustion chamber extending forward into the barrel. The grate length was nine feet, while the combined length of firebox and combustion chamber was 13 feet 4¾ inches. The rear part of the firebox crown had only a water space in the back end of the boiler, which saved weight and provided for a roomy cab.

The Mastodon did good work on the Sierra grades, hauling as many as 20 loaded boxcars, weighing 422 tons, on a grade lift of 116 feet to the mile.

In April 1885 the properties of the Central Pacific were taken over by the Southern Pacific system. However, in the meantime Mr. Stevens had been working out the design of a freight engine called El Gobernador—the Governor—a 4-10-0 type engine with ten drivers. El Gobernador carried 121,600 pounds on the driving wheels. With the exception of a change in the valve gear, this locomotive was practically an enlarged Mastodon.

El Gobernador sang its swan song in 1893. Came then, in the later nineties, a twelve-wheeled locomotive, built by the Schenectady Locomotive works, with a weight of 147,000 pounds on the drivers.

In 1900 the Southern Pacific began converting its locomotives for the use of fuel oil. It was one of the first railroads to capitalize on this "black gold" as a means of providing steam for its hungry giants, battering at the ramparts of the Sierras.

Because oil came to play so important a part in American railroading, we pause to examine something of its principle. In the early engines the burner was placed in the rear end of the firebox and under a brick arch, extending back some thirty inches from the front water leg.

This arrangement was not satisfactory, for when the engine was heavily worked the draft had a tendency to lift the flame over the arch, where it impinged directly against the crown sheet and back tube sheet, causing leaky stay bolts and tubes.

Further, it was difficult to prevent the arch from falling. The arch, in consequence, was replaced by a double flash wall, with "pigeonhole" openings. This in turn was backed by a solid brick wall, with an intervening space of about six inches.

The face of this double wall was located about forty-eight inches in front of the burner. In the meantime, the original burner was replaced by a type with an outside feed, designed by George von Boden, fuel supervisor. This von Boden-Ingles burner had two separate chambers running its entire length, with a corrugated lip in front of the steam outlet at the nose of the burner. This greatly assisted in atomizing the oil.

Followed, first, experiments with the arch; then with the double flash wall. It was discovered that by placing the burner at the front end of the firebox a more complete and uniform distribution of heat resulted, owing to the longer path traveled by the flame before entering the boiler tubes. At the same time the burner was moved to the front of the firebox, the vertical draft was changed to a horizontal method of drafting through the firebox door and around the burner. This method of burning oil, with a few minor modifications, became then the standard practice on the Southern Pacific.

Baldwin was now building Consolidation-type freight locomotives for the S.P. Later, with the introduction of the Mallet locomotive in the United States, the Southern Pacific quickly saw the advantage to be gained by the adoption of this articulated type of compound engine in hauling trains over the heavy grades of the Sierras.

Baldwin made a thorough study of batting heavy drags "over the hump." The rather startling result was two Mallets with a wheel arrangement of 2-8-8-2 and guaranteed to pick up exactly twice the tonnage hauled by the Consolidations and walk it across that last 7,000-foot pass in jig time.

There was, however, one slight flaw, and that was the result of cramming these snorting behemoths into tunnels and snowsheds, never in the world meant to receive so much engine all in one lump. The belching stacks poured out smoke and gases, which smashed at the roofs of these tunnels; then rolled back to suffocate and practically annihilate the gasping engine crews. The answer to this problem, nevertheless, was comparatively simple, and again Yankee brains licked it by an arrangement that placed the cab end leading, with the tender coupled to the smokebox end.

With oil as a fuel, this was possible.

Came then World War I, and the demand for a freight locomotive capable of handling heavy loads at higher speeds. The Southern Pacific acquired their first of a 2-10-2 type engine: two ponies, ten drivers, and two wheels on the trailer truck. These locomotives weighed 397,900 pounds and developed a tractive force of 75,150 pounds. These powerful 2-10-2 engines were designed primarily for fast freight, but they were also used in passenger service on this 2.6 per cent Sierra grade.

Followed a 4-10-2 type, with three cylinders, a feedwater heater and "booster" engine attached to a Delta-type trailing truck and with the throttle valve located in the smokebox. Because the Southern Pacific Company was the first to have built a 4-10-2 wheel arrangement, the type was designated as the "Southern Pacific type." These engines developed a tractive force of 84,200 pounds, exclusive of the booster, exceeding the 2-10-2 type locomotive in power by 12 per cent.

And now, rumbling out of the Baldwin works, we see with amazement a veritable mountain of iron and steel—a 4-8-8-2 single-expansion articulated locomotive, developing 112,760 pounds of tractive force, which was soon increased to 116,900 pounds of pulling power.

We mop a slightly feverish brow and mutter, "This is the end! The last word in motive power!" But it is not, as we shall see.

Refinements and improvements raised the tractive force to 124,300 pounds. And then came to Sacramento to stand beside the little C. P. Huntington, on exhibition there, one of these articulated locomotives, the firebox of which could have swallowed the Huntington, with its two driving wheels, in one easy gulp. The total weight of the C. P. Huntington, with tender, is 39,000 pounds. The weight of these Class AC-6, -7, -8, and -10 of the Southern Pacific, Nos. 4126 to 4250, is around 935,500 pounds. Multiply the Huntington by twenty-four and we have this monstrous 4-8-8-2 battle wagon of the rails.

And still, thrusting through the mists of things, we see the boiler front of another roaring Titan, crying its challenge to the world. A bigger engine even than this S.P. 4-8-8-2.

Storming at the grades of the snowcapped Wasatch between Ogden, Utah, and Green River, Wyoming, we find the Union Pacific Big Boy slamming a train down the road that General Grenville M. Dodge and his fighting Irishmen built. Murals are there against the sky, the story of yesterday, of red marauders in war paint, of gallant U. S. cavalrymen, of buffalo hunters, of scouts, of prairie schooners, of the handcart caravans of the Mormons. This is the old Overland Trail, the road of the Forty-niners, of the Pony Express, of the Concord stagecoach—the road of hope and of death.

Eyes are watching, the eyes of Grant and Dodge and Ames and Cody and the Casement brothers. A roaring train beats out its symphony, and these phantom figures see a locomotive of stupendous proportions hauling fast freight across this last frontier.

The railroads have pioneered in their own right. The iron horse has grown up. However, it was the silent watchers here who first hewed the path in the wilderness; they were the western trail blazers.

This Union Pacific engine is emblematic of the spirit of progress in America. It cries aloud the fact that there is nothing in the world that we cannot do, and do better than any other nation on earth.

The engine at the cannonading front of a long-trailing train of yellow "reefers"—refrigerator cars—is a simple articulated 4-8-8-4 type. It is the largest in size and the heaviest in point of total engine and tender weight of any single-expansion, eight-coupled locomotive ever built. This Gargantua of the rails has a length, over couplers, of 132 feet $9\frac{7}{8}$ inches. The weight—note it—is 1,197,800 pounds, with a tractive effort of 135,375 pounds. It is out of the shops of the American Locomotive Company and is distinguished by many outstanding features and refinements affecting its performance.

The basic design was developed by engineers of the Research and Mechanical Standards Department of the Union Pacific, headed by Otto Jabelmann, vice-president. Results of exhaustive road tests and experience gained in operating other simple articulated locomotives were imparted to the American Locomotive Company, collaborating with the Union Pacific. The idea was to originate a locomotive capable of hauling maximum tonnage and maintaining schedules over the Wasatch Mountains, on a ruling 1.14 per cent grade, without helper service.

Further, these locomotives can operate on any part of the line, and were designed for speeds up to 80 miles an hour and to produce maximum power output continuously at 70 miles an hour, which is moving tonnage with a vengeance. The design and running gear permits great flexibility when moving around curves, and at the same time provides for relatively high rigidity when operating on tangent track. The spring-rigging suspension of the locomotive also permits adjustment of the wheels to vertical curves with relatively little distortion of the weight distribution. The driving wheels are 68 inches in diameter. The axle journals have Timken roller bearings. Driving boxes and all other roller-bearing boxes are fitted with heat indicators. The side rods are of the articulated type. The pistons are light-weight alloy steel. The crossheads are manganese-vanadium-alloy-steel castings. The guides are carbon-steel forgings. Throughout, to every last small detail, material and workmanship are of the finest. Nothing was ever built with greater care and precision. To attempt to cover the general specifications would require pages. This is truly a locomotive builder's masterpiece.

Let's look at the cab for a moment, as an example. It is insulated with Fiberglas and lined with masonite. There are Prime clear-vision windows, with air defrosters at the front and windshield wings at the windows on each side. The seats of engineer and fireman are adjustable, both horizontally and vertically. There is a seat for the road foreman on the right and for the brakeman on the left.

This engine is a coal burner, and, of course, fired by a mechanical stoker. The stoker engine is installed in the tender.

A multiple throttle includes an auxiliary throttle, supplied with saturated steam from the dome. This is for drifting, and the handling of the locomotive by hostlers at the terminal. The engine is lubricated at 123 points by four 36-pint mechanical lubricators. A lubricator with eight feeds is mounted on the tender bed and driven from the stoker engine. This supplies oil to all tender-truck boxes and tender-truck center plate.

As we stand beside the rail and watch Union Pacific Big Boy 4-8-8-4 storming past, we take a deep and prideful breath and salute her going.

We have stressed the importance of freight, and the railroads and locomotive builders bear us out, in that more and more engines have been designed to haul both heavy passenger trains and freight.

We look to the New York Central and find this new trend in locomotive-power development well established. In its freight service, both for through and local trains, the Central uses Mohawk-type engines, classified as L-1, L-2, and L-3, as well as the Mikado type. Fifty Mohawk-type L-3 engines were delivered to the New York Central late in 1940 and the early months of 1941. Twenty-five of these giants were equipped for operation in both fast passenger service and fast and heavy freight service. The remaining twenty-five were designed primarily to haul fast freight. American Locomotive built some of these engines; the Lima Locomotive Works the rest. Like all Mohawk-type engines, they have a wheel arrangement of 4-8-2. You will remember that it was a 4-8-2 type locomotive that hauled the Merchant Prince. The tenders are mounted on trucks with a 41-inch wheel diameter, and are equipped with water scoops. Engine and tender of the dual-type locomotives weigh 381 tons; the engines for freight service have a weight of 384 tons, and both are 109 feet 6½ inches in length. The engine numbers range from 3000 to and including 3049. So successfully did these locomotives perform their allotted tasks that the New York Central ordered fifteen more for early delivery.

The Class L-3 engines were a refinement and development of the Mohawk L-2 locomotives, of which the Central has 300 in freight services. These L-2s have a steam pressure of 225 pounds and a tractive force of 60,620 pounds. The cylinders measure 27 × 30 inches. The tractive force is increased to 73,020 pounds by the booster, with which the engines are equipped. The drivers are 69 inches. These L-2 locomotives were an outgrowth of the first Mohawk-type engines of Class L-1. These first Mohawks were designed by New York Central engineers and built by the American Locomotive Company in 1916. There are 131 of these L-1s now in service hauling local freight.

In making comparisons between these New York Central engines and locomotives previously described, it must be borne in mind that those western engines were built for mountain iron and the whipping of heavy grades across high, snow-crowned ranges. The New York Central Lines operate largely at a little better than sea level, with fast, level straightaways, though there are plenty of heavy hauls in the Berkshires, which throw their tumbled ridges across western Massachusetts.

The New York Central also uses the Mikado-type freight locomotive in large numbers. They are employed principally on the Central's main line, the Big Four, and the Michigan Central. The first Mikado-type engine was built in 1897 for freight service on the Nippon Railway in Japan; hence their name. The early Mikados on the New York Central were converted from Consolidation-type locomotives in 1912; the first new engines were built by the American Locomotive Company in 1913, and subsequent engines by that company and the Lima Locomotive Works. These were a 2-8-2 type, with a large, deep firebox, great steaming capacity, and high boiler efficiency. Their high operating speed makes the Mikado type well adapted for fast freight service.

Their development led to the Mikado H-10 type, built in 1922. These engines carried a steam pressure of 200 pounds, with cylinders 28 × 30 inches and drivers 63 inches in diameter. They had a tractive force of 63,470 pounds, which a booster increased to 74,470 pounds. The New York Central has 281 of these engines in service today—numbered from 2080 to 2399. Of those earlier Mikes, the road has 265 on the roster.

A 1913 automobile is a museum piece, whereas many a grimy old freight hog of that period is still working on the railroad. The answer to that is constant inspection and maintenance, scrupulous servicing, and periodic overhaul.

Unique in many respects among railroads is the Richmond, Fredericksburg & Potomac, which connects the cities of Richmond and Washington and is known as the "Capital Cities Route." It forms the connecting link between the

Pennsylvania and the Baltimore & Ohio, terminating at Washington, D.C., and the Atlantic Coast Line and the Seaboard Railway, which terminates at Richmond, Va.

The Richmond, Fredericksburg & Potomac is one of the pioneer railroads of the country. Strategically, it is a line of vast importance, forming, as it does, a "bottleneck" between the North and the South. The road has a mileage of only 118 miles, practically all of which is main line trackage.

The Richmond, Fredericksburg & Potomac and its motive power is richly deserving of mention. Because the line has written its own page in American history, we give a little of its background. The road was granted a charter on February 25, 1834. Two years later the first train covered the twenty miles from Richmond to the South Anna River. In January 1837 the line was completed to Fredericksburg, whence connection was made to Washington by stage and steamboat. All-rail communication between Richmond and Washington was not established until July 1872. The original roadbed was laid with strap rails, spiked to wooden stringers, and weighing about 12 pounds to the yard. Later these were replaced with "edge" rails of around 40 pounds. Came then the iron T rails. Steel rails were another advance, weighing fifty pounds. The year 1890 saw rails of 67 and 75 pounds. Shortly after the turn of the century double tracks were laid, signals were installed, grades and curves reduced, and extensive yards constructed. Everything, in fact, was modernized, and today the track is of the most substantial construction, with rails weighing 130 pounds to the yard.

During the war between the states, the Richmond, Fredericksburg & Potomac changed hands many times, and, with such changes, was largely destroyed. But it came back and in recent years has established an enviable record in the handling of freight—fast freight.

A large portion of the road's tonnage is perishable, moving northbound. These manifest trains are handled from Acca Yard, near Richmond, to Potomac Yard, south of Washington, a distance of 108 miles. During the first six months of 1934, 1,033 trains of perishables moved north in the average time of 3 hours and 45 minutes. Between April 27 and May 22, 124 trains of North Carolina strawberries, filled out with miscellaneous tonnage, went roaring through in the average time of 3 hours and 15 minutes.

Here again we find fast freight storming the ramparts of the railroads.

Traffic and operating conditions on the Richmond, Fredericksburg & Potomac are such that it is desirable to use locomotives suitable for either freight or passenger service. The majority of road engines are the familiar 4-6-2 Pacific type. The first of these high-stepping locomotives was put in service in 1904. They were built by Baldwin and rendered fine service.

In 1924 the Richmond, Fredericksburg & Potomac bought four of the 4-8-2 Mountain-type freight and passenger power. In 1927 the most powerful Pacific locomotives ever built at that time were put in service on the road. These engines are stoker-fired, and their steam pressure has been raised to 225 pounds. Many of the older Pacifics have been partially rebuilt and modernized.

The latest addition to the motive-power equipment of the Richmond, Fredericksburg & Potomac is a group of seventeen locomotives of the 4-8-4 type. These engines have driving wheels 77 inches in diameter and are suitable for either fast freight or passenger work. Their tank capacity is sufficient to enable them to go through without stopping for water. Eight 2-8-4 type are expected shortly from the Lima Locomotive Works.

As long as twenty years ago the Pennsylvania Railroad, always progressive and forward-looking, began work on the development of a high-power steam locomotive that would handle either heavy passenger or fast freight. At that time passenger traffic was being handled by a locomotive known as a Class K-4 Pacific (4-6-2), with 80-inch drivers and a rated tractive force of 44,460 pounds. The heaviest freight locomotive on the road then was a Decapod 2-10-0 type, with 62-inch drivers, a steam pressure of 250 pounds, and a tractive force of 90,024 pounds. The general utility engine in freight service was a Mikado. These three groups are still in service on the Pennsylvania and continue to do fine work.

Looking around for a trial horse for high-speed, heavy-duty work, the Pennsylvania settled on an engine of the Mountain 4-8-2 type—the design of locomotive that handled our Merchant Prince so efficiently. However, the Pennsylvania wanted something a little heavier. In designing motive power, each road is confronted by problems raised by the physical characteristics of the country that it serves. Accordingly, a trial 4-8-2 type locomotive was built at the Altoona

Works. This engine had 72-inch drivers, cylinders 27 × 30 inches, and carried a steam pressure of 250 pounds. It had a rated tractive force of 64,550 pounds, against the tractive effort of 62,000 of the Merchant Prince motive power. This new locomotive was subjected to rigid tests on the road, as well as at the Altoona plant. As originally built, the engine was hand-fired.

Came certain refinements and improvements, and more tests. In the meantime, the locomotive had been given a road number of 4700. The 4700 really took a beating, but in the end designers and engineers were satisfied, and there had been evolved a highly successful piece of motive power, now designated as Class M-1.

In 1926 and 1927, 200 of these engines were built—175 by Baldwin and 25 by the Lima Locomotive Works. The high starting tractive force of these locomotives was backed by liberal boiler power, which enabled the engines to develop large horsepower for sustained periods.

The Class M-1 engines, while suitable for work on most of the main-line divisions of the Pennsylvania Railroad System, were specially intended for freight service on the Middle Division between Harrisburg and Altoona, Pennsylvania, a distance of 130.8 miles. This is a river-grade division, with three and four running tracks, carrying the entire east and west passenger and freight movement of the system. The westbound grade is ascending, with a rise from Harrisburg to Altoona of 862.5 feet, or 6.7 feet per mile. The last 30 miles has a grade of 0.47 per cent. The enormous volume of traffic over this section of the line and the increasing number of high-speed passenger trains made an increase in freight speed imperative.

Came then road tests for a Class M-1 locomotive numbered 6872, as well as exhaustive tests on the stationary plant at Altoona. This was in 1929. Out of these tests was developed an improved design known as Class M-1A. There were important improvements and refinements, including important change in the construction of the cylinders. One hundred of these new-class engines were built in the Altoona works of the company, beginning in 1930. An equal number were built by the Lima Locomotive Works, and fifty by Baldwin. The Class M-1A had twelve-wheeled tenders carrying 22,090 gallons of water and 63,000 pounds of coal.

Thus we find the Pennsylvania Railroad System equipped to meet demands for the handling of fast freight, and the result has been that practically all merchandise and perishable trains now move on regular schedules which are as dependable as passenger-train schedules and often approximate them in speed.

Limiteds of the Freight Service! And how they can roll!

"What's in a name?" asked Juliet. The Pennsylvania Railroad System has answered that with, "Tonnage! Increased business!" Freight, you see, is the gravy train.

The Pennsylvania, in naming many of its fast freights, attracted the attention of shippers. It proved a strong appeal. Thus we find the Bison handling livestock and perishables between Buffalo and seaboard cities. The Packer rushes refrigerator cars from Chicago to seaboard. The Thoroughbred is a stock train. The Yankee handles perishable and general

Photo by W. H. Thrall, Jr.

FIRST SECTION OF THE SOUTHERN PACIFIC'S MORNING DAYLIGHT leaving the magnificent Los Angeles Union Terminal, hauled by Engine 4425, Class GS-3, 4-8-4 type. The train was built by the Pullman Company.

OLD PICTURE OF THE BROADWAY LIMITED NO. 28 OF THE PENNSYLVANIA R.R. AND THE TWENTIETH CENTURY LIMITED NO. 26 OF THE NEW YORK CENTRAL, taken east of Englewood, Illinois, when they both departed from Chicago at 12:40 P.M. This time was adhered to for over twenty-four years. The Broadway is hauled by a K-4 and the Century by a J-1. Note the merchandise between New England and Chicago. And there is the Speedwitch, which we have already mentioned. This is one of the fastest of the group and operates between Baltimore and Boston, the New Haven road handling the New England end. The Speedwitch makes what is practically an overnight run in each direction and cuts approximately twenty-four hours from the previous running time. It is by far the fastest freight service ever provided between Baltimore, Philadelphia, and Boston and other New England points.

Playing a leading part in the handling of this speedy traffic, we find the cracking fast and powerful Mountain-type locomotive, the 4-8-2 of the Merchant Prince.

And we reiterate—fast freight is the king of America's railroads.

CHAPTER III

The Hiawatha—Speed Queen of the Milwaukee

THE STORY OF AMERICAN RAILROADING is a story of high adventure—and high speed. We have reached dizzy heights in safe, fast, and luxurious travel by rail. And still we look forward, watching for tomorrow's trains, exactly as we await tomorrow's sun.

We have been caught and held by the unfolding drama of the iron road. Color and romance are there; enterprise and hazard; conquest and daring. The railroads and the locomotive builders have thrilled and amazed us. We have seen the outreaching bands of steel, weaving their network across the nation; we have had a small glimpse of the development of the steam locomotive and the resulting rush of the fast freights. And now we turn, take a deep breath, and hold onto our hats, for this man-made meteor, coming with a rush and a roar, is a speed queen of the rails, a steam locomotive—streamlined to the ears—pulling the afternoon Hiawatha. We have come to accept speed of one hundred miles an hour as a matter of fact, and have, perhaps, credited it to Diesel-electric motive power. However, the steam locomotive a long time ago was demonstrating its ability to set records for men to shoot at.

Before we ride the famous Hiawatha out of Chicago on the Milwaukee, let's go back a little and take a look at some high-wheeling records. First, there was the locomotive Antelope, of the Boston & Maine, which made the run, Boston to Lawrence, Massachusetts, 26 miles in 26 minutes. That was in 1848.

And there was the Old 97, the pride of the Alton, a sleek little eight-wheeler. Came word that Chicago was burning. A call went to Bloomington, Illinois, for help. Bloomington had a good fire engine, and soon a special had been made up, with the fire apparatus stoutly secured to a flatcar. Chicago was 126 miles away. The special started. Engineer Lou Hawks was at the throttle of Old 97. Two hours and thirty minutes later the train pulled into the Chicago station. Engine 97, the Major Knowlton, had covered 126 miles in the amazing time of 150 minutes.

On October 26, 1891, came the inauguration of the Empire State Express on the New York Central, with a ten-hour schedule between New York City and Buffalo. This was the first high-speed, long-distance passenger service in the country. On May 10, 1893, the Empire State Express, drawn by Engine 999, covered a measured mile between Syracuse and Buffalo at 112.5 miles an hour.

Back in 1892, Delaware, Lackawanna & Western's Engine

134 hung up an unofficial record of eighty miles an hour between Binghamton and Elmira, New York, a distance of fifty-seven miles, averaging 66.59 miles an hour.

The turn of the century saw startling speed runs, with the Pennsylvania Special making the fastest recorded run in history at Elida, Ohio, where it covered three miles at 127.2 miles an hour. This was on June 12, 1905, and beat the record then held by the Florida Mail, which made five miles at 120 miles an hour between Fleming and Jacksonville, Florida, in March 1901.

In July of 1905 Death Valley Scotty came trekking out of the wasteland and waved a fistful of money at a high official of the Santa Fe in Los Angeles. Scotty wanted to go to Chicago, and he was in a powerful hurry.

That special between Los Angeles and Chicago not only hung up a record for long-distance, high-speed travel in its day, but scared the living daylights out of those who rode it. It was called the Death Valley Coyote, and it made the run to Chicago—2,265 miles—in 44 hours and 54 minutes. This beat the best time previously made between the two cities by about eight hours. The highest speed reached on this run was 106 miles an hour.

A further revelation in the possibilities of fast travel by steam-drawn trains came in June of 1927. The Lindbergh Special, running between Washington and New York, attained a speed of *115 miles an hour!* The engine was No. 460, a high-wheeled Atlantic type, 4-4-2, Class E-6. This was on the Baltimore, Maryland, Philadelphia Terminal, and New York divisions of the Pennsylvania Railroad. Including the change-over from steam to the electric engine at the Manhattan Transfer, the 226-mile run was made in 3 hours and 7 minutes, at the startling average of 72 miles an hour. And not once on the trip was the throttle wide open.

In July of 1934 a regularly scheduled train on the Chicago, Milwaukee & St. Paul traveled 85 miles in 67 minutes. This, remember, was steam, with people already declaring that the steam locomotive for high-speed travel was riding into the sunset. The answer to this has been a hoot and a snort from the iron horse.

This train on the Milwaukee maintained an average speed of 92.62 miles an hour for the 61.4 miles between Edgebrook, Illinois, and Oakwood, Wisconsin. The train averaged 76.07 miles an hour all the way between Chicago and Milwaukee—85 miles in 67 minutes! The engine was No. 6402, a locomotive of the 4-6-4 type, weighing 326 tons, with 79-inch drivers, 225 pounds boiler pressure, and exerting 45,822 pounds of tractive force.

This Milwaukee locomotive of the 6400 series was built by Baldwin, and these engines have hung up enviable records. Witness the 6415, delivered in October 1931. In November 1935 this engine ran 18,390 miles in regular service between Minneapolis and Harlowton, Montana. The 6415 made 360,000 miles without overhaul. At that time this class of engine on the Milwaukee averaged about 10,500 miles a month.

We come now to stand in the Chicago Union Station. It is a little before one o'clock. A streamlined train is waiting sleek and trim, from the winged emblem at the locomotive front to the final soft curve of the last car. The color scheme is maroon and gold. Regal beauty is there, queenly carriage, with every last line reflecting grace and speed.

This is the Hiawatha! Train No. 101.

The first Hiawatha was a great Mohawk chieftain of the sixteenth century who effected the confederation known as the Five Nations, or League of the Iroquois. Miraculous powers and deeds were ascribed to him in legend.

Here in symbolism stands another Hiawatha to which are ascribed deeds of endurance and swift flight. This Hiawatha effects the confederation of time and distance, welding close two centers of population—Chicago and the Twin Cities, on the Chicago, Milwaukee, St. Paul and Pacific Railroad.

Ten streamlined cars are coupled behind the last word in streamlined motive power—engine No. 1, the original Hiawatha oil-burning locomotive.

Like its train, the engine is painted in maroon and gold, with the shrouding above the running boards in light gray. We have to look twice to convince ourselves that this is really a steam locomotive. Gone is the familiar steam dome, the sandbox, the feedwater heater, the air pumps, the pipes and

Facsimile reproduction of tape (continued on succeeding pages) taken from the valve pilot of the Hiawatha's locomotive on an actual trip from Milwaukee to Chicago.

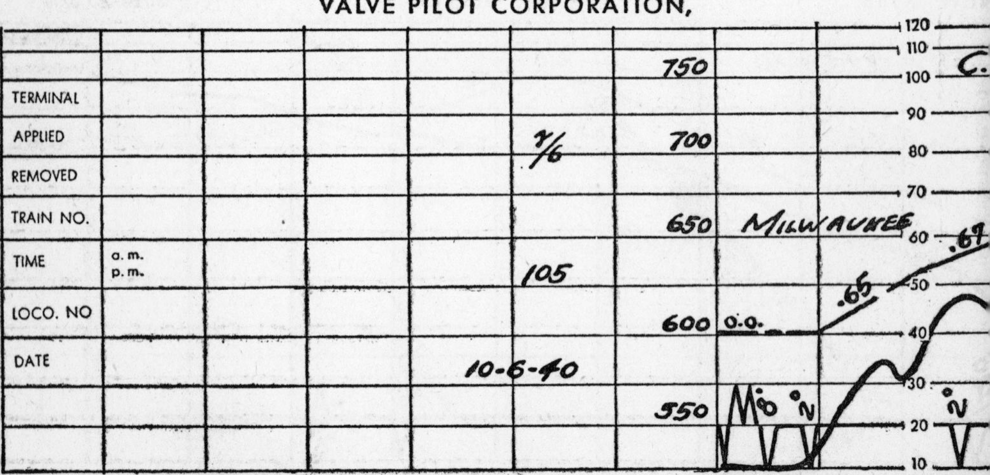

accessories that have always seemed so much a part of the steam locomotive with which we are familiar. Trim skirts drop modestly over the 84-inch drivers. The running board is there, and the handrail, but almost everything else has been covered by sheathing shaped to overcome the resistance of the air. The once-bold boiler front is rounded, from pilot to crown, presenting a smooth, curved surface. The streamlined effect is carried on past the tender, to blend in perfect, pleasing line with the cars of this modern speed queen of the rails. A worthy champion, this, of the proud name Hiawatha, carried on a sign on each side of the boiler.

Engine No. 1 has light reciprocating parts and a steam pressure of 300 pounds.

On the back head in the cab are mounted so many valves and gauges that one wonders how the builders found room for them all. Within easy reach of the engineer's seat are the automatic and independent brake levers, the operating valves to sludge removers, cylinder cocks, bell ringer, air siren and sanders, the acknowledging valve to the cab signals, operating handles of the injectors and steam whistle, and, of course, the main throttle and reverse levers. Equally convenient to the fireman's seat are the operating valves for the blower, smoke-

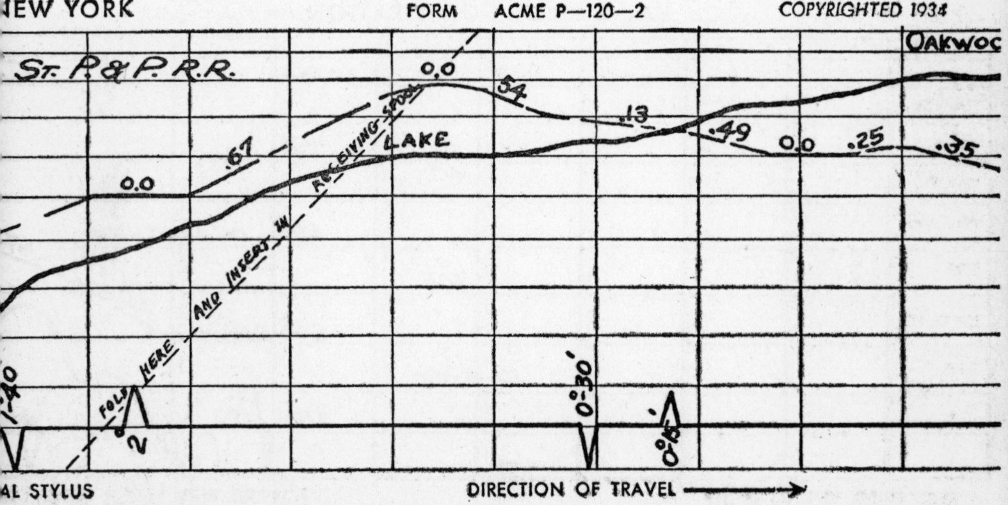

abating devices, feed-water pump, fuel-oil heater, atomizer, blowback, as well as others of less importance. Silver-faced gauges are there, their needles alive, quivering. By these dials the engineer and fireman read the pulse of the big locomotive.

Engineman and conductor have checked their watches. The minutes are running out; the time of departure is close. Comes the familiar, "All aboard!" Then that tense instant when the last good-bys are said.

There is the waved highball. The engineer says, "Let's go!" His hand reaches for the throttle. There is a hiss of steam, the slow movement of forward-turning drivers, a throaty cough in the stack—and the afternoon Hiawatha has begun her run to the Twin Cities.

White wings widen out with a rush, as accumulated condensation is cleared from the cylinders. The exhaust quickens. The train rolls smoothly behind the thrust of pistons and the muscular arms that are the side rods.

The engine emerges from beneath the Chicago Daily News Building at the west end of the train shed, and the fireman relays a clear signal. The engineer widens the throttle a little more. Now we are heeling to the sharp curve at Canal Street. Always our speed is increasing.

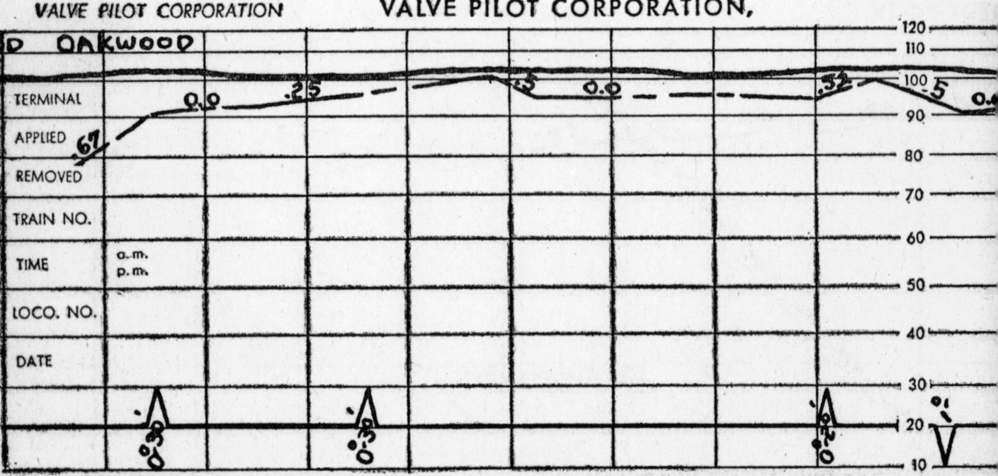

The tight-packed city drops behind us; the suburbs thin out. Never an instant that we are not aware of the still unleashed power packed in this locomotive at the thundering front of the Hiawatha.

We are traveling fast now on a clear railroad. The signals are called and repeated by engineer and fireman. This is important always, for not a split second must be lost if at any time a signal shows danger or the need for caution and it becomes necessary to take action. When the mileposts are passed at 36- to 40-second intervals, the train is covering 145 to 150 feet a second, and a hair-drawn instant of delay can mean the difference between assured safety and dark threat.

As the engineman works the throttle, the fireman gives close attention to the firing valve. They watch the steam gauge, the water glasses; now there is that quick call of a signal: "Semaphore clear!" And the instant echo: "Clear on the semaphore!" There is no time for unnecessary conversation.

The air siren is almost constantly sending out deep-toned warnings of our headlong approach. The engineer has the valve cut-off set at approximately 28 per cent; the throttle

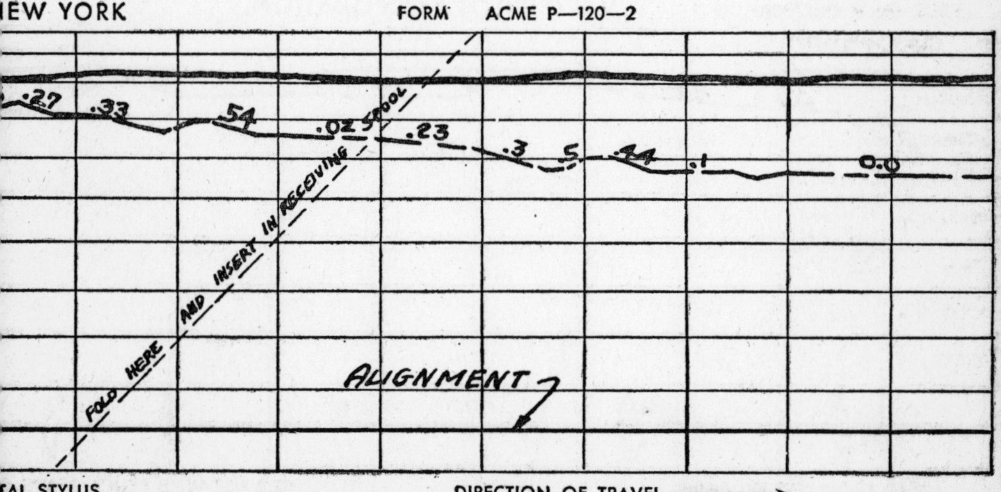

is almost wide open. The back pressure gauge indicates 275 pounds of steam in the valve chambers.

The speedometer has long since topped seventy-five. Eighty. Ninety. Ninety-five. We are riding a man-made comet across the world. One hundred! The exhaust is a seemingly unbroken roar. There is a gentle cradling motion in the cab. The landscape is a blur. Side rods and drivers lend to the orchestration that makes for the music of the rail. Its rhythm is sweet—fast.

One hundred miles an hour—with steam. And yet this breath-taking flight is merely a part of the day's work. It is routine with the Hiawatha.

And we come to the factors that have made the schedules of these so-called superspeeders possible. They did not just happen. There was more than the ability of the locomotive builders to create a whirlwind piece of motive power like engine No. 1, of the Milwaukee, capable of picking up a ten-car train and running like a winged god.

Engineers gave long study to every last mile on this main track, to every curvature, elevation, condition—every factor peculiar to the road and train operation of the territory involved. For instance, the speed permissible—the safe speed—

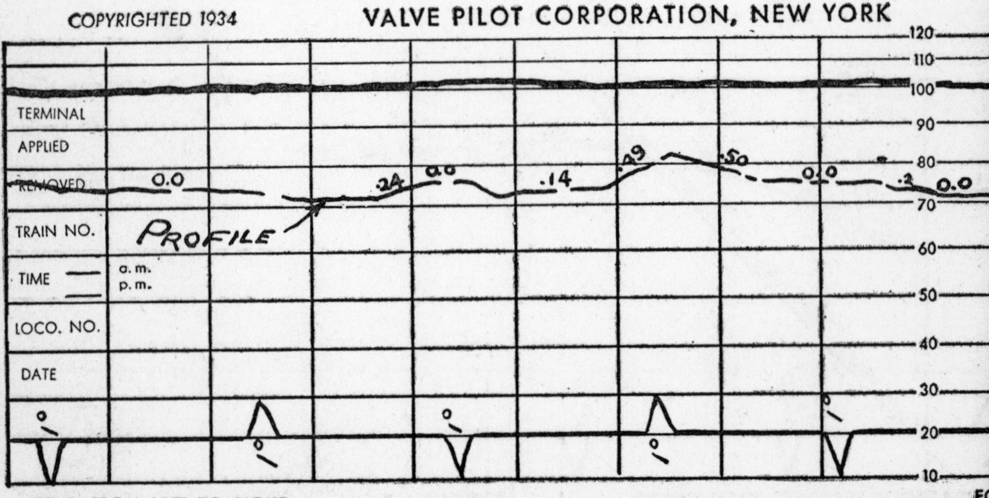

for a certain curve, say, was established at 70 miles an hour. That *meant* 70 miles an hour—not 75. Study had revealed that 70 miles an hour was the maximum speed at which a train could negotiate this curve without causing annoyance or discomfort to the passengers.

The saying that there is many a slip between the cup and the lip never originated on the Milwaukee road's diners. True, these engineers were looking for speed, a speed comparable to that of the Burlington's Zephyrs, which they matched mile for mile, but not at the price of uncomfortable riding. Every effort was made to provide smooth, luxurious travel accommodations. It entered into the design of equipment, construction, and maintenance of the roadbed, discriminating speed. When the Hiawatha's streamlined train service was introduced, the management made it clear that no speed violations would be tolerated, and from the inception of this service the speed of these trains has been rigidly policed by a daily check of the speedometer tapes from the engines.

This policy of policing the speed of the Hiawatha has been extended to all principal passenger and freight trains on the system, with most satisfactory results. To aid enginemen, so-called speed signs have been erected along the right-of-

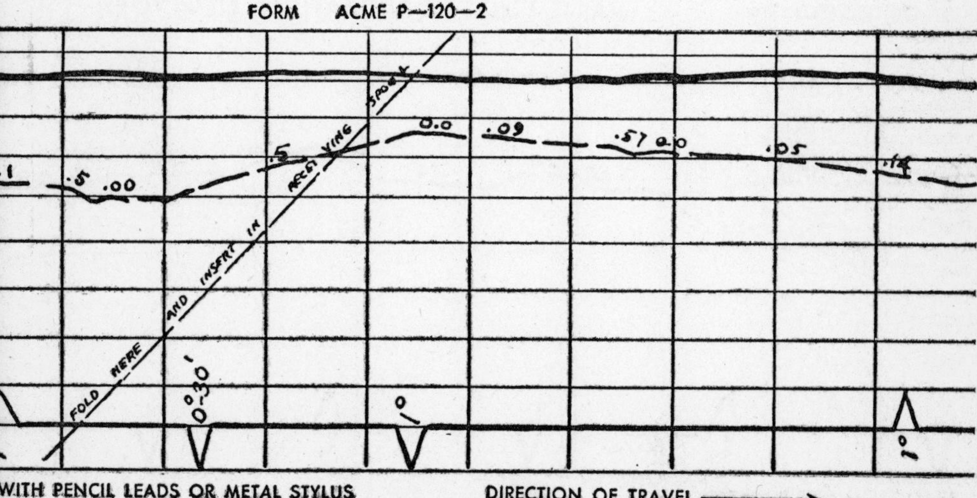

way, calling their attention to the permissible speed sufficiently far in advance to permit compliance. For instance, to insure smooth riding around curves, the speed must be reduced on the tangent, or straight track, allowing the train to come onto the curve with brakes released.

The engine is steaming beautifully. She has failed us only once, and that was back at Edgebrook. The pressure then fell away to 255 pounds. This in restricted-speed territory is not important, as the engine will make 70 miles an hour with this pressure. However, in those top speed brackets the needle must be on the pin.

This failure to steam properly indicated that the tubes were fouling up. The fireman immediately slowed down the feed-water heater to keep the pressure from dropping further. He checked the water level in both glasses, tried the gauge cocks to make sure the water level was correct, then prepared to sand out the flues. They call this "dusting her out." The fireman adjusts the damper for sanding position, then begins to pour dry sand into the firebox. The tremendous draft created by the exhausting steam pulls the sand through the flues, causing the accumulated soot to be dislodged and carried away by the stack.

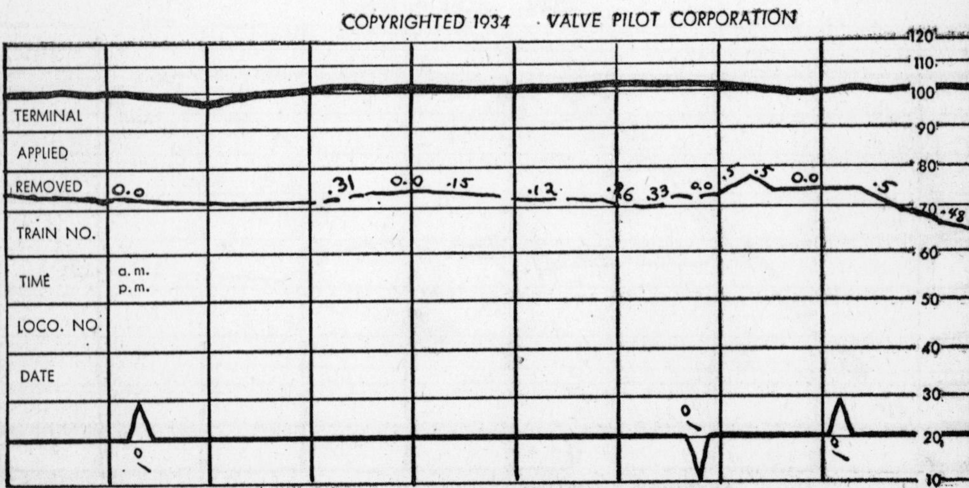

The smoke now is coal black, and as long as it remains black the fireman continues to pour in sand. Slowly the smoke clears. The damper is readjusted, the sand scoop is put away, and the needle of the steam gauge starts to climb, soon touching the 300-pound mark.

The Hiawatha is holding at 100 miles an hour. It remains at this speed for almost fifty miles, except for a slowdown to 90 miles at Rondout.

Approaching the Milwaukee yard-limit board, the speed is reduced and the train is held ready for a further reduction should the occasion arise. However, everything is clear, and at 2:10 we pull into the Milwaukee Station.

Eighty-five miles in 70 minutes! You will remember that in 1934 engine No. 6402, putting on a little extra flourish, made that run in sixty-seven minutes. But this 85 miles in 70 minutes is day-in-and-day-out running.

The engine of the Hiawatha has made an exact stop at the water crane. The tank is filled, and a new engine crew climbs aboard.

Again we get the highball and begin to move. We ease through the yards and on through the city of Wauwatosa, where we are restricted to 45 miles an hour. The engineer

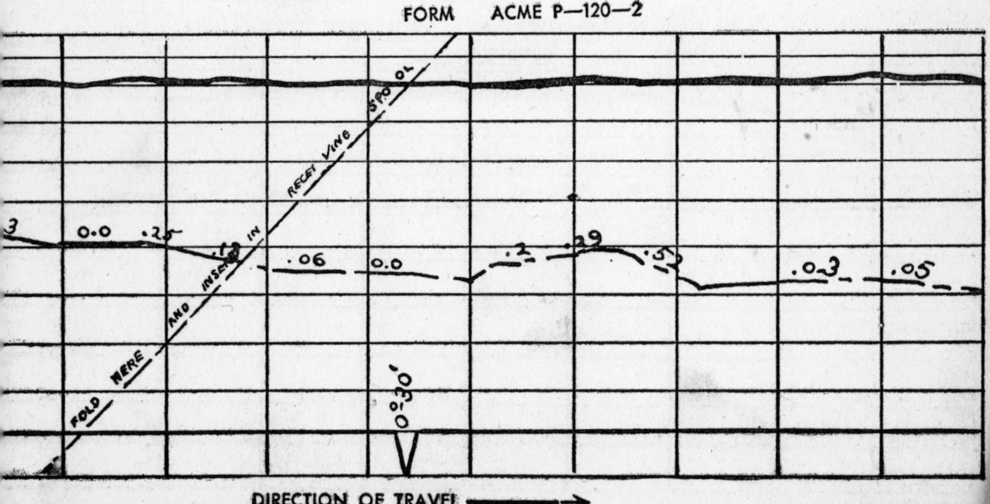

has a slow order for 60 miles an hour between Pewaukee and Hartland, and right now he sets about picking up a minute or so before he reaches this "slow order" district.

We execute this order absolutely, then wheel up to 90 miles an hour. The mileposts are dropping behind us; the telegraph poles flow away in quick flight. Ninety-five again. One hundred! We whip through Oconomowoc in a cloud of dust.

Approaching Watertown, we slow to a walk. We are restricted to 20 miles an hour for the North Western Railway crossing. Comes then the quick, sharp bark of our exhaust. The fireman adjusts his firing valve, as our acceleration is rapid.

Our maximum speed is cut to 70 for curves at Reeseville and East Rio. We grind to a stop at Portage at 3:33, right on the dot, and at 3:34 are under way again.

Now we enter cab-signal territory. A panel in the cab registers semaphore indications ahead. However, everyone respects the rights of the Hiawatha and the road is clear. The engineer handles the train with a fine, sure touch that stirs our admiration.

He makes a 30-pound brake-pipe reduction with the auto-

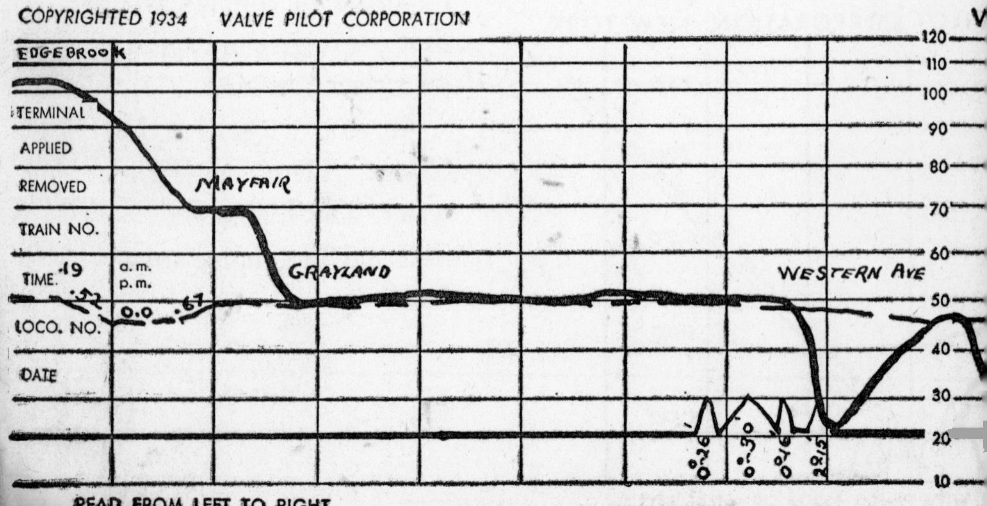

matic brake valve now, and the train decelerates quickly but smoothly. Then the brakes are released, and another slow-down operation is concluded by a wide-opening throttle, and, if necessary, the dropping forward of the reverse lever. This might be compared to shooting the gearshift lever of your automobile into second when you require the added power for quick acceleration.

On this run every split second is of tremendous importance, and the engineer is a master of the art of taking advantage of every last precious watch tick.

It is just west of Mauston that the fireman sings out, "Here she comes!" It is the eastbound Hiawatha. Both trains are wheeling at better than 95 miles an hour, and the impact of our meeting is brief and savage. The other track has swallowed our companion train in a twinkling. Tensed against the concussion of her going, we have glimpsed only a blur that is a maroon-and-gold lightning bolt.

We stop at New Lisbon at 4:07. Here passengers are exchanged with the North Woods Hiawatha, and at 4:11 we are rolling again. We slow to 45 miles through the tunnel at Tunnel City, then again touch the maximum permissible speed. We snap by Camp McCoy, doing a neat 90, and hundreds of soldiers take time out to give our speedliner their attention.

At 5:00 we stop at La Crosse. Here we take water. The engine is serviced and the engine crew

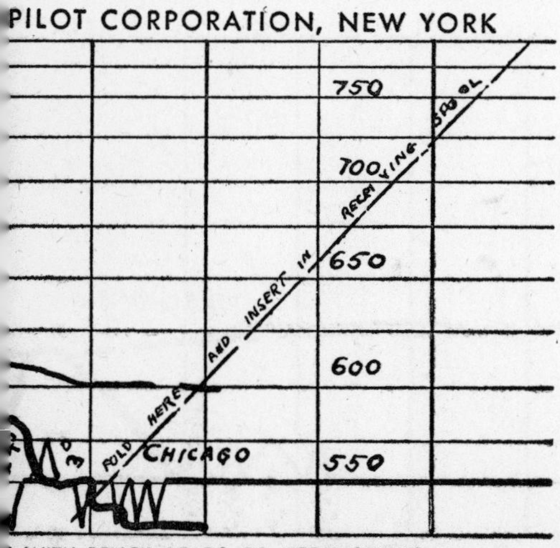
PILOT CORPORATION, NEW YORK
750
700
650
600
550
CHICAGO
FOLD HERE AND INSERT IN RECEIVING SPOOL
WITH PENCIL LEADS OR METAL STYLUS

is changed again. We highball out at 5:05. No hurry, no lost motion, no excitement—just clocklike precision by every man jack of them.

From La Crosse we follow the west shore of the Mississippi, the Father of Waters. This is as picturesque a right-of-way as a man could ask for. These past few years the physical characteristics along here have been changed. There are numerous dams now, and these have created a number of glimmering lakes, set like turquoise jewels against the bosom of the world.

The cruising speed at most places along the river is 70 miles an hour, and seventy it is: no more, no less. Occasionally there is a light brake application; again, when a stretch of straight track permits, we wheel a little faster.

We stop at Winona and Red Wing. At 7:14 we pull into St. Paul—one minute ahead of time. Here we discharge some two hundred passengers. And at 7:43 we are rolling into the Milwaukee Station at Minneapolis.

Watching, eager faces are there. People have come to meet friends and relatives, and we have not kept them waiting. The Hiawatha, a speed queen of the rails, has come through "on the advertised."

In railroad terminology, "on the advertised" means that a train has reached its destination exactly as indicated by the figures in the timetable, or better.

Courtesy of New York Central System.

MODERN VERSION OF THE TWENTIETH CENTURY LIMITED, NEW YORK CENTRAL'S NO. 25, westbound on the Hudson River Division, hauled by a streamlined J-3 4-6-4 Hudson-type locomotive.

Courtesy of L.&N.R.R.

STREAMLINED SOUTH WIND, LOUISVILLE & NASHVILLE'S luxurious coach train hauled by Engine 275, a modernized 4-6-2, just south of Louisville, Kentucky.

CHAPTER IV

Luxury Limiteds of the U.S.

ACE TODAY of the New York Central's fleet of crack passenger trains is the Twentieth Century Limited, probably the most famous train in the world.

When the Century first entered service on June 15, 1902, it operated on a twenty-hour schedule between New York City and Chicago. Subsequently it reduced this time to eighteen hours. Since it was streamlined in 1938 the time was further reduced to sixteen hours, so that it now averages a mile a minute, including stops, in its 960-mile flight each way.

This is a completely air-conditioned, all-room train de luxe, and equipped with bar lounge, two diners, and observation-lounge car. Including locomotive, it represents a cost of $1,384,000.

During a single run its crew comprises eight enginemen, eight firemen, three train conductors, six brakemen, three baggagemen, a train secretary, barber, tailor, and maid. There is one Pullman conductor, and as many Pullman porters as sleeping cars. The two dining cars have a crew of twenty-four.

The locomotive is changed only once between Harmon, New York, and Chicago. This is at the Collinwood Yard, east of Cleveland. Engineer and firemen change at Rensselaer (Albany), Syracuse, Buffalo, Cleveland, Toledo, and Elkhart. An engine crew change is also made at Harmon, where the motive power is changed from electric to steam.

Train conductors, brakemen, and baggagemen change at Buffalo and Toledo. All other members of the crew remain with the train throughout the run. The dining-car crews sleep in special dormitory quarters at the head end of the lounge car during the night.

The Twentieth Century Limited has run in as many as seven sections. Over the years, the train's total revenue has been greater than that of any other limited train in the world. Exclusive of dining-car receipts, its total revenue has exceeded $142,000,000.

The Mercury, offering daily service both ways between Chicago, Detroit, Toledo, and Cleveland, was the first luxurious streamlined day-coach train placed in operation on the New York Central System.

Like the Twentieth Century Limited, its equipment includes roller bearings on all trucks, air conditioning, tightlock couplers, automatic train-control apparatus, with all floors, walls, and ceilings of its cars thoroughly insulated against temperature changes and noise interference.

Every car in the Mercury is individually designed so that the interior of the train gives the impression of a succession of attractive rooms. Large, semicircular vestibules, colorfully decorated, facilitate exit and entrance and passage between the cars.

Both the Mercury and the Twentieth Century Limited are pulled by Hudson-type Class J-3A locomotives. These locomotives—numbered in the 5400s—have a 4-6-4 wheel arrangement.

The New York Central designers of this Hudson-type locomotive believe it to be an outstanding development in modern motive power for use in hauling fast trains over level tracks or low grades, such as exist on the Central's main line.

This Hudson-type engine has developed a cylinder horsepower of more than 4,700 at 75 miles an hour, and at a speed of 80 miles an hour it produced a drawbar pull of 17,500 pounds.

These Class J-3A locomotives are equipped with almost every approved modern device for safety and efficiency. Although of greater power than the Central's first streamlined Hudson locomotive, the Commodore Vanderbilt, which for three years pulled the Twentieth Century Limited between Toledo and Chicago, the J-3A weighs only $182\frac{3}{4}$ tons, or about $2\frac{1}{2}$ tons less than the Commodore Vanderbilt.

The use of aluminum cabs and running boards and of lightweight alloy steel for piston and rod assembly are among the factors contributing to weight reduction, despite the extra load imposed by streamlining features.

A notable benefit obtained from reduction in weight of the receiving and reciprocating parts is the decrease of more than 50 per cent in the dynamic augment, or pound on the rail, imposed by the driving wheels at higher speeds. This is highly beneficial from the standpoint of both track and locomotive maintenance.

Class J-3A locomotives are distinguished for a number of advances over the earlier design Hudson-type locomotives first developed in 1927 by the New York Central and American Locomotive Company. These since have been adopted by many railroads all over America as an improved design for fast passenger service.

Late in 1941 two new stainless-steel streamlined trains replaced the former equipment of the famous Empire State Express, thus honoring the fiftieth anniversary of this, the oldest express train on the New York Central System.

For these two trains, thirty-two cars were specially built by the Edward G. Budd Manufacturing Company. They consisted of tavern-lounge cars, parlor cars, dining cars, coaches, and observation cars, and their cost was approximately $2,500,000.

The construction of the new streamlined Empire State Express trains embodied all the advanced principles of modern railroad engineering. They are almost one-quarter lighter in weight than former trains, because of the use of the patented welding process employed by the Budd company.

These trains start and stop as a unit, the cars being equipped with twin-cushion rubber draft gears and tight-lock couplers. The cars have extra-wide, non-frosting windows, reclining seats, individual lights for each seat, large lounge and wash rooms at the end of each car, and are air-conditioned. The interior arrangements, decorative plan, and furnishings are the most luxurious ever installed in day-coach trains.

Hudson-type J-3A locomotives were rebuilt for the trains and were given the individual streamlined treatment of the Empire State Express.

The Pennsylvania Railroad proudly points to its inauguration of the first de luxe all-Pullman limited train in America, the Pennsylvania Limited. This train has been operated daily between New York and Chicago since 1881, and was the forerunner of the Broadway Limited.

The Broadway Limited is one of the present leaders in an era epoch-making in travel enjoyment. From the standpoint of luxury, comfort, speed, safety, and regularity, none exceed and few equal this colorful and glamorous speed queen of high iron.

Famed, indeed, are the trains on the Pennsylvania. The names, Broadway, General, Congressional, Liberty, American, Spirit of St. Louis, are almost household words. Ten great trains between New York and Chicago. Six to St. Louis. Three to Detroit. Seven to Cleveland. Twenty-four to Pittsburgh. And twenty-three to Washington, led by the Congressional—226 miles in 215 minutes. Between New York and Philadelphia there are fifty trains every twenty-four hours.

These, in addition to the two new coach trains, Trail Blazer and the Jeffersonian, operating between Chicago, St. Louis, New York, and return, represent the backbone of the Pennsylvania fleet of passenger trains, producing one fifth of the passenger service of the country.

To better understand what this means, let us stand for a little in the Pennsylvania Station in New York City. Here we learn that a passenger train arrives or departs every fifty-one seconds between the hours of eight and nine o'clock each morning. For three continuous hours, from 7 to 10 A.M., the average is almost precisely one train a minute, and this exactly one block from Broadway, in the heart of America's greatest metropolis!

The Broadway Limited, named for the teeming thoroughfare beloved by every New Yorker, has long been the fair-haired child of the Pennsylvania system. Its equipment was designed by company engineers, working in collaboration with the Pullman Company and Mr. Raymond Loewy. It provides for the traveler in this, a country of travel-loving people, a speed train that furnishes safe, sure, and comfortable transportation. This all-room train offers complete privacy over the shortest east-west route between New York and Chicago, with a running time of sixteen hours.

The Trail Blazer is a luxury, all-coach train, running daily in each direction between New York and Chicago. It combines low-cost, high-speed service, with comforts and conveniences afforded by coaches of the most advanced and improved types.

The trains flying the banner of the Trail Blazer were first inaugurated by the Pennsylvania on July 28, 1939, and were the first long-distance exclusive coach trains established by any eastern road.

The running time of the Trail Blazer between the two cities is seventeen hours, or just one hour longer than the Broadway Limited. In the first two years of operation the Trail Blazer carried over 300,000 passengers. During the first five months of 1941, the patronage showed a jump of 60 per cent, compared with the like period of 1940.

The special features of the Trail Blazer, in addition to ultramodern reclining-seat coaches, with all seats reserved and adjustable, include observation buffet-lounge cars, club-lounge cars, and "twin-unit" diners, with popular-priced meals and refreshments.

The Jeffersonian, luxury, all-coach train between New York and St. Louis, substantially duplicates the fastest schedules in effect on the Pennsylvania Railroad. The run is made practically in twenty hours each way.

The coaches accommodate fifty-six passengers each. Each coach has spacious dressing rooms for men and women, with washstands, a sofa, and an abundance of full-length mirrors. The women's dressing rooms are furnished with mirrored vanity tables with chairs.

In the observation-lounge-buffet there are a radio and restful armchairs for thirty-one passengers, while sixteen more can be accommodated at tables located in the buffet section of the car.

From the shining and spotless stainless-steel kitchens of modern-type dining cars, table-d'hôte breakfasts are served at fifty cents, luncheons at sixty-five cents, and dinners at seventy-five cents, with a liberal choice of à-la-carte selections. A complete range of beverages is available.

At a suitable hour each evening the overhead lights in the coaches are turned off, but a soft illumination of the aisles is maintained by floor lights located beneath the seats. Prior to this, the through-ticket "lift" is completed, so that passengers are not disturbed during the night. The observation-buffet car is kept open as long as passengers desire.

Passengers on these trains pay only the regular low coach fares, with no additional charges for the special features of equipment and service.

This is, indeed, a far cry from the day when a journey of a thousand miles for the coach passenger was something of an ordeal. Then, because the traveler usually felt that the prices in the diner were out of his reach, he either carried a lunch in a paper sack or he joined the rush for a place at some railroad eating-house counter. Here he bolted his food, each instant fearful that the train would go off without him. He arrived at his destination hot and grimed, with cinders in his hair and a generally wilted appearance, as he breathed a sigh of relief that the dreary hours of accumulating discomforts were at an end.

For a woman with children, yesterday's coach travel was a trying experience, at best. For her the coach of today's streamliner offers every comfort and convenience.

On the west coast, the Southern Pacific Company's Daylight streamliner, operating daily between San Francisco and Los Angeles, is an outstanding example of the results that can be obtained in restoring travel to the railroad through the operation of modern, comfortable, high-speed streamlined trains.

Following the romantic El Camino Real—the King's Highway that linked the chain of early California Missions—this train traverses the rich Santa Clara Valley, famous for its prunes and apricots; the Salinas Valley, known as the "Salad Bowl of America," where is grown much of our lettuce; passes through the Santa Lucia Mountains; and winds down to San Luis Obispo, which means "St. Louis the Bishop."

South from San Luis Obispo the train skirts the Pacific Ocean for nearly a hundred miles, with blue water breaking on white sands and surging against sheer cliffs. Then, leaving the sea, the Daylight passes enormous orange groves. Arriving at Los Angeles, the traveler's eye is taken by the magnificent new Union Station, high-ceilinged and spacious, its motif entirely that of early California.

Here, again, is an example of what the railroads are doing to earn the good will of the traveling public. The seats are of the overstuffed-chair type, upholstered in soft leather. The main waiting room seems more like the lobby of a fashionable hotel than a part of a railroad station. There are patios and walks, orange and olive trees and stately palms, with the atmosphere and charm of an exclusive resort. The Los Angeles Union Station is as much a mecca for sightseers as it is a clearing house for train passengers.

Since its inception, the Daylight has proved extremely popular and more than justified its cost. The Southern Pacific has spared no expense in making this train the most luxurious means of travel on the west coast.

The Daylight consists of fourteen attractively styled and splendidly appointed streamlined passenger cars, hauled by specially designed steam locomotives of sufficient power to handle the trains adequately over the mountain grades, yet capable of sustained high speed on level track. These locomotives, built by the Lima Locomotive Works and known as GS-3-4 classification, or Golden State type, are streamlined and capable of a maximum speed of 106 miles an hour, although as a practical matter of operation their train speed is limited to around 75 miles an hour. The wheel arrangement is 4-8-4.

Advanced features of these engines include the Valve Pilot Corporation's speed and cut-off indicators to guide the engineer in a better and more economical operation of his engine; Boxpok driving-wheel centers; an air-draft smoke lifter to carry smoke up and over the train; and the General Steel Casting Corporation's high-initial, low-constant resistant leading and trailing trucks, permitting the locomotive to negotiate curves smoothly and safely at high speeds.

Among the safety devices used on these locomotives are boiler drop plugs, applied in the crown sheet of the firebox, and tire-retaining clips, securing the driving and trailing wheel tires to the wheel centers. Both of these safety devices were developed on the Southern Pacific Lines and were made standard equipment on all their locomotives.

The cars of the Daylight were built by the Pullman-Standard Car Manufacturing Company and have welded frames of Corten steel, sheathed with high-tensile stainless steel and Waughmat Twin-Cushion Draft Gears.

The exterior color scheme of the train is Saxony red and

orange. The aluminum striping, extending over its entire length, including locomotive and tender, emphasizes sleekness and streamlining.

The interior of the Daylight coaches offers the most restful accommodations that modern transportation can provide. Varying color schemes, combining shades of apricot, jade, and Nantes blue with ceilings of warm ivory, give an individual touch to each car. Reclining chairs, upholstered with curly mohair and cushioned with soft sponge rubber, can be turned to face windows of exceptional width, providing for maximum visibility.

The tavern car features a semicircular bar, backed with mirror walls and flanked by large, deep leather lounges. Particular interest centers about the dining service, provided in either the coffee-shop car, which furnishes low-priced meals, or the dining car, where the Southern Pacific's well-known "Meals Select" are served on flower-decked tables.

Parlor and observation cars are furnished with revolving chairs and roomy settees, placed to give passengers the feeling of a comfortable living room or club. It goes without saying that the entire train is completely air-conditioned.

Particular care has been exercised to assure a high degree of riding comfort. Car trucks are of special design, with triple instead of single bolsters for superior riding qualities. Brake equipment is of the most modern design, incorporating features for safety and the smooth retardation of trains.

As a result of the popularity of this means of travel between San Francisco and Los Angeles, an additional Daylight has been added: the San Joaquin Daylight, which traverses the fertile San Joaquin Valley for more than two hundred miles, climbs the Tehachapi Mountains, and crosses the Mojave Desert. The San Joaquin Daylight, also, is powered by steam locomotives of the big 4-8-4 type.

North, south, east or west—it makes little difference which way the traveler turns today, for there is always one of these speed queens of the rail waiting and eager to serve.

The Louisville & Nashville's passenger service, although greatly overshadowed by its freight traffic in producing revenue, is always good and, in many cases, luxurious.

The road looks with especial pride on its splendid safety record of not having had a passenger killed in a train accident for some twenty-four years.

The principal all-Louisville & Nashville passenger trains are the Pan-American and the Azaalean, operating daily both ways over the main line between Cincinnati and New Orleans. Other famous-name trains, which use Old Reliable* trackage for varying but considerable portions of their journeys between Midwest and Deep South and Florida points, include the Southland and the Flamingo (Cincinnati to Atlanta on the L.&N.); the Dixie Flyer, the Dixie Limited, and the Dixiana (Evansville to Nashville on the L.&N.); and the Jacksonian and Florida Arrow (Louisville to Montgomery on the L.&N.).

The Crescent and the Piedmont Limited, which operate between New Orleans and New York, use the lines of the

*The name by which the Louisville & Nashville is affectionately known in the South, where it has served the public for nearly ninety years.

Louisville & Nashville between New Orleans and Montgomery. Of the trains mentioned, the Jacksonian, Florida Arrow, Dixieland, and Dixiana are winter-season trains and operate over the Louisville & Nashville only every third day.

Mention has been reserved until the last of the two streamlined, all-coach luxury trains which were inaugurated in December 1940 and which travel between Chicago and Miami and other Florida points, using Louisville & Nashville lines for a portion of their journeys. These trains are the Dixie Flagler and the South Wind. Each train operates every third day, each following a different route. The Dixie Flagler operates between Evansville and Nashville, and the South Wind between Louisville and Montgomery. These streamlined trains were originally inaugurated as winter-season trains only, but they proved so popular that they were retained permanently. Their schedules called for 29½ hours between Chicago and Miami. The Louisville & Nashville was now confronted by two problems. First, the streamlining of motive power to harmonize with other exterior appointments of these trains. Second, the maintaining of the fast schedules established.

At that time the Louisville & Nashville had no streamlined locomotives, but its mechanical department attacked the problem at its South Louisville shops. Soon there emerged engines numbered 277 and 295, streamlined and ready to hit the high iron trail. Subsequently No. 275 had its face lifted—in the spring of 1941. The 275 was assigned the task of hauling the South Wind, with the 277 powering the Dixie Flagler. The 295 was transferred to other service.

The 275 and the 277 are K-5 Pacific-type engines, with a 4-6-2 wheel arrangement and 42,210 pounds of starting tractive effort. They were built by the American Locomotive Company.

To meet the schedules established for the South Wind and the Dixie Flagler, the Louisville & Nashville hauls the trains over its lines at high speeds (an average of about 55 miles an hour for the South Wind; about 52 for the Dixie Flagler) and has eliminated all unnecessary stops.

The Dixie Flagler operates non-stop between Evansville and Nashville, and the South Wind non-stop between Birmingham and Montgomery. The non-stop run between Birmingham and Nashville, a distance of 205.4 miles, is said to be the longest such run made by a coal-fired train in this country.

To enable the engines to make these non-stop runs, the Louisville & Nashville outfitted them with oversize water tanks. For example, the big 12-wheeled tender on the 275, which pulls the South Wind on its record run, has a tank capacity of 20,000 gallons of water and 27½ tons of coal, almost double the capacity of the average tender on the road.

In addition to the trains mentioned, the Old Reliable has many more. They serve a large section of the central South. All principal trains are air-conditioned and offer dependable, comfortable, and economical service.

Like other American roads, the Louisville & Nashville believes in advertising. This is done through a variety of mediums. However, the L.&N. employs one form of publicity that is unique, in that it allows the crack Pan-American to speak for itself. High and shrill, the whistle of the locomotive pulling the southbound Pan-American sends its triumphant cry to the world in a radio broadcast—daily except Sunday. Just south of Nashville, a microphone placed beside the track picks up the sound of the train. The listener who has tuned in on Station WSM, Nashville, Tennessee, late in the afternoon hears the sound of an approaching train, building in pitch. Then there is the scream of the whistle—coming straight at you. The full-throated roar of the train pours from your loud-speaker—the drumming thunder of trucks and wheels and clicking rail joints. Then it is fading. Gone.

Year in and year out, this program does not change its script. Never in the more than eight years of its existence has this broadcast lost its novelty and charm for a vast listening audience. People in every walk of life, eyes bright, listen to the whistle scream of the Louisville & Nashville's southbound Pan-American. Fans in nearly every state in the Union and in neighboring countries tune in this strange broadcast regularly. Many have their favorite engineer and can tell who is at the throttle prior to his identification by the announcer. There are those who have actually named the number of cars in the train correctly by counting the clicks of the wheels on the rail joints!

For many it is a minor tragedy when the train arrives at the "pick-up" spot too late to be broadcast, though, to the honor and glory of the Louisville & Nashville, this seldom happens. On a few occasions when the train has been late there have been scheduled revisions at the broadcasting station to meet this contingency.

And so again we find the pioneering spirit of America reflected by this road of the South, where the Pacific-type passenger engine of the justly famed Pan-American—the largest radio star in the world—rides the air waves.

Photo by Robert Dudley Smith.

PENNSYLVANIA RAILROAD'S EASTBOUND GOLDEN ARROW NO. 42, rounding the curve at Radnor, Pennsylvania, descending grade on the electrified Philadelphia Division. The locomotive is the justly famous P.R.R. GG-1. Note position light signals standard on the Pennsylvania.

Courtesy of the Milwaukee Road.

CHICAGO, MILWAUKEE, ST. PAUL AND PACIFIC'S WESTBOUND OLYMPIAN NO. 15 on the Clear Creek Bridge, showing upper tracks in the Bitter Root Mountains, east of St. Paul's Pass Tunnel, Montana.

CHAPTER V

Electrification

ELECTRICITY has played an important part in solving certain transportation problems on American railroads. From the day in 1887 when the first electric street railway began operation in Richmond, Virginia, until the present time, the electric motor and the electric locomotive have done much to facilitate the handling of trains.

It was the electric motor that made possible the construction of rapid-transit subway lines in cities like Boston, New York, Philadelphia, as well as in London and Paris.

Under certain conditions, electricity readily demonstrated its superiority over the steam engine. Particularly was this true in metropolitan districts, and never more so than underground, in tunnels, feeding steam trains into the heart of great congested areas like New York City.

Already mention has been made of the fact that steam

takes over at Harmon, New York, and at the Manhattan Transfer in New Jersey. Days were when steam engines ran under New York. Before the electrification of the Grand Central Tunnel, coal- and coke-burning engines handled trains there, coming out of the tunnel at Ninety-sixth Street. The smoke and fumes made the tunnel a veritable hellhole for engine crews. Came then electric locomotives, first introduced by the Baltimore & Ohio in 1895—clean, smooth-operating, powerful. The New York Central and Pennsylvania railroads electrified the tracks leading to their passenger terminals. The New York, New Haven & Hartford extended electrification to New Haven.

In 1911 the Boston & Maine electrified its long Hoosac Tunnel. The "juice" engines hauled Michigan Central trains through the bore under the Detroit River. Suburban trackage on the Long Island Railroad, some three hundred miles of it, was electrified. The Delaware, Lackawanna and Western has electrified its system in the vicinity of New York.

The Chicago, Milwaukee, St. Paul and Pacific Railroad spanned the Rocky Mountains with thin copper wires and set great electric locomotives to the task of hauling trains across the backbone of the continent. Here we find one of the longest electrified steam lines in the world—some seven hundred miles in length.

The Great Northern whipped the mighty Cascades with electricity. Its electrified line is seventy-three miles in length. Clean, smoke-free power here for the haul through its 7.8-mile-long tunnel. Again a godsend for engine crews.

Third-rail electric power was first used by the New York

Central in its Grand Central Terminal district in 1906. This road has 168 electric locomotives in service.

The Pennsylvania Railroad's initial electric operation was put in service in 1910 in connection with the New York tunnel and terminal development. This was a direct-current, low-voltage, third-rail system, which at that time appeared to be the most satisfactory for the tunnel operation, and extended from Sunnyside Yard to the Manhattan Transfer. Soon after the completion of the New York terminal it became apparent that the electrification of a part of the Philadelphia terminal area was necessary to relieve congestion. After extensive research and experimentation it was decided to adopt the overhead-trolley, or catenary, high-voltage, alternating-current system for this and future installations.

The first electrification of the Philadelphia district was from Broad Street Station to Paoli and was completed in 1915. This was followed by the Chestnut Hill branch in 1918 and the line to White Marsh in 1924. Came then the main line to Wilmington, and the branch to West Chester in 1928. Also, in 1930, the main line to Trenton and the branch to Norristown in 1930. This completed the electrification of all Philadelphia suburban lines.

In the meantime study had indicated the economic advantages of electrification in the dense traffic territory between New York, Philadelphia, and Harrisburg, and in 1928 it was announced that a program of electrification to include lines in this area would begin. The difficult financial situation following October 1929 interfered somewhat with the prosecution of this work, but the program was advanced continuously, and in 1933 electric operation of through passenger service was started between New York, Paoli, and southward to Wilmington.

Desiring to co-operate with the Federal Government in providing employment and endeavoring to assist industrial recovery, as well as obtain the full benefits of the work already done, the railroad company in 1933 made arrangements with the Federal administration to secure funds necessary for the completion of this program of electrification south to Washington and the Potomac Yard. A construction force of 11,000 men was recruited from furloughed employees of the Pennsylvania road, and the electrified service from Wilmington to Washington and Potomac Yard was put in operation early in 1935, thus completing electrification of the main route from New York to Washington and the South and the Philadelphia suburban district.

In 1937 work was started on electrification of the east-and-west lines between the Atlantic seaboard and the Harrisburg district, including the low-grade freight line from Morrisville to Enola, the main line from Paoli to Harrisburg, the Columbia and Port Deposit branch, and the branch lines between Lancaster and Columbia, and Columbia and Royalton. This part of the project was completed and placed in service in 1938, finishing the electrification program as set up for that part of the railroad east of Harrisburg.

From New York to Harrisburg and Washington, the electrified line now includes 675 miles of line and 2,195 miles of track and operates 284 electric locomotives and 504 multiple-unit cars. It contemplates speeds of 100 miles an hour, and speeds in excess of this figure have been made in actual tests. It is an 11,000-volt catenary-type trolley-wire system, supplied with electric power over a network of high-voltage transmission lines, feeding from the main power connections to substations distributed along the lines. Single-phase, 25-cycle current was selected as the most satisfactory type for the movement of heavy transportation units at high speed over a system with traffic as dense as exists in this electrified territory.

An indication of the enormous traffic handled by these electrified lines is at once revealed by the following figures.

In passenger service, 125,000,000 car-miles are made per year, which is the equivalent of a 10-car train circling the earth five hundred times a year.

In freight service, 7,300,000 locomotive-unit miles are made per year, hauling approximately fifteen billion ton-miles of freight cars and their contents, the equivalent of a train of *one hundred* 40-ton cars circling the globe 150 times a year.

In addition to this service handled by electric locomotives, nearly fifteen million car-miles are made by multiple-unit cars in suburban passenger service. The foregoing figures represent traffic corresponding to the business of 1940.

As astronomical as these figures seem, they represent but a small cross section of what American railroads are doing in the world of transportation, of the cars handled by steam locomotives, by electric engines, as well as by the comparatively new child of the iron road, the Diesel-electric power plant.

It has been forecast that by 1950 New York's metropolitan district will have thrust itself thirty miles or more into New Jersey and an equal distance out on Long Island and will embrace a population of thirty million. Other questions weighed are the growth of the Philadelphia and Baltimore areas and of other communities served, the key position in the nation of the city of Washington, and the importance of the electric route as the principal highway for passengers and freight between the South and the north Atlantic seaboard, together with eastern Canada and the West.

Electrification of the eastern part of the Pennsylvania road affords the most desirable solution of operating problems peculiar to this dense traffic territory, where the number of trains is so great.

Under electric power, substantial savings are possible in train-operating costs. It is more efficient, where many train units are moved and the flow of traffic is continuously heavy, to generate power at a central source and distribute it in the form of electricity than to produce power separately on each train.

Under these circumstances it becomes more economical to increase the capacity of the railroad for the future by electrifying than by building additional trackage through congested areas, with enormous outlays for property and construction. Equally important are the great public benefits to be gained.

On the Pennsylvania there are two general types of electric locomotives in use. One type, known as the P-5A, is a 4-6-4 locomotive having three driving axles, with 220,000 to 229,-

000 pounds total weight on these axles. Each axle is equipped with a twin motor, geared to a quill shaft, and equipped with flexible spring members engaging the spokes of the driving wheel for propulsion. The nominal rating of the locomotive is 3,750 horsepower, and it is capable of producing 6,400 horsepower for short periods of time. The locomotives of this type are assigned to freight service and are geared for a maximum speed of 70 miles an hour.

The second type of locomotive, known as the GG-1, is of the 4-6-6-4 type, with articulated chassis and single cab unit extending over the complete running gear. The six driving axles are each equipped with twin motors, driving through a quill, as in the case of the P-5A locomotive. The total weight on driving axles is 300,000 pounds. Normal rating in horsepower is 4,620, with the ability to develop, for short periods of time, 8,520 horsepower.

Fifty-seven locomotives of this type are equipped with 90-mile-an-hour gearing, and the remaining fifty-two with 100-mile-an-hour gearing. These GG-1s with 100-mile-an-hour gears are used at all times in the passenger-locomotive pool. Those with 90-mile-an-hour gearing are used in both passenger and freight service, the number available for the freight-locomotive pool depending on the demand for locomotives to handle adequately the passenger service. The relative number used in the two services varies from day to day.

An outstanding characteristic of electric-locomotive operation has been the ability to obtain a high availability factor. In addition to their inherent reliability, the comparatively short time required for regular inspection is largely responsible for this result. The required daily inspections are being performed within a period of less than an hour. Few special facilities are required, and these daily inspections are scheduled largely while the locomotives are at terminals awaiting transfer return movement. Therefore, inspection does not appreciably affect the locomotive availability.

The regular monthly inspection on road locomotives is performed at two locations—Enola, Pennsylvania, and Wilmington, Delaware. This inspection requires from eight to sixteen hours each month. Heavy inspections and repairs are performed on the basis of total locomotive mileage. As a result of operating experience it has been possible gradually to increase the mileage operated between heavy repair periods, and the final limit has not yet been reached. On the basis of the present mileage it is equivalent to approximately three-year intervals on passenger locomotives and five years on electric freight locomotives. The locomotive is out of service for this work of heavy inspection and repair for approximately two weeks.

Typical of the improvement brought about by the operation of electric locomotives in passenger service is the schedule of the Congressional Limited, running between New York and Washington, a distance of 226 miles, in 215 minutes, as compared with 255 minutes under steam operation with a shorter length train.

In the freight service the running time has been improved an average of two hours between the New Jersey terminals and Enola Yards to the west, and in the north and south service one to two hours have been cut from the running time, depending on the weight of train and type of service.

We have seen the important part electrification has played in metropolitan areas, where it has met and done much to solve operating problems on these dense traffic arteries. Now let us turn west to the Rockies and the Continental Divide.

Here is mountain railroad, and nowhere in the world can we find a finer example of main-line electrification than that offered by the Chicago, Milwaukee, St. Paul and Pacific Railroad on its justly famed Rocky Mountain Division, as well as its Coast Division.

It was in 1915 and 1916 that the General Electric Company and the American Locomotive Works built for this road the first group of electric locomotives, forty-two in number. Thirty were intended for freight service and were geared for a maximum operating speed of 30 miles an hour. The remaining twelve, intended for passenger service, were geared for a maximum operating speed of 60 miles an hour. Apart from this distinction, and the fact that the passenger locomotives were equipped with oil-fired boilers for train heating, and with train lighting panels, all locomotives were alike.

Each of the freight locomotives thus put in service consisted of two units, symmetrical in arrangement and coupled together back to back. There was control equipment at the front end of each unit. Viewing the locomotive as a whole, we find a four-wheeled truck at each end, with eight pairs of driving wheels, arranged in four groups of two pairs each.

There were two sets of frames under each unit, or four

sets under the complete locomotive, and these were connected by articulated joints. The frames were placed outside of the wheels, and the two cabs floated on the frames. In this manner the cab structures played no part in transmitting pulling of buffing stresses. With a total wheel base of 102 feet 8 inches, the rigid wheel base was only 10 feet 6 inches.

Each of these locomotives had eight motors, twin-geared to their respective axles. The torque was transmitted from the gear-wheel rims to the spiders through springs, which absorbed shocks in starting under heavy loads. This was an important feature in an electric locomotive developing the high starting tractive force of 113,000 pounds.

These locomotives were placed in service on the Rocky Mountain Division as rapidly as they were received from the builders. This extended over a considerable period of time, during which traffic was handled by both steam and electric locomotives.

The General Electric Company had a number of representatives on the line, and the steam-enginemen were instructed in the art of handling the electric locomotives as rapidly as the latter were placed in service. The change-over was made without serious difficulty or confusion, and traffic delays were remarkably few.

Though slight changes were subsequently made in certain details of the locomotives, their performance, all things considered, has been highly satisfactory.

Before further examining the locomotives of the Chicago, Milwaukee, St. Paul and Pacific's electrified territory, let us look at the physical characteristics of this Rocky Mountain

Division. The name itself savors of high adventure. Here are the ramparts of the Rockies, with thrill-packed romance in every mile. New and startling panoramas unfold as we turn the corner of each upthrust mountain face. There are high passes and deep-slashed river gorges, threaded by gleaming bands of steel—the steel of the railroad builders.

From the day the first engineer lined his transit and settled those thin cross-hairs on the distant leveling rod until the last spike was driven home, man, the pygmy, matched brain and endurance against these burly, blustering bulwarks here on the roof of the continent.

And the construction crews slowly won through. The roadbed they carved across the Rockies was shaken down finally into a permanent right-of-way, and whistles screamed their defiance to the high, cloud-shrouded peaks. Air horns hooted the announcement of the going of peerless trains down the road of high iron.

The Chicago, Milwaukee and St. Paul road joined with the Northern Pacific, the Great Northern, and others, recording valiant deeds of conquest, as their rails reached out to the far Pacific. And now it was the Chicago, Milwaukee, St. Paul and Pacific Railroad.

The Rocky Mountain Division extends from Harlowton, Montana, to Avery, Idaho. The length of the electrified line of this division is 442.7 miles. Leaving Harlowton westbound, the line crosses the Belt Mountains, climbing 1,625 feet in a distance of 46 miles. The maximum grade is 2.1 per cent, with frequent curves, the sharpest being ten degrees.

The maximum descending grade is 1 per cent, with several

tunnels and frequent curves. From Lombard to Piedmont, at the base of the Continental Divide, a distance of 54.5 miles, the grades are light and gradually ascending westbound. Here again are many curves of six degrees or less; a few as sharp as eight degrees.

At Piedmont begins the climb over the Rockies. The ascent is 1,978 feet in a distance of 21 miles, on a maximum grade of 2 per cent. At the summit is the Pipestone Pass Tunnel, 2,290 feet in length, in which the grade is 1 per cent, descending westbound. The line then drops sharply to Butte on a maximum grade of 1.66 per cent, with winding curves all of the way.

From Butte to St. Regis, 196.2 miles, the road is located in the valleys of the Hell Gate and Missoula rivers. The grades here are light and generally descending, with considerable curvature.

It is west of St. Regis that the ascent of the Bitter Root Mountains begins. From St. Regis to Haugan, a distance of 19.1 miles, there is a rise of 470 feet, with a maximum grade of 0.8 per cent. The country is wild. The mountains are jumbled and broken by high ridges and deep-hewn gullies. The curvature is almost constant, as the railroad feels its way through a rugged, tempestuous world. The road climbs 1,020 feet in 15 miles on an average lift of 1.7 per cent.

The St. Paul Pass Tunnel drives its bore 8,771 feet through the high rims at the summit. Follows a steady descent to Avery, at the end of the electrified section.

Hydroelectric power for operating this division is purchased from the Montana Power Company and is delivered to the railroad substations located along the line at a tension of 100,000 volts alternating current. There are fourteen of these substations, spaced on an average of 32.8 miles apart.

Static transformers, located in the substations, reduce the high-tension current to 2,300 volts, and this current is then transformed, by means of motor generators, to direct current for use on the line. Each motor generator is of the three-unit type, with one three-phase, synchronous motor direct-connected to two direct-current generators. These operate in series at 1,500 volts. Thus the current is furnished to the line at 3,000 volts.

An overhead-trolley system is used to supply current to the locomotives. Over the main track there are suspended two No. 4/0 B.&S. grooved copper trolley wires, hung side by side. A single wire is suspended over side tracks.

The trolley wires receive current from feeder wires, to which they are connected at suitable intervals. The feeder system consists of one or more 500,000-circular-mil or 700,000-circular-mil copper cables, carried by the same poles which support the trolley wires.

The normal height of the trolley wire above the rail is 24 feet 2 inches, and the minimum height is 17 feet. At intervals the trolley line is broken by "air gaps." Thus power can be cut from a section on which there may be trouble without disturbing the distribution on the remainder of the division. The wiring is carried on cedar poles, spaced at distances not exceeding 150 feet.

The Coast Division of the Chicago, Milwaukee, St. Paul and Pacific Railroad extends from Othello to Tacoma, in the state of Washington. The physical characteristics of this line are in many respects similar to those of the Rocky Mountain Division. The distribution equipment used on this division covers 229.8 miles of line.

Power is purchased from the Washington Water Power Company and is distributed through eight substations approximately twenty-eight miles apart.

From Othello westbound to Beverly, near the crossing of the Columbia River, there is a drop of 505 feet in a distance of 38.5 miles. Here the country is largely desert. West of the river the road lifts sharply to the summit of the Saddle Mountains, amounting to 1,910 feet in some 18 miles. The maximum grade is 2.2 per cent, and the sharpest curves are six degrees.

The line then drops into the Kittitas Valley, which is prosperous and fertile. Crossing the valley the track is almost level, but from Cle Elum to Hyak, at the summit of the Cascades, there is a rise of 617 feet in 29.7 miles. The maximum grade is 1.74 per cent, with frequent curves, the sharpest being ten degrees.

From Renton, at the foot of the grade of the western Cascade slopes, to Tacoma via Seattle, a distance of 49.3 miles, the line is practically level and the curvature light.

The electrification of the Coast Division necessitated the purchase of additional locomotives. It was decided to change the gear ratio of the then existing passenger locomotives, to fit them for freight service, and to order new passenger locomotives for both the Rocky Mountain and Coast divisions.

Ten locomotives were ordered from the Westinghouse Electric & Manufacturing Company for service on the Rocky Mountain Division. The mechanical parts were built by the Baldwin Locomotive Works.

The wheel arrangement was 4-6-2-2-6-4, and the locomotives operated in either direction with equal facility. Two sets of frames were connected by a drawbar, thus forming an articulated joint. The total wheel base was 79 feet 10 inches; the rigid wheelbase, 16 feet 9 inches.

Twin motors connected in series rotated each of six driving axles, the full voltage on each motor, when operating at maximum running speeds, being 1,500 volts. The axle was surrounded by a quill to which the motors were geared. This quill transmitted the torque to the wheel centers through coiled springs acting on spring pads formed in the spokes of the driving wheels.

Forced ventilation was provided for the motors. The frames were placed outside of the wheels, and the loads carried by driving and truck wheels, equalized as in steam practice.

These locomotives, at the time of their construction, were considered to be of extraordinary capacity, as they were designed to develop a maximum of 4,200 horsepower for a period of one hour and to handle trains of 12 cars, weighing 960 tons, up a heavy mountain grade of 2.2 per cent at a speed of 23.8 miles an hour. They were placed on an exceedingly difficult run, covering what, under steam operation, were four engine divisions, and crossing three mountain ranges, with steep grades, many tunnels, and an excessive amount of curvature.

Electricity, "the juice hog," was on the way to licking Old Man Mountain.

It was found necessary to strengthen some of the structural parts of these locomotives before they fully met the rigorous conditions of mountain railroad. This was done, and they then fully measured up to their difficult operating requirements.

In the meantime the General Electric Company built five locomotives for service on the Coast Division. The American Locomotive Company built the mechanical parts.

These locomotives were of an entirely different type from the ten built to haul trains on the Rocky Mountain Division. They were carried on twenty-eight wheels, of which twenty-four were driving wheels, arranged in four groups. Each of the center group had four driving wheels, while each of the end groups had two pairs, with a single pair of guiding wheels.

The design of this locomotive is popularly known on the road as the "bipolar," since there are twelve bipolar motors, with their armatures directly mounted on the driving axles. All gearing is thus dispensed with. The motors were designed to operate at a maximum of 1,000 volts, so that, when running at full speed, the four groups, each consisting of three motors, operated in series.

These locomotives develop a maximum horsepower of 3,517. They have required comparatively few alterations since being placed in service and have proved most satisfactory on the Coast Division.

Four switching locomotives are in service on the electri-

Courtesy of C.R.I.&P.R.R.

CHICAGO, ROCK ISLAND & PACIFIC'S DIESEL ELECTRIC NO. 629, built by the General Electric Company, hauling the westbound Rocky Mountain Rocket No. 7, en route to Denver, Colorado, near Wyanet, Illinois.

Courtesy of Florida East Coast Ry.

THE ATLANTIC COAST LINE'S ALL-COACH LUXURY STREAMLINER, THE CHAMPION NO. 1, southbound on the Florida East Coast Railway, crossing the Saint Lucie River, near Stuart, Florida. Diesel built by Electro-Motive Company.

fied divisions, each weighing 164,000 pounds. These locomotives, built by American Locomotive and General Electric, are of the double-truck or 0-4-4-0 type, with a central cab. They have geared motors of a combined capacity, on an hourly rating, of 670 horsepower and develop a maximum starting tractive force of 41,000 pounds.

Some years ago the railroad company issued a report covering the results obtained with electrification up to that time. This report was in the form of an exhaustive study and presented a large amount of valuable information.

It showed that the total cost of the facilities provided for electrical operation was about $23,000,000, as compared to $7,400,000 for the steam plant formerly used. However, the operating cost with electricity was so much less than with steam that, even allowing for increased interest and depreciation charges, electrical operation at that time showed a net saving of $1,271,793, as compared with steam operation.

Fifty-nine electric locomotives handled a volume of business which would have required 166 steam locomotives. The fuel saved during the year amounted to approximately 32,600,000 gallons of oil and 237,000 tons of coal.

From the beginning of electrical operation in 1916 to the close of 1924, reports showed that the total net saving effected by electrification amounted to $12,400,000. In working up this figure, all costs were adjusted to those obtaining in 1923.

In mountain railroading, one of the greatest advantages possessed by the electric locomotive, as compared with the steam engine, is the ability of the former to regenerate on descending grades. This is accomplished by reversing the action of the motors and using them as generators, thus forcing energy back into the line and assisting other trains that are on ascending grades. If the power developed while regenerating cannot be used in this way, it is returned to the mains of the power company, and the railroad is credited accordingly.

In handling passenger traffic over mountain grades, a notable feature is the smoothness with which the train is operated and controlled. A practically constant speed can be maintained on both the ascent and descent, and there is no running in and out of slack or grinding of brakes.

In steam operation the speed of a descending train is of necessity controlled by train brakes, resulting in a great deal of wear on brake shoes and car wheels. The principle of an electric train coming down a grade might be compared to that of the control of an automobile when the driver drops into second gear. If it is necessary to bring this electric train to a stop, the air brakes must, of course, be used after the speed has been reduced to a point where regeneration is no longer possible. Enginemen have attained to a high degree of skill in handling the train brakes in combination with the regenerative feature.

Under former steam operation, a large amount of helper service was necessary in handling passenger traffic, but this has been almost entirely dispensed with, as the electric locomotives handle practically all through trains over the steepest grades without helpers.

From an operating point of view, the advantages of electrification are most apparent in the handling of freight traffic.

As compared with steam operation, the tonnage per train has been practically doubled, as well as the speed on ascending grades, while the absence of wear and tear on the brake equipment, due to the regenerating feature, greatly reduces maintenance and at the same time increases the safety of operation. Furthermore, when the electric locomotives are properly handled, heavy-tonnage trains can be started more smoothly than with steam locomotives, greatly reducing the liability of break-in-twos and damaged draft gears.

Trains weighing 4,500 to 5,000 tons, frequently made up of 100 or more cars, are moved over the steepest grades with one road locomotive and two helpers. The latter are cut into the train and are so located that each locomotive has approximately one third of the tonnage back of it. After making an ascent it is the regular practice to keep the helpers in the train on the succeeding downgrade, so that they can assist in controlling the train by regeneration.

Co-operation on the part of the engineman on the road locomotive and the helpers is essential if heavy-tonnage trains are to be started and stopped without serious shocks or damage to equipment. By watching the ammeter in the cab, which indicates the load on the motors, and observing the slack action of the cars adjacent to the locomotive, the skilled engineman can make a start without slipping the drivers or transmitting heavy shocks to the train. This is constantly demonstrated on the electrified sections of the Milwaukee road.

On both the Rocky Mountain and the Coast divisions it is the practice to run passenger and freight locomotives through, changing crews at what were formerly intermediate locomotive terminals.

Passenger locomotives average about 7,000 miles a month, and there are frequent instances where individual locomotives exceed 10,000 miles a month. If the traffic were more dense, the monthly mileage could be easily increased.

As with steam locomotives, the electrics are subject to Interstate Commerce Commission inspection. Repairs and replacements are, of course, made when necessary, but it is not the practice to give the electric locomotives classified repairs at regular intervals. Some of these locomotives have made as much as 500,000 miles without a general overhauling. All the repair work on the locomotives operating on the Rocky Mountain Division is done at Deer Lodge, Montana; the locomotives operating on the Coast Division are maintained by the shop at Tacoma, Washington. Both shops are equipped to handle not only the mechanical parts but the electrical apparatus as well. Much of this work is very exacting, requiring special equipment and men thoroughly trained to handle it. A few spare armatures and other parts are kept in stock, ready for immediate application to a locomotive, as the repairs to such equipment often take a long time for completion.

In addition to maintaining the electrical locomotives, the shops at Deer Lodge and Tacoma handle a considerable amount of steam-locomotive work. Particularly is this true of the Tacoma shop, which maintains the steam locomotives used on the Idaho Division and on the branch lines of the Coast Division.

The main line of the Idaho Division, which is interposed between the two electrified divisions, extends from Avery, Idaho, to Othello, Washington, a distance of 225.7 miles. The Idaho Division, which also includes several important branch lines, is operated entirely by steam locomotives.

CHAPTER VI

Diesel-Electric Streamliner

DIESEL-ELECTRIC MOTIVE POWER, like the neighborhood brat in pigtails, grew up without attracting any particular attention of a favorable nature. And then, all at once, folks were rubbing their eyes at sight of a sleek, slim-hipped platinum blonde—an alluring young thing—crashing the stiff portals of high railroad aristocracy.

A great many years ago there were gasoline-driven motor units propelling noisome and jolty cars in outlying districts and providing service of a kind for local residents.

We then became aware of bobtailed trains on small branch and suburban lines of the steam roads. They had husky-voiced air horns and trundled into town to the accompaniment of the familiar *punka-punk, punka-punk* of internal combustion engines. Folks said, "Here comes the Galloping Goose." Or perhaps it was the Hinky Dink, or the Bungaloo. Their motive power was a combination of Diesel engine and electric motor.

In the meantime Yankee brains were once more hard at work, and powerful Diesel-electric units were engineered. Dr. Oskar Tietjens, of the Westinghouse Research Laboratories, began fooling around with train models in a wind tunnel.

And then this railroad brat, like Cinderella, the scullery maid, acquired a new dress and went to a party, where she met a charming Prince. The Prince was really a hard-bitten individual, more commonly known by the name of John Q. Public. John promptly fell for this silver-clad Cinderella, little dreaming then that the lady was on her way to setting the world—the railroad world—afire with her motif modern.

Meanwhile, a lot of the highborn ladies of the clan of the iron horse uttered a few hoots and sneers, indulged in a little roundhouse and back-shop gossip; then rushed away to take a beauty treatment themselves. In fact, a lot of them fell all over each other in attempting to copy this new dame's latest style creation.

And, all opinion to the contrary notwithstanding, they really did a job of it; for there is nothing under the sun as stunning and blood-pulsingly alive as a streamlined steam locomotive. The Empire State Express will take your breath away, as will the Broadway Limited, the Century, the Hiawatha, the Daylight, and the Chief east of La Junta, Colorado.

The Union Pacific sent a dazzling Diesel-electric streamlined train flashing down the iron road. Came the Burlington Zephyrs; the Boston & Maine's Flying Yankee; the Champion, of the Atlantic Coast Line, and others.

People became streamlined conscious, and a new era was born.

For a fine example of a modern Diesel-electric-hauled train, let us look at the present-day Florida Special. This beautiful speed queen is a justly eminent successor to the original Florida Special, which was inaugurated on January 9, 1888.

At that time it constituted the first all-Pullman, electric-lighted, vestibuled, and steam-heated train in the world. It was the first through train ever to be operated between New York and Florida.

In 1888 the southern terminal of the Florida Special was Jacksonville, Florida, which was reached in slightly more than thirty-one hours—and that, fifty-four years ago, was breath-taking speed.

Ever since its inception, the Florida Special has set the standard of trains for Florida-resort travel, and today its late-styled counterpart continues to set the pace.

In reality there are three Florida Specials in daily operation over the Atlantic Coast Line Railroad. In addition to the first east-coast Special, there is the Florida Special of the west coast, running between New York, St. Petersburg, Tampa, Sarasota, Orlando, Fort Myers, and other interior and west-coast points.

There is then that section of the Florida Special in operation between Boston and the South. These three Specials combine to provide accommodations for more than five thousand passengers a week, or about thirty-five times as many as did that original train of 1888.

The schedule is approximately twice as fast as it was then, as the Florida Specials whirl chilled northerners to the land of sunshine and palms deep down that great peninsula of perpetual summer. Smooth and fast they ride over double-tracked, rock-ballasted roadbed, protected by block signals all the way, and with electric train control over most of the distance.

Between New York and Washington, these Florida Specials are powered by Pennsylvania Railroad electric engines, previously described. South of Washington, the motive power is provided by Diesel-electric engines. These sleek locomotives represent the last word in sturdy and dependable power plants. There are two types in the Coast Line's Diesel fleet. "A-Units" are fitted with cab, nose, and headlights. "B-Units" are without these features but develop the same 2,000 horsepower.

"A-Units" are used in light trains requiring only one power unit. "B-Units" are used in connection with "A-Units" to make up the "engine" where two or more units are required to handle heavier trains. (The Interstate Commerce Commission has ruled that, regardless of the number of units pulling a train, the motive power shall be called or classed as "the engine.")

Each Diesel unit is basically an independent power plant, generating its own electric current and using this electrical power in its own traction motors to pull the train.

Each unit has two 12-cylinder Diesel engines, generating and developing 2,000 horsepower, or 1,000 horsepower apiece. This power is applied to the moving train through two traction motors on each truck. There are two trucks for each Diesel-electric unit.

Each unit is equipped with an oil-fired boiler for heating and air-conditioning the cars and for providing hot water for the passengers. The boiler is fitted with a photoelectric eye which keeps an automatic watch on the fire in the boiler furnace. Another essential mechanism is the air-pressure pump and the apparatus for the application of train brakes.

An instrument board in the cab enables the engineman to tell at a glance the train-operating conditions.

Each locomotive is equipped with a steam-ejector, water-transfer system. By the manipulation of valves either locomotive unit can be filled by drawing water from the other or from the baggage-car tank, provided that the anti-freezing drain valve is closed and the pump valve is open in the baggage car.

All units are under multiple control and are operated by the engineman.

The brake equipment is of the electro-pneumatic type, and the engineman can change over to the automatic pneumatic brake by the operation of a small lever on the automatic brake valve. In either application, brake pressure can be reduced or released on the locomotive by manipulating the independent brake valve.

In an emergency application of brakes, wheels on forward locomotive are sanded automatically. In making a service application, sand can be applied by depressing the handle of the automatic brake valve; and sand can be applied to the rail at any time by pressing the bail on the automatic valve.

The engineman keeps his foot on the "dead man" pedal at all times when the train is running. This is a further safety feature, for, should the engineman die suddenly or become incapacitated, releasing the pressure on this pedal would instantly cause the application of the train brakes.

The control room is equipped with a system of lights and an alarm bell which immediately notify the engineman when trouble develops in any part of the equipment. Hot journals, an overheating engine, low oil pressure, steam-generator failure, etc., are promptly indicated in the cab.

The engineman also has a call bell close at hand by which he can summon the fireman should the latter be attending to duties back in the motor compartment.

An electrical maintainer makes up the third member of the crew on this Diesel-electric locomotive.

Before slipping away from New York, let us take a look at the equipment of this limited, sunshine-bound.

First behind the big electric engine, here in the Pennsylvania Station, is a well-equipped dormitory car, with berths for the dining-car crews and staterooms for the stewards. Next is a full-length baggage car; then a ten-section Pullman with two drawing rooms. There are two Pullmans of fourteen sections each; an eight-section Pullman with three drawing rooms; a lounge car, with a drawing room and three compartments. There are two dining cars and a recreation-entertainment car. Come then a six-compartment Pullman, with three drawing rooms; an eight-section Pullman, with drawing room and three double bedrooms; a fourteen-section Pullman; and, finally, a ten-section Pullman with an observation end.

The recreation-entertainment car deserves special mention, because it is to be found only on the Atlantic Coast Line Railroad—or was the only one when this was written. The car is a masterpiece of decorative art and is equipped with comfortable movable seats. There are musicians to entertain the traveler. Tables are provided for bridge and other games. A train hostess contributes much toward making the trip a pleasant one, particularly for women traveling alone, or for women with children.

Frigid blasts are lashing New York; snow is falling. The streets are slippery with a brown slush. Passengers board the Florida Special bundled in great coats and furs. We hear the conductor calling "All aboard!" Vestibule doors close, and this big, all-Pullman train gets under way. We rush through the tunnel beneath the Hudson. Newark, Trenton, and industrial New Jersey make up the panorama of our going.

We are in Philadelphia almost before we know it and come to a stop in the Pennsylvania Station at Thirtieth Street.

The lights of Baltimore gleam in the evening dusk. Snow is still falling, mantling the world. Once more we are moving to the urge of that big GG-1 electric locomotive and its better than 4,000 horsepower, and traveling fast.

Then the brakes ease us to a stop in the great Washington Union Terminal. Men move in quickly to break the couplings up ahead, and now a huge Diesel-electric engine slides up to take the Florida Special in charge. This engine will haul us all the way from Washington to Miami.

Highball! Smoothly we start to roll, threading through the tunnel, with Capitol Hill somewhere above us. Now we glimpse the lights of Potomac Park, gleaming there like diamond dust. Darkly the waters of the Potomac flow beneath us, carrying wavy streamers of reflected lights.

This is Virginia now, and from the east windows of our Pullman we have our last look at the dome of our nation's Capitol.

Deep night. The Diesel-electric whirls us on across the Carolinas, across a corner of Georgia, in our magic flight. Dawn cracks open a black world, and new, strange vistas unfold. It is still snowing in New York. Muffled men are clearing the streets. There are frosted panes and icicles in that far-away North.

From the windows of the flying Florida Special golden sunlight gleams on stiffly marching long-leaf pines. Palmetto leaves sway to a soft, warm breeze. Pickaninnies wave at us, and we know that this is the deep South. Winter seems a million miles away as we come to a stop in the Jacksonville Union Terminal.

Again this speed queen rolls on. The sand and pines of the Florida landscape are rushing past. There are more palmettos now. The vegetation of the Temperate Zone has given away to semitropical.

Here is St. Augustine, the cradle of white civilization in the United States. This, the oldest city, still carries many traces of its ancient Spanish origin and is the mecca yearly for thousands of sight-seers. We are told that each year more visitors come to this ancient city than annually view the Statue of Liberty.

We pause at Daytona Beach, a year-round resort, with

beaches almost as crowded in July and August as at the peak of the winter season in January and February.

From Jacksonville we have been traveling on the tracks of the Florida East Coast Railway. The big Diesel is moving easily but swiftly on a rock-ballasted roadbed. Fort Pierce, and the first cocoanut palm. West Palm Beach, and off there across the blue waters of Lake Worth the one and only Palm Beach.

Fort Lauderdale, resort and beach town, and, beyond the shore line, the warm waters of the Gulf Stream. Hollywood and suburban Miami. Miami itself now, and the crushed shell walks of the Florida East Coast Station, gleaming whitely in the sunshine of the Florida afternoon.

We alight and walk up past the purple-and-silver Diesel-electric engine that has wheeled us south so effortlessly. Tomorrow morning at eight o'clock it will be ready to pick up the task of that northbound run to Washington.

This is, indeed, a modern miracle of fast railroad transportation. For in twenty-four hours we have been delivered from the teeth of a blizzard in the making and set down in a flower-bowered world that for tropical beauty outrivals Tahiti of the South Pacific.

Twenty-four hours! Except for that haul by the electric motive power of the Pennsylvania, this Diesel-electric engine has transported us all the way from North to South with never an instant's hesitancy. This, then, is the princess of flight, the new member of the American railroads' royal family.

CHAPTER VII

Diesel-Electric Freight Hauler of the Santa Fe

FAST FREIGHT was not to be denied a part in this whirl of modernism. Came at last the Big Brother of the trim streamliners. Creeds and dogmas went by the board, and out of the yards at Shopton, Iowa, a night in February 1941, glided Diesel-electric freight engine No. 100, flying the banner of the Santa Fe.

Romance has cloaked the Santa Fe Trail always—the Trail of Holy Faith, so named by the padres, the brown-frocked priests who had left their footprints across the Southwest over a hundred years before the Confederation of the New England colonies.

The pueblo of Santa Fe had been founded 171 years when the Declaration of Independence was signed. It seems, then, entirely fitting that the Santa Fe railroad should pioneer the unveiling of a huge Diesel-electric locomotive, dedicated to the hauling of fast freight.

For this is the first regular road freight trip on any American line—the first freight train to be wheeled swiftly across the long miles by Diesel power.

Train crews on American railroads go about the day's work with a matter-of-fact disregard for frills and sentiment. With them there is a job to be done, and its accomplishment is an accepted fact before they highball out.

Here is a train of three thousand tons of freight to be moved, or perhaps it is a passenger train's job, with mail and express and two or three hundred passengers. Cars are rolling, night after night, day in and day out—across endless prairies, over dizzy trestles, across rockbound reaches of mountain iron.

Tonight the moon casts its sheen on the rails. Tonight the headlight is cutting a ghostly cone in blinding snow.

Railroad men, cool, competent. Steel-nerved, tight-lipped, these sons of the railroad. And yet now, aboard locomotive No. 100, of the Santa Fe, you sense a new feeling of tenseness. Nerves are wound just a little tighter. Eyes are fired with hope and determination, as were the straining eyes of those conquistadores of long ago.

Among these men, from the division trainmaster in the cab to the last brakeman, a new something is smoldering. The road foreman of engines put it into words when he said:

"History is in the making tonight!"

There was no symbolic turning of that first spade of earth; no golden spike hammered home. Here was simply a prosaic string of freight cars, coupled behind us—furniture and

Courtesy of Santa Fe Ry.

EASTBOUND SANTA FE FAST FREIGHT hauled by Engine 3173, 2-8-2 type, snapped from the cab of the Diesel hauling No. 11, Kansas Cityan, west of Marceline, Missouri.

Courtesy of Santa Fe Ry.

SANTA FE'S NEW 5,400-H.P. FREIGHT DIESEL-ELECTRIC LOCOMOTIVE built by the Electro-Motive Company, ascending Cajon Pass, California. Note the green fruit on the head end.

dishes, suits and overcoats, sugar and flour, canned goods—and bound for the Pacific coast.

The only foreign thing about this train was the dynamometer car, with its maze of intricate recording instruments and machines, manned by a crew of skilled technicians.

Squat little Diesel engines have long been proving their dependability and economy in switching operations. Those who had come to accept the streamliners and their Diesel-electric motor units as an established forward step in the world of transportation—these men were still skeptical about the substitution of an internal-combustion motor for the big, black dignity and well-nigh irresistible force of the high-pressure steam locomotive in freight service.

Locomotives of a type similar to No. 100 had been tested, up and down the land, for a full year or more. But now, for the first time, a Diesel-electric freight locomotive was going to have to prove her mettle.

No. 100 has a rating of 5,400 horsepower. It consists of four sections, each containing one 1,350-horsepower Diesel engine. The overall length is 193 feet. It stands 14 feet 1½ inches, rails to cab roof, and has a fuel capacity of 4,800 gallons.

The locomotive's starting tractive effort is 220,000 pounds, and its total weight, fully loaded, on the drivers is 923,600 pounds.

The welded car-body framing of No. 100 is of bridge-construction type. At the cab end the collision framing above the platform consists of a combination of posts, plates, and braces. The large front posts are fastened to the platform and a deep anti-telescoping plate, the ends of which tie into heavy diagonal braces, and are anchored in the side framing.

The elevated cab-floor supports, the front bulkhead, and the rear partition members add strength to the front end. There are roof hatches for easy installation and removal of engines, generators, and other equipment.

The outside finish consists of panels of plywood covered with galvanneal steel. Underframe construction is supplemented by welded floor plates, acting as a foundation for anti-skid runways. Body center plates are of steel casting. Wear plates are applied to bottom and outside surfaces.

The control cab is over the front bolster. The floor is elevated above the platform to provide maximum vision. Front windows have windshield wipers and defrosters. Swivel, adjustable upholstered seats, with back and arm rests, are provided for the engineer and the fireman. The cab is soundproofed against the engine-room and track noises. Safety plate glass is used in windows and doors.

Each of the 1,350-horsepower engines is direct-connected to a 600-volt direct-current generator. A supplemental 10-kw. generator, for storage-battery charging, is mounted above and driven by V-belts from each main generator. The main generators are used as motors for engine starting. Each main generator feeds four direct-current roller-bearing-equipped motors directly geared to driving axles. Motors are cooled by clean air delivered from blowers.

The cooling system for the engines consists of two 200-gallon-per-minute engine-driven water pumps and forced air circulation through radiators in the ceiling. Each engine has a separate water-supply system with a capacity of 225 gallons.

And this is the Big Brother of the Diesel-driven streamliners, waiting now at the head of 60 loaded freight cars—3,150 tons. We are waiting for the highball, waiting once more to prove that fast freight is king of railroads, but this time with a new Diesel-electric freight engine.

Spread around us are the vast freight yards of the Santa Fe—the Kansas City freight yards at Argentine, Kansas. Pale faces are there, winking lanterns, signal lights—a thousand smoldering eyes. Colored eyes—red, green, purple.

Comes at last the flash of an official lantern—high, over, and back in its brief, jerky arc. We have been aware of the steady, low throb of the Diesels. Now the tone changes to a deeper note; the pulse quickens. No. 100 is moving. There is the clank and clatter of slack running out; car wheels are turning. The train is rolling.

The headlight's silver beam points the way down the rails toward the far horizons of the Pacific coast—1,782 miles away.

No. 100 has exactly 28 minutes' leeway on the Super Chief, passenger-train pride of the Santa Fe—the Super Chief that will be thundering on our tail at 80 miles an hour; the speed queen with superior rights, proud of her ability to "run on the advertised"—hold her breath-taking schedule.

It is a cardinal sin for a train made inferior by class or direction to knock out—delay—a fast limited train like the Super Chief, and every man aboard No. 100 is fully aware of it.

The question is, can No. 100, hauling 3,150 tons of general freight, make Emporia, 108 miles away, ahead of the Super Chief? Nobody on No. 100 wanted to have this fast freight humbled by crawling "into the hole"—taking a siding—for the flying streamliner behind us.

So those 5,400 work horses of the No. 100 strained into their collars, fiercely determined to show a clean pair of rear marker lights to the pride of the Santa Fe.

No cracking thunder of an exhaust tonight, no battling roar from a squat stack splitting the heavens, no whipping side rods, no white plume waving at the dome. Instead, a mounting roar from the motor compartments—Diesel power, churning up electric energy in those 600-volt generators. Fluid forces, invisible but with the awesome energy of lightning, spilling brute strength into those big motors geared to the driving axles.

No. 100 was out to show the world that Diesel-electric power has what it takes, not, perhaps, to move mountains, but to bat fast freight across the plains and the Continental Divide between the Big Muddy and the Coast.

No. 100 went to work, smashing at grades, tearing around curves, streaking down long tangents at speeds ranging up to 60 miles an hour. Men in cab and caboose thumbed their watches, anxiously watched the signal lights ahead, and visioned the nearing glare of the headlight on the Super Chief, whipping time behind us.

No. 100 cleared the Super Chief at Emporia with exactly eight minutes to spare, which is shaving it pretty fine, if we look too closely at the book of rules. But we were there, and never once had the streamliner caught even a faint cautionary glimmer on a signal behind us.

There was never any question of power on that long, mauling grind. Always the grades of the Great Plains were lifting, climbing higher toward the Continental Divide, but the No. 100 took them in stride.

Where the practice had always been to double-head trains pulled by steam locomotives, No. 100 had no trouble at all in pulling those 60 loaded cars.

Once Chief Engineer Dilworth, of the Electro-Motive Corporation, builder of No. 100, announced that one of the motors was "sick." What he meant was that one of the 1,350-horsepower engines of the No. 100's four power units was out of commission.

Repairs were made while we traveled at close to top speed. With a quarter of its total power temporarily out, there was never a sign of limping, and the big Diesel carried on without the slightest trouble. An hour later the disabled engine was again in shape and was cut back in. From there on, all was serene in the well-lighted corridors of the locomotive units.

Particular interest centered around the operation of the new retarding brakes. To the layman, the big problem in railroad operation is, perhaps, the hauling of heavy trains up long, steep grades. The railroad operating man, however, knows that the retarding of the movement of a train on a downgrade is equally important—perhaps more important.

The cost to the railroad in worn wheels, worn brake shoes, and lost time in general in downgrade operation is enormous. Possibly no single invention was of so great help to a railroad as that of the air brake. Nevertheless, while the air brake reduced the manual labor of retardation and its hazards, it did not reduce the cost.

The designers of No. 100 attacked the problem from a new angle. So powerful and efficient a hauler as the great Diesel locomotive, they reasoned, ought also in some manner be made to take care of the braking job. It is common knowledge that the compression of an automobile engine can be used to hold the speed in check on downgrades, and something of the kind might be worked out in the Diesel-electric locomotive, the engineers decided.

Indeed, this was already being done on electric locomotives operating from power lines. We have seen an example of it on the Chicago, Milwaukee, St. Paul and Pacific Railroad. Here this was accomplished by reversing the action of the motors and making generators out of them. Of course, the electrical energy thus developed had to be taken care of. As has been explained, in electrified territory the practice was merely to feed this excess energy back into the power line itself.

However, a Diesel-electric locomotive does not have such means at its disposal. It has been demonstrated how the Diesel-electric engines turn generators, which, in turn, feed power to the motors connected with the wheels. It was a simple matter to disconnect the motors from the generators and reverse their action, thus making generators out of them. The problem was what to do with the power thus generated.

This was solved by building into the roof of No. 100 huge resistance grids. Into these was fed that surplus power, and our electric brake was in service. True, these grids became hot, and this heat had to be dissipated. This was done by means of a fan blowing air over and through the grids.

Much interest centered around this new type of brake on the initial run of No. 100. The first real test came in the early morning, as the train dropped down the grade from Mountainair to Belen, New Mexico. Here the right-of-way falls about 1,700 feet in a little over 40 miles. The descending grades for 26 of these miles is 1.27 per cent.

There was a tenseness as the engineman first threw in the retarding brake. This was constructed so that there were two stages of braking operation. The first position of the brake is at 30 miles an hour; the second at 20 miles an hour.

This second stage of the electric brake was first cut in at a speed of 15 miles an hour. When the speed of the train increased to 23 miles, a warning light flashed, notifying the engineer that the automatic brake must be used to assist in retarding the train.

With the speed of the train choked down to about 15 miles an hour, the automatic brake was released. The first position of the electric brake was then cut in. Gradually the speed increased to 30 miles an hour, at which speed the brake is designed to hold the train. Only once or twice in the 40 miles of descent was it necessary to use the automatic air brake to assist the electric brake in controlling the speed of the train.

There were other severe tests: 23 miles of downgrade from Louise to Yucca; 19 miles between Supai and Ash Fork, Arizona, where the right-of-way drops 1,806 feet at an average of 1.8 per cent.

And then the stiffest test of all—22.5 miles of 2.2 per cent grade from Summit to San Bernardino, California. Here, as earlier, the performance of the electric brake was all that could be asked. Not once had this method of braking failed to measure up to expectations, which speaks well for the engineers who designed it.

For the entire trip, the brakes were in operation over a distance of 83 miles, about 5 per cent of the total distance from the Argentine yards to Los Angeles, California. When in operation, they generated from 2,500 to 2,750 horsepower, which was dissipated through the grids into the desert and mountain air.

The saving of wear and tear on wheels and brake shoes had been great. Where normally the heavy freight drags had had to stop periodically to permit wheels to cool—where sometimes on dark nights the wheels glowed cherry red—the wheels of the cars behind the No. 100 never got over a few degrees warmer than the surrounding atmosphere. Consequently never was it necessary to replace worn brake shoes.

Fifty-three hours was the running time of the No. 100 and its train from the Argentine yards to Los Angeles—1,782 miles. The maximum speed was 65 miles an hour; the average 33.6 miles an hour. And that is wheeling long-distance fast freight with a vengeance.

The train consisted of cars varying in numbers from 49 to 68—plus the business cars and the dynamometer test car.

In terms of work done at the drawbar, the No. 100 exerted 197,600,000 foot-pounds. For the run, 10,750 gallons of fuel oil were used, at an average cost of 4½ cents a gallon. Comparing this performance with that of steam locomotives over the same distance, and hauling the same tonnage, the cost of fuel for the Diesel would be considerably less.

On the regular freight runs between Chicago and the Coast, nine steam locomotives are used. These make eighteen or nineteen stops for fuel, and from thirty-four to thirty-six stops for water. From the Kansas City yards, No. 100 made but five stops for fuel. Water was added to the radiators at these points, but actually the run could have been made without adding water. And this is important on the long desert runs where water must be conditioned, and where, not infrequently, it must be hauled long miles by tank cars.

Without a doubt, the running time and the fine performance of the No. 100 presages a further cut in the freight running time between Chicago and the Pacific coast, and this is of tremendous importance, not only in the handling of general freight but also in the rush of the fruit trains.

Ten of these big Diesel-electric freight haulers are now operating or under construction, with an additional ten on order.

In viewing the rapid advance made by various transportation agencies, it is often asserted that the airplane is faster than the railroad; that busses and trucks are more flexible, and that the barge lines can haul greater loads. On the face of them, these statements are true.

However, the railroad still stands as the only agency in the country that can pick up some 3,000 tons of freight and move it over 1,700 miles in one fell swoop in 53 hours.

True, this was only a test run, but the flight of Diesel-electric locomotive No. 100 between Kansas City and Los Angeles marks the passing of another milepost in fast freight hauling and the dawn of a new day for through-tonnage trains. And the Santa Fe is now making runs like this a daily occurrence.

CHAPTER VIII

The Pacific Fruit Express

THE DEVELOPMENT OF TRANSPORTATION in America is nowhere more strikingly illustrated than in the shipment of perishables, conceived in 1885 with a few experimental carloads of strawberries and oranges, and now grown to such a volume that today over 360,000 carloads of fresh fruits and vegetables are moved annually from the Pacific coast alone to eastern markets, and under conditions not duplicated or even approached in any other part of the world.

Nowhere else does any district of intensified production attempt to spread its products over a continental area and make them conveniently available to over 125,000,000 people. In no other branch of agriculture would failure of transportation bear so heavily on the grower, mainly because of the perishable nature of the produce.

Four transcontinental railroads, the Southern Pacific, Santa Fe, Union Pacific, and Western Pacific, handle this perishable-freight movement, which begins with cantaloupes from the Imperial Valley of California and Salt River Valley of Arizona in the spring and summer, reaches its height with the grapes from the San Joaquin Valley in the late summer and autumn, and continues through the winter months with orange and lettuce shipments.

These are the heavier crops, moving through the greater part of the year. In addition to these there are many other vegetables, mainly celery, asparagus, carrots, peas, beans, cauliflower, and even fresh flowers, which are handled in iced express cars.

The rapid transportation of these perishables creates a complicated and stupendous problem and involves an elaborate system of handling. And once more fast freight—this time long-distance fast freight—plays a prominent part.

Already we have had a glimpse of the Union Pacific's Big Boy wheeling a long train of yellow reefers across the Wasatch Mountains. This train was one of the fruit blocks. However, before we travel east with one of these Red Ball trains, let us first see what happens before this green fruit highballs for those distant markets.

As the various crops begin to ripen, pickers swarm over the fields. Swarthy Mexican families, making their livelihood "following the fruit," arrive in overburdened flivvers and set to work.

Carloads of box shooks are piled high in the packing sheds. The busy hammers of crate makers pound incessantly as these boxes are put together. Switch engines work endlessly. Buyers from eastern markets are busy bargaining, buying, rejecting. The packing centers are a beehive of activity.

The Santa Fe has developed a special Refrigerator Department, organized for the purpose of providing adequate and efficient protective service for the handling of these crops. The railroad owns over 18,500 refrigerator cars. In addition there are icing plants and many special facilities peculiar to the swift and efficient handling and prompt dispatch of perishable freight.

At San Bernardino, California—often referred to as "Santa Fe Town"—are located the railroad's classification yard, pre-cooling plant, "reefer" sheds, car and locomotive shops, and various other units that comprise the system's western terminal facilities.

The Pacific Fruit Express, organized in 1906, and owned jointly by the Southern Pacific and the Union Pacific systems, furnishes refrigerator cars for these roads and the Western Pacific. Today the Pacific Fruit Express has some 40,800 refrigerator cars, with shops located in Idaho, California, and Arizona.

Typical of these shops is the one at Roseville, California, situated at the foot of the western slope of the Sierra Nevadas, where the rails of the Southern Pacific and the Western Pacific begin the climb over this mountain iron.

Roseville is strategically located at the junction of the great Sacramento and San Joaquin valleys, which extend north and south through the heart of vast fruit-growing districts. The plant here is used exclusively for the rebuilding and repairing of refrigerator cars, and covers an area of 110 acres, with over seventeen miles of trackage.

In addition to its refrigerator cars and shops, the Pacific

Fruit Express owns eighteen ice-manufacturing plants, together with several natural-ice plants, which have a possible production capacity of 2,000,000 tons of ice annually.

A typical refrigerator car weighs about 52,000 pounds and has a carrying capacity of approximately 32 tons. Walls, floors, roof, and doors are all heavily insulated. The prevailing method of obtaining refrigeration is by means of naturally circulated air, cooled either by contact with ice or a mixture of ice and salt contained in ice bunkers located at each end of the car.

Air circulation is assisted by bulkheads so placed in front of the ice bunkers that the relatively warm air passes over the top to reach the ice; then, becoming chilled and therefore heavier, it sinks toward the floor, where it reaches the body of the car by passing through a space beneath the bulkheads.

Before a refrigerator car is delivered to a packing shed or loading station, it is first pre-cooled with slightly over five tons of ice placed in the bunkers at each end. This pre-cooling is an important feature, as the fruit has a normal temperature of about 80 degrees when brought from the field, and considerably higher during summer months.

If the field heat is not promptly withdrawn, the ripening process continues at an accelerated pace. If this was not checked the fruit would either spoil en route or reach its destination in such a condition that the market value would be greatly reduced.

The extraction of the field heat rapidly melts the ice in the bunkers, and for this reason it is imperative that loaded cars be switched promptly to an assembling point, where they are classified, re-iced, and made up into solid trains, often of 100 cars or more.

Our rolling icebox, loaded with perishable fruit, is now ready to start for the eastern markets, and it is dispatched on fast schedules with a precision equal to that of passenger-train service.

According to the railroad's agreement with the shipper, his car will arrive at Chicago the seventh day after loading. From the Imperial Valley, the schedule is one day shorter, and from Arizona, two days. This is a big accomplishment, in that the work must be carried on in all kinds of weather, and it necessitates the co-operation and co-ordination of large staffs of trained men and equipment costing nearly half a billion dollars.

Fresh fruit and vegetables must arrive at their various destinations as crisp and fresh as when they left the fields and groves. The rush of perishables over 3,000 miles to market is one of the major problems of the railroads. Failure to maintain those hot-shot schedules may result in serious loss.

An example of the magnitude of this train movement is revealed by the fact that as many as 111 trains have passed through the Southern Pacific yards at Roseville in a single day.

Roseville boasts the largest refrigeration-icing station in the world. Here there are platforms and equipment capable of icing 254 cars at one time. During the peak year of 1929 it required 200,000 tons, or 400,000,000 pounds, of ice to take care of shipments moving through that gate alone.

The cars must be iced quickly and efficiently, for every

minute counts heavily. After a train has been spotted at the icing plant, the operation consists of opening the hatch covers, removing the hatch plugs, and chopping down the ice crust that may have formed with long bars. New ice is then packed in until there is barely enough space for the hatch plugs.

A foreman and his several assistants go over the train then, making a final inspection before closing down the hatch covers. An inspector on the ground moves along the train, checking the drains and seeing that the doors are properly closed and sealed. An average of one minute a car is allowed for the icing operation, although the actual time is frequently less than fifty seconds, and there have been occasions when eighty cars or more have been re-iced in twenty to twenty-five minutes.

The business of the railroad is more than simply picking up a train of fruit and delivering it at some distant destination, for a shipper of perishables receives a great deal of special service. For example, the railroad will allow him to change the destination of the car while in transit. A shipper can divert a car four times without paying for the privilege. The changing of the billing of a single carload five or ten times is not uncommon, and there have been instances of twenty-five or more successive changes. The reason for this is to avoid flooded markets and to allow the car to be diverted to points where there is a greater demand for the shipment and, consequently, higher prices.

The quality of this diversion and reconsignment work is maintained at a high standard always, and it has been systema-

Photo by W. H. Thrall, Jr.

SANTA FE'S EXTRA 3831, 2-10-2 TYPE, hauling an eastbound green-fruit block on the second district of the Arizona Division west of Daggett, California.

Courtesy of Union Pacific R.R.

UNION PACIFIC'S NO. 4000, 4-8-8-4 TYPE, world's largest locomotive, built by the American Locomotive Company. Takes water at the coaling station at Evanston, Wyoming.

tized to the last degree of perfection, necessitating, as it does, the prompt location of cars rolling in all parts of the country. It requires the utilization of the telegraph, the telephone, and special messenger service.

A further service of vast importance to consignees is the notification of the arrival or passing of a car at certain points en route.

When a carload of fruit is turned over to the railroad, this fruit becomes the nursling of the carrier. If the weather is hot, the car must be cooled. If the weather is cold, there must be precautions against freezing.

A fruit train may leave California under summer conditions. However, before reaching Chicago cold and frigid temperatures may be encountered and heaters may have to replace the ice in those bunkers.

Every minute of the journey the temperature must be watched with the same solicitude a mother shows for a newborn babe. Carriers maintain regular and emergency icing stations along the route. At certain points cars are opened and the fruit is given a careful inspection.

Sometimes the weather conditions or a desire to change the condition of the contents of the car make it advantageous to have the perishables "top-iced." The car is then switched out and set in at the top-icing platform. Here machines shave the ice into snow, and this is blown over the load in the car, burying it under a snow bank six to eight inches in depth.

The fruit traffic is of such importance and demands such rigid observance of schedules, icing, and reconsigning en route that the railroads have entered into certain carefully observed agreements, to the end that unfair and destructive competition is entirely eliminated.

Let us look at the schedules observed by the Southern Pacific / Rock Island lines between Colton, California, a Coast concentration point, and Chicago. The time is 139 hours and 30 minutes, based on the departing time from Colton at 3:00 A.M. and arrival at Chicago at 12:30 A.M. the seventh day. This insures a 3:00-A.M. delivery to the Chicago Fruit Auction, and 3:30-A.M. delivery on the "Team Tracks." It further insures a 4:00-A.M. delivery to intermediate switching tracks for outbound 7:00-A.M. trains of eastern lines and provides ninth-morning delivery on Atlantic seaboard points.

A faster schedule is provided for trains leaving the Colton zone after 3:00 A.M. This is known as the "16-hour run-off schedule." As its name implies, this schedule provides for trains leaving the concentration point as much as sixteen hours after the basic-schedule train departure at 3:00 A.M. the first day, but arriving at Chicago for the same delivery as the basic-schedule train.

These later trains consequently must run much faster than the first train; the minimum schedule being 123 hours and 30 minutes, and insuring arrival on the same time the seventh morning. Further, this run-off must be completed before the trains arrive at Kansas City, as this is a point where part of the traffic is delivered to eastern connections.

The same situation, as concerns guaranteed schedules, prevails on traffic originating in the Imperial Valley and Yuma, Arizona, districts. However, here the minimum schedule on the run-off blocks is 103 hours and 30 minutes, compared with the basic schedule of 109 hours and 30 minutes.

From the Salt River Valley districts of Arizona, with Phoenix as the concentration point, there is a basic schedule of 95 hours and 30 minutes, with a three-hour run-off, making the minimum schedule 92 hours and 30 minutes.

All of this perishable traffic, regardless of the origin or the hour at which it was started, is due in Chicago at 12:30 A.M., with the Colton perishable arriving on the seventh morning, the Imperial Valley on the sixth morning, and the Salt River Valley on the fifth morning.

There is also a very substantial seasonal movement of ripe tomatoes from the west coast of Mexico, which is received into the United States through the Nogales, Arizona, gateway. These trains go to Tucson, from which point they are handled by the regular fruit blocks and given the same schedule.

The Southern Pacific delivers these fruit trains to the Rock Island at Tucumcari, New Mexico, and they roll in at all hours of the day and night.

Tucumcari being an "off-going" junction point for the inbound carrier, an extensive recording must be made of waybills covering each car—in order that the delivery line may know just what their revenue is to be on the cars delivered.

In this day of fast transportation, the teletype and a machine called the "Recordak" play an important part. Waybills are run through the Recordak, which takes two pictures of both the front and the back of each waybill on a moving-picture film for future record.

Each of the loads in this train of perishables at Tucumcari now receives an individual symbol number. This is recorded by teletype and transmitted to the next receiving terminal, as well as to Kansas City, Chicago, and other possible points of destination.

Thus the receiver at any of these points is informed that certain perishables are leaving Tucumcari. He immediately knows at what time to expect this shipment. With this information at hand his sales organization can start selling the contents of the car, which, perhaps, has not as yet rolled out of Tucumcari, 1,137 miles away.

Let us say now that we have a car billed to Chicago, but the shipper decides that he wants to try the market at Minneapolis, Minnesota. In this case he instructs the carrier to add to the waybill, "Stop at Minneapolis." Although Minneapolis is out of the direct line to Chicago by 650 miles, this is contributed by the carrier as part of the modern method of distribution of perishable freight.

If the shipper decides to sell the car at Minneapolis, well and good. If, on the other hand, he belatedly finds it to his advantage to receive the car in Chicago, he simply orders the "Stop" removed from the waybill, and the car moves back into the direct line of haul and continues to its originally billed destination.

If a shipper finds the markets slow and the prices falling and desires to delay the arrival of the shipment, the carrier again comes to his aid and the car is diverted to a "slow schedule," which permits the shipment to be taken from the regular schedule and held at certain designated points for a total of seventy-two hours.

In the meantime, if the shipper is confronted by a sudden demand for the perishables in question he can immediately order the car taken from the slow schedule and rushed forward on the next hot shot.

Before all the cars of our train of perishables have been lined up in their proper current of traffic for their various destinations, the original train may have to be broken up into fifteen or twenty separate units.

Thus the final classification of the train may read as follows:

For:	Rock Island destinations	15 cars	7 switches
	Rock Island Road haul	24 cars	22 "
	Wabash Railroad haul	26 cars	13 "
	Missouri Pacific haul	15 cars	12 "
	Alton Railroad haul	13 cars	10 "
	Burlington haul	2 cars	2 "

So this train has been absorbed, while another one is being built up of the road hauls from the inbound train, plus the same class of traffic reaching the line from various connections.

When our Chicago train arrives at the Silvis Yard, 158 miles to the west, it receives a final going over. So that there may be no failure of the guaranteed train in making points east of Chicago, the perishable freight for the Indiana Harbor Belt Railroad (the line handling the bulk of perishables between the western and eastern roads at Chicago) is classified on the rear of the train.

This is done so that if the time is short on arrival at the Blue Island Yard the train does not have to pull into the yard, but stops at the point of connection with the Indiana Harbor Belt Railroad. Here those cars for the East are cut off and sent hurrying to be made into those limiteds of freight service bound for the Atlantic seaboard and way points. The balance of our fruit train from the Pacific coast then pulls into the yard for regular handling.

The housekeeper living in the populous middle-western and eastern states naturally gives little thought to the story behind that head of crisp lettuce or the cantaloupe she purchases at the neighborhood market. That it is there, and in good condition, is enough.

And yet the scene backstage has been one of sweat and toil, of perfect co-ordination of schedules and handling by American railroads, of thrills and high adventure.

Fruit pickers laboring in sweltering heat, hurrying trucks, puffing switch engines, tanned college men wrestling with heavy blocks of ice, busy clerks, trainmen and enginemen, hot telegraph wires, the fast-rolling wheels of long white and yellow reefers—all and more have played an important part in giving Mrs. Jones a fine assortment of fruits and vegetables from which to select her day's menu.

Fast freights at her service. Giant locomotives storming down the rail. The huge 4-8-8-2 type articulated engines of the Southern Pacific; mighty freight locomotives of the Union Pacific, the Santa Fe, the Rock Island. Fast freights of the Central and the Pennsylvania. The Merchant Prince.

CHAPTER IX

Handling Perishables on the Atlantic Coast Line, Southern Pacific, and Union Pacific

Endlessly they roll, a marching legion of our railroads, those reefer cars of the Fruit Express. Yellow trains with helper engines climbing toward the notched summit of El Cajon, hewn between the San Bernardino Mountains and the Sierra Madre Range; rushing cars pounding along the "Gila Monster Route," the "High, Dry, and Windy," between Yuma and Phoenix; crawling drags storming at the grades of the High Sierras; fleet northbound perishables wheeling swiftly over the Atlantic Coast Line from far down the lower Gulf coast.

In mid-January, deep on the Florida Peninsula, there begins the gathering operation which brings together one of the most notable railroad movements of fresh winter fruits and vegetables within the scope of present-day commerce.

Day after day various sections of the fruit trains make

what is one of the fastest-scheduled long-distance freight runs in the United States. Oranges and grapefruit which may have been on the trees in the vicinity of Fort Myers, Florida, on Sunday morning, in many instances, may be in the hands of New York consumers Thursday afternoon. Boston gets its Florida oranges and grapefruit one day later.

During the weeks and months that Florida is sending forward its tremendous production of citrus fruits, the Atlantic Coast Line maintains breath-taking schedules, as section after section roars north with clocklike precision.

Not only has the Atlantic Coast Line proved its ability as a carrier, but it has further aided in the pioneering of the production of citrus fruits and winter vegetables on a huge commercial scale on the Florida Peninsula.

Year by year, and step by step, it has expanded its services, as it has constantly speeded up the handling of the perishables of this rapidly expanding industry.

Let us watch the movement of a fruit train, making up at Fort Myers, close down to the Big Cypress Swamp. There are several modern citrus-packing plants in this area, and here now are assembled a certain number of carloads of oranges and grapefruit. These form the nucleus of the train moving north to the consuming centers. More loads are added at Punta Gorda. In succession, the packing houses at Arcadia, Brownsville, and Wauchula provide other loaded refrigerator cars. Bartow contributes to the make-up of the train.

Upon arrival at Lakeland, terminal for gathering operations, certain cars are switched to the ice platform for reicing. Beginning here, a predetermined classification is maintained, traffic for certain destinations or junction points being kept in one block, while that for other junctions or destinations is held in another.

So far as possible, cars which will later require icing at Waycross, Georgia, Potomac Yard, or elsewhere are held in one block. Switching operations at Lakeland are carried out with swiftness and precision. The crews are well drilled from long experience, and everything moves in perfect time.

Leaving Lakeland in the early evening the train highballs northward for High Springs, 140 miles away. Packing houses at Dade City contribute more cars; likewise Trilby, which has been gathering cars from St. Petersburg, Clearwater, and other points on the Pinellas Peninsula.

There are more perishables waiting at High Springs, gathered on other divergent lines of the Atlantic Coast Line. Some cars are re-iced. This about finishes the pick-ups, and we head for Waycross, running extra, arriving there at 9:30 A.M.

Waycross is the concentration point for fast perishable traffic moving northward. Here are gathered cars that have rolled in from the east coast and the central portion of the peninsula.

Already the refrigeration supervisor at Waycross is in possession of information concerning the cars to be iced or re-iced and has varying instructions from the numerous shippers involved. Waycross is, further, a diversion point, and many shippers have simply consigned their fruits and vegetables to themselves at this point.

Telegraphed diversion instructions now await the cars. Destinations and routings are supplied which will distribute these fruit cars to markets all over the eastern half of the country.

From Waycross to Acca Yard at Richmond, Virginia, the distance is 591 miles, and this perishable really rolls, maintaining an average speed of 39.4 miles an hour. There are intermediate stops for fuel and water and to change crews. At Southover Yard, Savannah; Florence, South Carolina; South Rocky Mount, North Carolina, and at Falling Creek, Virginia, cars may be set off for various destinations or for handling by other roads. And then again the highball, and the continuing rush north.

There is a fixed limit of fifty cars for each train section, and the number of sections, of course, varies. But always between mid-winter and early spring they are thundering down the rails and at the maximum allowed speed of 60 miles an hour on every last stretch of railroad the man at the throttle finds safe and clear.

We pull out of South Rocky Mount and wheel the 125 miles into Acca Yard at Richmond, traveling through the darkness at close to passenger-train speed. Monday morning it was when we pulled out of Fort Myers. This is Wednesday morning—4:45.

Now one of those big Mountain Type locomotives of the Richmond, Fredericksburg and Potomac takes over, or, perhaps, one of the "Generals." The Atlantic Coast Line's job is done.

At 9:30 our fruit train pulls into the Potomac Yards just south of Washington. Here is one of the great classification and switching yards of the country. There are further diversions, and the fruit train speeds on its way for the Jersey shore. Thursday morning the cars are on the New York piers for the regular market and those early-hour auctions. And if Friday morning's Fort Myers or Indian River grapefruit slyly squirts you in the eye, remember it is only exuberance, possibly, because it has traveled so far so fast.

Perhaps nowhere are the odds so greatly against the fruit trains as the battling climb over the Sierras between Roseville, California, and Sparks, Nevada. The maximum grade is 2.5; the maximum curvature, 10 degrees 30 minutes. This, you will remember, is a stiffer climb than that found on the Rocky Mountain Division of the Milwaukee Railroad.

From an elevation of a little less than two hundred feet above sea level at Roseville, the line lifts to close to seven thousand feet. The snow belt begins at Gold Run at an elevation of 3,228 feet and extends on over the summit to Sparks, where the elevation is 4,426 feet. In this territory it is reported that snow reaches as great a depth as anywhere in the Northern Hemisphere. During the winter of 1890 the snow on the level in many places was twenty to twenty-five feet, with drifts in these mountain valleys varying from fifty to two hundred feet. On the east slope of the Sierras some of the coldest weather in the United States is also encountered.

To help combat these snow conditions, the Southern Pacific constructed snowsheds between Emigrant Gap and Andover, a distance of 28 miles. These sheds were above the 5,000-foot level. Within this 28-mile stretch there were 20 miles of sheds, called the "longest house in the world," which required 100,000,000 feet of lumber, at a cost of $3,000,000.

Openings arranged on the downhill side served the double purpose of providing ventilation and allowing passengers on the limiteds a rapid-fire glimpse of some of the finest scenery outdoors. So they may view it better, most of these snowsheds have now been dismantled. The modern rotary snowplows and big engines can take care of the snow satisfactorily.

Storming up the grade now we see a Red Ball freight—a fruit train—with the cannonading engine at the front assisted by two giant helper locomotives cut into the drag at suitable intervals behind. And this is but one unit of the Big Parade.

Today, for example, the general yardmaster at Roseville started 720 cars up the mountain, and tonight 500 more will be roaring after them. The tonnage lift for the 88 miles, Roseville to Norden summit, is some 6,800 feet straight into the clouds. And this, indeed, is mountain railroading, and in the author's opinion the finest individual operation in the country. Believe me, there are some great railroaders on the S.P. Sacramento Division; they have to be. It takes strong, tough, and clearheaded men to perform the job they do so well.

The reverse levers of those powerful AC-class engines are right down in the corner, as they go snorting upward. On the ruling grade of 1.5 per cent between Roseville and Colfax the speed is between 20 and 25 miles an hour; 10 to 12 miles an hour on the 28-mile pull up the grade of 2.2 to 2.5 per cent between Colfax and Emigrant Gap.

The helper engines are cut out at Norden, and the train engine takes over the task of dropping the fruit train down to Truckee. Though it required plain brute strength to bat the drag over the hump, now it takes the nicest kind of handling to nurse it down.

The standard practice is to set the retaining valves at ten pounds on the first 60 to 65 cars; then, by using the short-cycle method of brake application, the heavy train is held at a uniform speed of 20 miles an hour, with the slack at all times bunched against the engine.

From Truckee to Sparks, owing to the fact that retainers are not used, the braking procedure is somewhat different. After the speed picks up close to the maximum allowable, the engineer makes a brake-pipe reduction not exceeding six pounds, and, if necessary, follows it with another light reduction. With driver brake released and working a drifting throttle, the engineman, as the speed starts to decrease, builds up sufficient driver-brake-cylinder pressure on the engine to prevent a run-out of slack. He then charges the brake system, after which he graduates the driver-brake cylinder off, permitting the slack in the train to move out gently. This procedure is continued to the foot of the hill. It is necessary always to maintain careful handling to control the slack on the different variations of grade prevailing between Truckee and Sparks.

We have now seen the start of the run of a fruit train across the High Sierras. The navel oranges start to market early in November and keep rolling until April. There is, too, the Valencia crop, keeping the refrigerator cars occupied through the spring and summer and into the early fall. There are lemons and grapefruit, and those vegetable harvests, mounting to enormous proportions, that come out of that "Salad Bowl of America" around Salinas, California, and from the great delta country of the Sacramento.

Because of varying conditions and temperatures, the transportation of these perishables entails many difficulties. For part of the run of the fruit trains normal car ventilation may be sufficient. Again ice may be necessary in those bunkers we have described. Or perhaps there will have to be charcoal heaters to prevent freezing.

This fruit train that pulled out of Roseville is in Nevada now and streaking east through vast reaches of desert. Imlay and Carlin are behind. It rolls into Ogden, Utah. In the meantime, another fruit block has been moving out of Colton, California. It whips the grades of El Cajon and wheels across the Mojave and nips a corner of Nevada. Las Vegas, gateway to Boulder Dam; Milford, Utah; Provo and Ogden.

CN symbol covers Union Pacific green fruit originating at Colton, and RV is the symbol for Southern Pacific green fruit originating at Roseville. In this case, the first-named train arrives at Ogden with thirty-nine loads; the latter, with 66 loads and 14 empties. There is the usual inspection; bills are checked at the yard office, and the Ogden Union Railway sets about the consolidation of the two trains.

The eastbound drag is ordered to leave with 3,100 to 3,200 tons and not to exceed 70 cars. When the train is finally made up a big simple articulated 4-8-8-4 locomotive backs on. This is Union Pacific Big Boy.

A complete inspection is made of running gear and understructures, as well as roofs, where watchful eyes look for loose running boards, loose top grab irons, and so on. The air brakes have been tested now; the conductor has his waybills and train orders, and we highball out.

Across the rugged Wasatch we roll, with the powerful engine doing a beautiful job of handling our train. We wheel into Green River, Wyoming, and here a big 3,900-class engine takes over. We storm away for Bitter Creek, Rawlins, Hanna, Rock Springs, Laramie, the Black Hills, Sherman Summit, and Cheyenne, the capital.

At every stop there is a careful inspection of brake rigging and all running parts. Eternal vigilance always. Telegraph operators also make "running inspections," as they watch for smoking journals or anything that might be dragging and throwing fire under the fast-traveling train. They signal the watching face in the cupola of the caboose.

We leave Cheyenne and soon enter Nebraska. Kimbal, Sidney, Julesburg–Julesburg, Colorado, famous in history as one of the toughest towns of the old frontier. We slow for Ogallala and stop. The head brakeman hurries to a switch. The streamliner, hot-footing behind us, must have a clear railroad.

We snake into a siding, and soon train No. 104, the sleek and trim streamliner, City of Los Angeles, of the Union Pacific, streaks past. Again gleaming rails are rushing under our pilot. Prairie cities come swimming out of the miragelike haze on the horizon. North Platte, Kearney, Grand Island.

This is the old Oregon Trail–the Great Medicine Road. The trail of the pioneers and the bull trains, with their plodding oxen and heavy-laden Conestoga wagons. In the dim mists of yesterday we can see those caravans, and campfires glowing in the dusk.

Because these trail blazers broke the raw western frontier, the fruit trains now are rolling to the marching rhythm of the exhaust and the echoing chorus of fast-spinning wheels.

We are in the yards at Council Bluffs now, and switch engines tear the train apart. There are cars for the Chicago & Northwestern; cars for the Milwaukee road; cars for the Rock Island, the Chicago, Burlington & Quincy, the Illinois Central.

New trains are made up and go rushing north, south, and east to eager, waiting markets—to the breakfast and dinner table and you.

To avoid monotonous detail and repetition we have reviewed but briefly the runs of those two fruit blocks, originating at far-separated points in California. We have seen them consolidated at Ogden, Utah, and the subsequent flight of this green-fruit express across the vast reaches of Wyoming and Nebraska.

There have been necessary stops for coal, water, and servicing of motive power. Engine and train crews have swung off; new crews have climbed aboard. Locomotives have been changed; other engines have rushed the train eastward. Endless routine, precision, and timing have been involved. Hundreds of railroad employees have performed their duties with sureness and accuracy—alert and resourceful train dispatchers, efficient clerks, vigilant operators, ready call boys, grimy mechanics, keen-eyed car inspectors, and others, down to the last lowly track walker, patrolling his lonely beat of the rails.

Photo by W. H. Thrall, Jr.

SOUTHERN PACIFIC'S EXTRA 811 WITH ENGINE 4110, CLASS AC-5, passing through one of the many tunnels before rounding Tehachapi Loop on the San Joaquin Division.

Courtesy of P R.R.

PENNSYLVANIA'S FW-8 MAN-O'-WAR CRACK STOCK TRAIN, hauled by a Class M-1 engine, scooping water from the track tank on No. 2 track at Wilmore, Pennsylvania, on the Pittsburgh Division. Note the snapper pushing on the hind end.

Perfect synchronization here, like that of a great machine driven by complicated gears. And yet we have witnessed the movement of but one of an endless parade of fast-wheeling perishable trains. This is the systematized and unerring thoroughness of America's modern railroad transportation, an intricate but powerful organization that as readily adapts itself to serving our country in a national emergency as to delivering the needed fruits and vegetables that mean so much to our health and well-being.

CHAPTER X

"King Coal"

As IMPORTANT as are the green-fruit trains and other limiteds of the freight service to the people of the nation, "King Coal" still maintains its foremost rank in the list of commodities transported by American railroads. In 1940 lines in the United States originated 298,315,270 tons of bituminous coal, or 27 per cent of all the freight handled.

Well up among the leaders in this tremendous haul of "black diamonds" is the Louisville & Nashville, with 31,-474,575 tons—or over 10 per cent of the total bituminous shipment—moving over its lines. This is an impressive showing for a carrier which has only 2 per cent of the nation's rail trackage.

Before examining the enormous coal haul of the Louisville & Nashville, let us give our attention for a little to the growth and development of the road and its relationship to the mining industry in its tempestuously rugged back yard.

The Louisville & Nashville sprawls over an area embracing thirteen states, from the Ohio River on the north to the Gulf of Mexico on the south, and from the Mississippi on the west to the Cumberland Mountains on the east. The major portion of its some five thousand miles of track is located in the central southern states of Kentucky, Alabama, and Tennessee. The story of the road's growth is, in a substantial measure, the story of its development in these three states.

In the early part of 1840 there was an ever-increasing sentiment on the part of residents of Kentucky and Tennessee for a railroad connecting the metropolis of the one with the state capital of the other. It was felt that a railroad between the cities of Louisville and Nashville would not only benefit and develop the territory intervening, but would also do much to expedite the flow of traffic and commerce between the North and the South, a development which had been retarded by entirely unreliable transportation facilities.

After much agitation and many torchlit mass meetings, charters were granted the Louisville & Nashville Railroad by the states of Kentucky and Tennessee. This was early in 1850. Actual construction, however, was not begun until May 2, 1853. Once under way, all the evils to which man is heir beset the undertaking. There were financial difficulties, droughts, crop failures, and cholera. Further, in Europe the Crimean War was in progress.

And yet, in spite of all this, the L.&N., or Old Reliable, as it was to be known, went ahead and built a railroad, which was completed between Louisville and Nashville in the fall of 1859, with the regular operation of trains beginning in October of that year.

By the end of 1905 the lines of the Louisville & Nashville had spread their iron network as far as New Orleans, Mobile, Pensacola, Memphis, Evansville, Cincinnati, Knoxville, St. Louis, and Atlanta. Communities like Birmingham, Alabama, literally sprang into being following the arrival of the L.&N.'s iron horse.

The Louisville & Nashville long has been influential in the affairs of the South, and it was personified at that time by its famed president, Milton Hannibal Smith, who was a worthy successor to such titans as James Guthrie and Albert Fink. Mr. Smith was the road's chief executive from 1884 until 1886 and from March 1891 until his death on February 22, 1921.

Milton H. Smith proved to be one of the real railroad giants of the nation, and under his guidance the L.&N. made few mistakes, and these were overshadowed many times by his leadership and judgment.

Milton Smith was responsible for the development of the Birmingham district, for the creation of the Cincinnati-Atlanta line, and the opening up of the eastern Kentucky coal fields, centered in Perry, Letcher, Bell, and Harlan counties, as well as other coal-mining operations.

As early as 1888 the Louisville & Nashville had placed itself within striking distance of the coal fields of Harlan County by the construction of a line from Corbin to Pineville, Kentucky. At this point, after hot and furious debate,

Courtesy of New York Central System.

NEW YORK CENTRAL COAL TRAIN on the Pittsburgh & Lake Erie, east of Youngstown, Ohio, triple-headed with two L-2s and an L-1. The train consists of 95 cars with 8,469 tons and is en route to the Ashtabula coal docks.

Photo by Robert Dudley Smith.

P.R.R. COAL TRAIN hauled by Engine 6746, 4-8-2 type, Class M-1A, with a 22,000-gallon tank on the Trenton cut-off of the Philadelphia Division, eastbound.

it was decided to build the line into Norton, Virginia, for connection with the Norfolk and Western Railway. The route chosen was by way of Middleboro and along the southern base of Cumberland Mountain.

Milton Smith, although not president at the time, was strongly of the opinion that the proposed line to Norton should go along the northern base of the mountain barrier, following the Cumberland River through Harlan County. Weight was given his belief by a special report, prepared at the behest of the L.&N., on the mineral resources of southeastern Kentucky and southwestern Virginia. This was compiled by Andrew S. McCreath and E. V. D'Invilliers, mineralogists, of Philadelphia, who recommended the Cumberland River route as the most advantageous for the location of a railroad designed to develop the mineral resources between Pineville and Big Stone Gap, Virginia, some fourteen miles from Norton. However, other factors, chiefly lower construction costs, prevailed, and the road was built via Middleboro and through Virginia.

In consequence, it was not until the latter part of 1909 that the Louisville & Nashville entered Harlan County, and then through the medium of the Wasioto and Black Mountain Railroad. The line was completed to Harlan, the county seat, in July 1911. In September of the same year it moved on "up the hollow" to Benham.

The first carload of coal left Harlan County on August 25, 1911. Almost simultaneously, the L.&N. proceeded with the acquisition and construction of what has since come to be known as its Eastern Kentucky Division. Already it had acquired the Louisville & Atlantic and the Lexington & Eastern railroads, both of which made partial penetrations of the eastern Kentucky coal fields.

These purchases followed investigation of the coal deposits in Breathitt, Perry and Letcher counties, and resulted in the building of the North Fork Extension of the Lexington and Eastern Railway. This 100-mile line from Jackson to McRoberts, Kentucky, was completed on November 23, 1912.

Following the completion of this basic trackage, and for many years afterward, the Louisville & Nashville's efforts were directed towards the building of supplementary branches, designed to tap the vast coal deposits of the areas it served. The L.&N. further spent millions of dollars in the relocation of line, the reduction of grades, and the construction of freight yards.

Year by year traffic increased, with coal ever solidifying the position and importance of the L.&N. From the first, coal, as a revenue producer, has been an important factor in the road's development.

Since coal comprised nearly 60 per cent of the total tonnage handled by the Louisville & Nashville in 1940, it obviously required the full-time attention of much of the road's personnel. The L.&N.'s relation to coal might be divided into three major parts: its handling by the transportation department, its use by the mechanical department, and the promotional work and associated activities of the company's general coal-and-coke department.

The coal haul is one of the transportation department's biggest jobs, with some 370 train-service employees concerned almost exclusively with this movement over the L.&N. to such strategically located coal-handling terminals as Corbin, Loyall, Hazard, and Ravenna, Kentucky. At these and other points long 120-car coal trains are made up for movement northward through the outlet gateways.

The crews of these trains are known as "mine run" crews, and the 370 mentioned do not include crews on the through freight trains, who, obviously, play an important part in delivering the coal to the ultimate consumer. In addition to the train-service employees, there are many yard clerks, switchmen, section men, operators, and others, all playing a vital part in the movement.

The *modus operandi* of these mine-run crews is for each to leave the home terminal at an established time with an engine and a string of empty coal cars and caboose to cover a particular assignment. The loaded coal cars are picked up at or near the various mines' tipples. The coal, of course, has been screened and graded.

The locomotive returns to its terminal with its armada of heavy-laden cars, trundling grimy gondolas and whale-bellies. These cars are then consolidated and classified. Within a short time after leaving the mines, the bituminous is speeding to the ever-hungry furnaces of the nation in long trains of 100 cars or more. Here is fuel for heating, for factories, for the creation of power and light.

The coal industry is delicately adjusted and highly competitive, and in no phase of its many ramifications is precision handling more important than in rate making. On the Louisville & Nashville these and other duties are handled in its general coal-and-coke department, where a corps of rate and division clerks, statisticians, stenographers, coal freight agents and executives see that rates are adjusted to the constantly changing picture in coal production, transportation, and consuming fields.

The rates from the various groups of mines to competitive destinations must be correlated with one another and with the producing areas on other roads in the same general producing sections. The rates by groups are not necessarily the same, however, some being higher or lower than others, but they are carefully adjusted nevertheless, and these differences have either been made by the Interstate Commerce Commission directly or have been indirectly approved.

The L.&N.'s coal traffic department must, naturally, work in close collaboration with such bureaus or committees as the Southern Coal and Coke Committee, the Illinois-Indiana Coal and Coke Committee and the Central Freight Association Coal, Coke, and Iron Ore Committee, the personnel of these being drawn from the various railroads themselves. All advances and reductions in rates are subject to the approval of the Interstate Commerce Commission or other regulatory bodies.

The Louisville & Nashville also employs a mining and a combustion engineer. The former is concerned with the development of new mines. The latter assists coal and coke users with their various problems, demonstrating the scientific application of coal and coke to their various requirements.

The coal freight agents might be regarded as salesmen, though in reality they are "customers' men," and they render a real service not only to the railroad but to coal operators and users as well.

Thus we see that coal looms large in the scheme of things on the Louisville & Nashville, as it will continue to do for a long time to come, and this despite recent adverse influences, over and above the depression years.

Obviously, competing forms of power and light and heat, notably the hydroelectric developments of the past decade and the increasing use of fuel oil, have curtailed coal consumption. However, new uses for coal are being developed constantly. Witness its use in the manufacture of Nylon, perfumes, medicines, chemicals, dyes, and plastics. Moreover, a more scientific consumption of coal for domestic use has reduced the amount necessary to the average home, while, at the same time, it has made the use of coal more attractive to a greater number of people. Hence the gains thus enumerated have largely counterbalanced the losses, and the demand for coal is comfortably certain to continue for a great many years, with the mines, in so far as the L.&N.'s producing territory is concerned, having an estimated available supply that will last hundreds of years.

Of course, the transportation of these millions of tons of coal is not all clear profit for the railroad. A great deal of money is spent for wages, fuel, stores, and supplies. A large sum is tied up in coal-carrying equipment and in other facilities. At the present time the L.&N. has nearly 35,000 coal cars, representing an investment of almost $69,000,000.

Until 1939 the Louisville & Nashville's 900 locomotives were powered exclusively by coal, and, with small exception, that is true today. In the fall of 1939 the company placed two Diesel-electric locomotives in switching service in its East Louisville yards. Subsequently it authorized the purchase of twelve more. And now eight Diesel-electric passenger locomotives have been added to the road's motive-power equipment.

In 1940 the fueling of the L.&N.'s steam motive power required 2,711,573 tons of coal, at a cost of something like five million dollars. The road is constantly striving to reduce its coal consumption. This is being done in many ways. For example, the cost of stopping and starting was taken into consideration, and a great many stops once considered necessary have been eliminated. This was accomplished by the use of larger coal tenders and water tanks, permitting longer non-stop runs, through schedule revision, through the installation of spring switches, and finally through the gradual elimination of hot boxes and bearings.

There has further been a more scientific firing of engines, related changes in coal-consuming equipment, and a closer inspection of coal to remove foreign matter which might hinder the operation of stokers. This intensive effort to reduce the company's coal bill has resulted in a consumption of only 125 pounds of coal for each 1,000 gross ton-miles of haul (1,000 gross ton-miles is a statistical unit representing freight and equipment moved one mile). This as of 1940, and in comparison with 181 pounds for the year of 1923. The difference of 56 pounds, when integrated with the 10,-

984,990,798 ton-miles handled in 1940, runs into a large amount of money saved by improved efficiency in locomotive operation and design.

The Louisville & Nashville's export and import business represents an important phase of its operation. At Pensacola, Florida, it has a $700,000 mechanical coaling plant and wharf, which can pour coal or other bulk material from the freight cars into the waiting holds of vessels at the rate of 750 tons an hour.

The L.&N. maintains a coal wharf at Mobile, Alabama, and this is used in the bunkering of harbor vessels mainly. Here, too, through the facilities of the Turner Terminal Company and the Alabama State Docks and Terminals, both of which are served by the Terminal Railway, connecting with the L.&N., the road handles many export goods originating on its lines and in addition receives import goods for widely separated destinations.

Thus we see the Louisville & Nashville as a great coal-hauling aristocrat, and yet not by coal alone does it maintain its high place among American railroads. In fact, the show could go on without the black diamonds, though in a much less pretentious manner.

For instance, in 1940, in addition to wheeling Old King Coal, the L.&N., among the more important items, hauled 14,361 cars of cement, 21,880 cars of fertilizer, 27,000 cars of iron and steel, 46,018 cars of lumber, 32,834 cars of oil, 33,370 cars of iron ore, 10,970 cars of potatoes, 16,387 cars of rock phosphate, 12,514 cars of tobacco leaf, 14,000 cars of stone, and 12,410 cars of livestock.

One of the "mighty atoms" of the Louisville & Nashville trackage is its 35-mile Foley Branch, which extends from Bay Minette to Foley, Alabama, through the rich agricultural area of Baldwin County. In 1941, 8,719 carloads of fruits and vegetables originated on the Foley Branch. This line is always maintained at tiptop shape for the handling of this traffic.

In Baldwin County we find an American success story on a big scale. Prior to the turn of the century, most of the county's 1,595 square miles was covered by an immense forest of virgin yellow pine. And then, in September 1906, one of the most destructive tropical hurricanes that ever struck Alabama tore through the county, leveling billions of feet of standing timber. Only a small amount of this timber was saved.

After salvaging what they could, many of the lumber companies owning tracts in the devastated area, aided by the Louisville & Nashville, which in May 1905 had completed the building of the Bay Minette and Fort Morgan Railroad to Foley, and the L.&N.'s Industrial and Agricultural Development Department and other sources, began to introduce immigration. The stumps and worthless timber were cleared from vast areas when it was found that the soil was productive for the raising of a great variety of crops. Here in Baldwin County was a growing season of 320 days, which in itself was a natural advantage. With the arrival of the settlers, the Louisville & Nashville's agricultural agents assisted them with the problems of planting suitable crops, which included sweet potatoes, cucumbers, radishes, roasting-

Photo by R. H. Kindig.

DENVER AND RIO GRANDE WESTERN'S NO. 3705, CLASS L-105, 4-6-6-4 TYPE, running 60 m.p.h. with second No. 61 near Mack, Colorado, at sunset. The emblem on the utility sandbox is not the Japanese Rising Sun but a warning to trespassers and motorists.

Photo by R. H. Kindig.

RIO GRANDE'S NO. 3401 AND NO. 3607, Class L-95 and L-131, 2-8-8-2 type, climbing the 2 per cent grade near Fireclay, Colorado, on the Denver & Salt Lake Moffatt Tunnel route with the Ute. Note the utility water car behind each engine.

RIO GRANDE'S NO. 3615, CLASS L-131, 2-8-8-2 TYPE, helping No. 1526, 4-8-2 type, Class M-67, on an eastward C.C.C. special, climbing Tennessee Pass, near Mitchell, Colorado.

Photo by R. H. Kindig.

ear corn, and pecans. More and more acreage was cleared. In the meantime potatoes, plain Irish potatoes, proved to be the "big money" crop, and in 1941 Baldwin County had 24,000 acres planted. It is still increasing its acreage in this commodity alone. Baldwin County, Alabama, like the phoenix, arose from its ashes, and, with the fires of stumps and dead trees still burning, laid the foundation for a new and lasting empire of the soil.

At New Orleans the Louisville & Nashville tracks connect with the Public Belt Line, which serves the vast state-owned waterfront wharves. Here we see, bound for export in normal times, export items from the L.&N. They include iron and steel products, lumber, naval stores, and cotton. Import items are largely bananas and coconuts.

To meet the demands of national defense, the Louisville & Nashville by the early part of 1941 had approved or incurred expenditures aggregating over $15,000,000, of which sum $11,800,000 or more were invested in new equipment, including locomotives, coal and box cars and passenger cars, with the remainder spent in making varied improvements all along the line.

As we look back down the years, we find locomotives of the L.&N. chanting their high call of the iron road almost ten years before the wedding of transcontinental steel there at Promontory, Utah. And again the builders of a vast transportation system have demonstrated their right to a place on the country's roll of honor. The Louisville & Nashville, empire builder of the South. Old Reliable.

CHAPTER XI

Steel Across the Colorado Rockies

THE DENVER & RIO GRANDE WESTERN has engraved its name in steel across some of the most glorious scenery out of doors—the Colorado Rockies. Threading this world of deep-slashed canyons and cloud-shrouded peaks, here on the roof of the North American continent, are the rails of two scenic routes, the rugged beauty of which unfolds with each passing mile.

The Denver & Rio Grande Western is a system operating 2,551 miles of line in the states of Colorado, Utah, and New Mexico. Originally the road was the Denver & Rio Grande, and it began operation as a narrow-gauge road away back in 1871. There are some 560 miles of the first three-foot-gauge line still in operation.

It was brave little narrow-gauge locomotives that first whipped the grades of the Colorado Rockies, and they are still hauling trains over Marshal Pass, 10,856 feet in the clouds.

Small-gauge roads played an important part in the railroad history of America, and be it to our everlasting shame that we have allowed these charming and picturesque lines to be sold down the river.

The rails and the chuffing little engines that rode them have, for the most part, bowed out as junk, going to Japan these past years as scrap metal. We saved the redwoods and, belatedly, spread our guardianship over the vanishing buffalo, but, except in a few isolated instances, the narrow-gauge roads of the country are gone and forgotten.

We see, in thumbing back the pages of time on the old Denver & Rio Grande, something of the important part the narrow-gauge played in transportation development in America.

The story of the Denver & Rio Grande Western is one of pioneering achievement, the conquering of what once appeared to be an insurmountable barrier in the form of a frowning mountain range thrust up into the sky. With the completion of the Dotsero Cut-off and the James Peak route in 1934, the road took its rightful place in the ranks of transcontinental carriers, with fast freights storming through the Colorado Rockies and crack passenger trains wheeling over this grand railroad.

However, it was the narrow-gauge that led the way, and those little trains, crowding hard on the heels of the construction crews, richly deserve a place in the railroad hall of fame.

When the final chapter has been written, and the last narrow-gauge locomotive whistles for the board of the Terminal at the end of the Glory Road, there will be at least one of those small-gauge engines occupying a shrine in the heart of an American city. On the day in August 1938 when Colorado celebrated the sixty-second anniversary of its admission to statehood, the Denver & Rio Grande Western presented narrow-gauge engine, No. 168, to the city of Colorado Springs as a permanent monument to the early railroad builders, the empire builders of the Colorado Rockies.

No. 168 was built by Baldwin for the Denver & Rio Grande in 1883 and proudly it played its part in the handling of the first passenger train to run from Denver to Ogden on May 21 of that year, with the thin, far cry of its whistle stirring echoes from mountain and canyon fastness as it challenged the ramparts of the Rockies.

When the first transcontinental road was building through —the road of Dodge and Huntington and Stanford—men shied away from the Colorado Rockies as they would have from a place of pestilence and death, and the territory of Colorado was completely left out of the railroad picture.

But there were men of courage and vision in Colorado, and they were not to be denied a part in the making of western railroad history. As far back as the first year of the Civil War, William Gilpin, Colorado's first territorial governor, predicted that one day steel would conquer the Rockies, with a railroad tunnel somewhere through the mountains in the vicinity of James Peak.

James Evans, the second territorial governor, tried unsuccessfully to interest eastern capital in the venture. Following his death, the battle was continued by David Moffat, but without immediate results. However, here again was a railroad builder who didn't know when he was licked, and today the name Moffat is engraved forever in these same Colorado Rockies.

The Denver & Rio Grande was first projected by General William J. Palmer as a trunk line extending from Denver to Mexico City, along the Rio Grande del Norte, from which it took its name. Grading was started in March 1871, and by 1874 the railhead had reached the banks of the Arkansas River at Pueblo. But by now the trend of gold seekers westward into the Rockies was so strong that the Mexico City objective was abandoned and the steel was diverted into the Grand Canyon of the Arkansas, "The Royal Gorge Route," which was to win acclaim as America's most scenic line.

After a stirring fight for right-of-way, the railhead continued on deep into the heart of the Rockies, where miners were already uncovering undreamed-of wealth. Not only was this great mountain range to yield rich treasures in mineral form, but there were opened up grazing lands for cattle and sheep, and fertile valleys capable of producing an amazing variety of agricultural products.

Here, too, in this country back of beyond, was a land that was one day to stand prominently as a playground of the nation, with rushing streams filled with trout, forests alive with game, and more rampant scenery than the human eye could properly digest at one sitting.

The first crossing of the Continental Divide in Colorado was by this undaunted little narrow-gauge railroad through

Marshal Pass. A little road and little engines, manned by men of brawn and steel nerves, but they tamed the Rockies. And all down the years they have been panting over this original Denver / Salt Lake main line and are still there hauling tonnage, the bark of their exhausts crying defiance to those high crags.

But in 1890 a standard-gauge line over Tennessee Pass was placed in operation, joining Denver and Salt Lake City. However, efforts to secure a railroad directly through the front range immediately west of Denver still persisted. The Denver & Salt Lake Railway, known as "The Moffat Road," and crossing the Divide at Corona Pass, was built early in the twentieth century, but lack of finances prevented it from reaching Salt Lake, its projected terminus.

The Moffat Road's operation over Corona Pass was costly and uncertain and focused attention on the necessity for the construction of the tunnel prophesied by William Gilpin. Denver's attempt to finance the venture ran into difficulties; nevertheless, in 1922 a state bond issue was authorized by a special session of the Colorado legislature.

The great bore known as the Moffat Tunnel was completed in 1927 at a cost of close to $18,000,000. The tunnel is 6.09 miles long and pierces the Continental Divide at an elevation of nine thousand feet. The summit of the grade is in the center of the tunnel, with a grade of 0.3 per cent to the east and 0.8 per cent to the west.

The eastern portal of the tunnel, approximately fifty miles west of Denver, is approached by a long 2 per cent grade, combined with frequent curves, the sharpest being 10 degrees. There are thirty tunnels in this distance, twenty-eight of which occur in a span of eleven miles, and new and startling panoramas unfold constantly.

The Moffat Tunnel itself ranks sixth in length among the great tunnels of the world and is second in the United States, being exceeded only by the Cascade Tunnel on the Great Northern.

The Dotsero Cut-off was projected as the next step in the realization of Denver's dream for a rightful place on a direct transcontinental railroad. More, after the completion of the tunnel, the cut-off became an immediate necessity, if the huge investment involved was to be safeguarded. Despite depression hardships and retrenchment, and despite the loss of business to unregulated competitors, the Denver & Rio Grande Western courageously undertook and carried to a successful conclusion the only major new-line railroad construction in North America during this depression period.

So the Dotsero Cut-off came into being. It was thirty-eight miles in length and was completed at a cost of nearly $3,750,000. The Cut-off follows the valley of the Colorado River and entails a number of severe reverse curves. There are two bores of 1,084 and 650 feet respectively, with ten bridges, nine of which span the river. The line is single-track throughout, with no intermediate stations, although there are sidings at several points for the convenience of the numerous ranches in this high mountain valley. Improved business for the Denver & Rio Grande Western, as well as improved transportation service for Denver, western Colorado, and Utah, has fully justified the construction of the

Dotsero Cut-off. Denver was now 175 miles closer to Salt Lake City than in the old days, with Rio Grande schedules between the state capitals eight hours faster. Fast freights rolled across the Rockies. The crack Expedition Flyer of passenger service reduced its time between Chicago and San Francisco by a full eighteen hours.

The Denver & Rio Grande Western, with the building of the Dotsero Cut-off and the James Peak Route, has thus kept in step with the forward march of American railroads and has added another gallant page to the history of the railroad builders.

So the "baby" road grew up, and the Rio Grande road made good an early boast that it would go "through the Rockies—not around them"—with the result that this universally acclaimed "Scenic Line" maintains two routes across the Colorado Divide that are unequaled for grandeur anywhere: one by the way of the Royal Gorge, the other via the famous Moffat Tunnel.

Because of the unusually rugged characteristics of the territory traversed, Denver & Rio Grande Western locomotive requirements differ widely from those ordinarily hauling trains over the mountains.

The old Denver & Rio Grande began operations with narrow-gauge engines built by Baldwin. These were of the 2-4-0 type for passenger service and the 2-6-0 or Mogul type for freight. It soon was found that these small locomotives were of inadequate capacity, and larger engines of the 4-4-0, 4-6-0, and 2-8-0 types were purchased.

With the coming of standard gauge on portions of the

line, the Denver & Rio Grande Western introduced locomotives of greatly increased capacity. The motive-power equipment of the road now includes fine examples of the 4-8-4 type for passenger service and single-expansion articulated designs for freight. Most recent purchases include five locomotives of the 4-8-4 type and fifteen of the 4-6-6-4 type, built by the Baldwin Locomotive Works. Both types were specially designed to meet the unusual operating requirements of the Rio Grande road and include special features.

The 4-6-6-4 type represents a new wheel arrangement on the Denver & Rio Grande Western. The purpose was to provide a locomotive of sufficient power to handle hauls over these heavy grades which would balance with those of other districts, and, at the same time, be capable of sustained high speeds.

These engines replaced locomotives of the Mountain (4-8-2) type, of smaller capacity, and also those of the Santa Fe (2-10-2) type, which were limited in power and curving ability.

The class designation of the 4-6-6-4 type is L-105, the numeral representing the maximum tractive force in thousands of pounds. These engines are intended for service on grades up to 3 per cent. The sharpest operating curve is 16 degrees, but the design is laid out for a 22-degree curve.

In spite of their great size, the Class L-105 locomotives have a rigid wheel base of only 12 feet 2 inches and are actually more flexible than many smaller units. They have driving wheels of seventy inches. In either fast freight service or on passenger runs they really go to town. They are coal-burning, stoker-fired. Their design is of particular interest and will be treated in detail after we have a look at these engines in action.

For preference-freight work, the 4-6-6-4 handles 2,750 adjusted tons from Salt Lake City to Grand Junction, Colorado, with a pusher over the 30 miles of 2 per cent grade, Thistle to Soldier Summit, Utah, at a comparatively high speed for mountain road. From Helper, Utah, to Grand Junction, Colorado, a distance of 177 miles, the 4-6-6-4 locomotive wheels this 2,750 tons in 5 hours and 40 minutes, with one stop for coal and two for water. Further, these locomotives have actually handled 2,870 tons on this stretch in 4 hours and 50 minutes. It is a common occurrence for them to make the run in thirty minutes less than their two-fisted schedule calls for.

In passenger service a 4-6-6-4 locomotive will handle 15* cars westbound and 16 cars eastbound on the following schedule. The author has made up fifteen minutes riding the 3705 on train No. 2, the Scenic Limited, from Salt Lake City to Helper, with sixteen cars.

WESTBOUND

District	*Miles*	*Ruling Grade*	*Average Speed*
Helper to Kyune	12.8	+ 2.40	21.95
Kyune to Soldier Summit	12.1	+ 1.00	33.00
Soldier Summit to Thistle	29.5	— 2.00	31.00
Thistle to Salt Lake	64.2	— 0.65	44.20

*Time was when it required four engines and a pusher to put an 11-car passenger train over the hump west of Helper.

EASTBOUND

District	*Miles*	*Ruling Grade*	*Average Speed*
Salt Lake to Thistle	64.2	+ 0.65	43.30
Thistle to Soldier Summit	29.5	+ 2.00	28.60
Soldier Summit to Kyune	12.1	— 1.00	38.20
Kyune to Helper	12.8	— 2.40	19.70

The Denver & Rio Grande Western 4-8-4 type locomotives were designed to incorporate the maximum power obtainable in this type with an axle load of 70,000 pounds, in order to fill out the quota for fast heavy passenger service and reduce the necessity for double-heading. These 4-8-4 engines are used on the crack Scenic Limited passenger trains between Denver and Salt Lake City, via the Royal Gorge, a distance of 745 miles. This line crosses the Continental Divide at Tennessee Pass, Colorado, at an elevation of 10,240 feet.

Eastbound from Minturn to Tennessee Pass, a distance of 21 miles, there is a rise in elevation of 2,415 feet, with a maximum grade of 3 per cent. Westbound from Pueblo to Tennessee Pass there is a climb of 5,568 feet in the 162 miles, with a maximum grade of 1.42 per cent.

In the Salt Lake district these locomotives operate at speeds up to eighty miles an hour. On arrival at Salt Lake they are turned the same day for the return trip to Denver.

The specifications covering the construction of the five 4-8-4 type locomotives recently purchased are in many respects similar to those applying to the 4-6-6-4 type. These specifications will be set down as a conclusion to this chapter.

The new 4-8-4 type, designated as Class M-68, represents

the second design with this wheel arrangement built for the Denver & Rio Grande Western. The first design, Class M-64, was represented by ten locomotives, built by Baldwin in 1929.

The Class M-68 has a weight of 279,172 pounds on the drivers, as compared to 252,000 for the M-64. The tractive force of the newer M-68 is 67,200 pounds against 63,700 pounds. It further has an increased grate area of 21 per cent; increased water-heating surface of 21 per cent, and increased superheating surface of 4.5 per cent. It has 73-inch driving wheels as against 70-inch on the M-64 class.

The working pressure is 285 pounds. The valve gears are controlled by a Baldwin-type C power reverse, and, as on the 4-6-6-4 engines, are designed to give a lead varying from 0 in full gear to 3/8 inch at 25 per cent cut-off. The maximum valve travel is 7 inches, and the valves have a steam lap of 1 1/4 inches and an exhaust clearance of 1/8 inch.

These Class M-68s are a lot of engine, as they have to be to cover a 745-mile run across the Colorado Rockies and turn the same day. However, this kind of performance is rather the rule than the exception on American railroads today, and it is a striking example of the advancement made by both the railroads and the engine builders. Time was, not so many years ago, when a locomotive was changed at every division point, after having traveled anywhere from 100 to 150 miles, by which time the old gal was more than willing to call it a day.

Both the 4-6-6-4 and 4-8-4 type locomotives make a striking appearance in their severe dress of black paint, with all numbers and lettering standing out sharply in aluminum paint. The Rio Grande's monogram appears on the sides of the tank in red and blue, and the beauty of these queens of the mountains is further enhanced by Baldwin Disc driving-wheel centers.

Let us examine a little of the material and design of these locomotives of the Denver & Rio Grande Western. This is one of the 4-6-6-4 type, the Class L-105.

The boiler has a straight top, but the second ring in the barrel is sloped on the bottom to provide ample water space under the combustion chamber. The boiler shell is built of silicomanganese steel, and this material is also used for the welt strips and shell liners. The working pressure is 255 pounds, and the boiler was tested with steam at 275 pounds and with water at 319 pounds.

An idea of the proportions of this boiler can be formed from the fact that the firebox length is 224¼ inches, and the length of the combustion chamber is 109½ inches. The tube length is 22 feet. The combustion chamber is electric-welded to the crown and inside throat sheets. The seams on the bottom of the combustion chamber and around the firebox door are also welded.

The grate has a length of 182 inches and terminates at the front end at a transverse wall of firebrick. A cinder hopper is placed between the brick wall and the front of the firebox. The arch is supported on two thermic siphons, and there is a third siphon in the combustion chamber. The grate is divided into three longitudinal sections, with three shaker bars to each section.

A Standard Modified Type B stoker is installed, with seven

control valves, and the stoker engine is placed on the tender. The ashpan is built of steel plates and has two large hoppers with air-operated slides. Superheated steam is used in the ashpan blower, with a separate operating valve for each side.

There is a Hancock non-lifting type K-NL injector of 12,000 gallons capacity. Nine of the fifteen 4-6-6-4s have Elesco feed-water heaters, located on the smoke-box front above the two air compressors, with the pump on the left side of the locomotive. The other engines have Worthington Type SA heaters and exhaust steam injectors.

The cylinders are 23 × 32 inches. Steam is distributed by 14-inch piston valves operated by Walschaerts gear. The maximum valve travel is 7¼ inches; the steam lap is 1⅜ inches and the exhaust clearance 1/16 inch.

The locomotives have two Baldwin Type C power-reverse gears, one for each unit. The gear for the front unit is supported on a bracket cast on the bed, and that for the rear unit is supported on the boiler. By means of a connection between the reverse shaft on the rear unit and the floating lever of the gear operating the forward valve motion, the two gears are synchronized to provide the same cut-offs on both the front and rear units. The connection is fitted with two universal joints and one slip joint, so that it can accommodate itself to the swing of the front unit when traversing curves. Application has been made for a patent covering the device.

The piston heads are of nickel cast steel, and the guides and crossheads are of multiple-bearing type. A "Slide Guide" connection is used on the back cylinder heads. The guides on the front unit are placed about three feet back of the cylinders, being supported by brackets cast on the bed. With this arrangement, the same length of main rod is used on the front and back units. The back cylinder heads are separate, instead of being cast in one piece with the beds.

The driving-wheel centers, as has been pointed out, are Baldwin Disc type. They are 63 inches in diameter. The material used is Special Double Anchor High-tensile Steel. Forty per cent of the reciprocating weight is balanced, and the main wheels are cross-balanced. The driving axles are of hammered carbon steel and are fitted with S.K.F. roller bearings.

The front engine truck is designed for a swing of six inches on each side of the center line. It is fitted with the American Steel Foundries Roller-bearing Unit, and with Standard rolled steel wheels, quenched and tempered. The rear truck, of the Delta type, is also fitted with Roller-bearing Units. It is designed to swing 8½ inches on each side of the center line at the rear wheel.

The locomotive has six Detroit Model A lubricators of 30-pint capacity, three for each unit. Two lubricators for each unit are mounted on the left side and one on the right side, all being operated from the valve motion.

These lubricators feed oil to the valves and cylinders, main guides, valve-stem crossheads, lead changers, driving and engine truck box pedestals, front engine truck center pin, articulated hinge pins, waist bearer saddle, ball and expansion joints in steam and exhaust pipes, and radial buffer between engine and tender, as well as other points.

There is also one Chicago K-23 hydrostatic lubricator of

3-pint capacity in the cab. This is for the feed-water pump and stoker engine. Flange lubricators, arranged in accordance with the railroad company's standards, are applied to the leading driving wheels of each unit.

There are two sandboxes, each of 20-cubic-feet capacity, on top of the boiler. The front box feeds sand ahead of the second and third pairs of drivers of the front unit, and also back of the third pair. An auxiliary sandbox, placed over the front deck, delivers sand ahead of the first pair of drivers. The rear sandbox on the boiler delivers sand ahead of all driving wheels of the rear unit and also back of the third pair. Graham-White sanding equipment is applied.

Westinghouse brake equipment, Schedule No. 8-ET, is in use, with two 8½-inch cross-compound pumps mounted on the smokebox front. An air reservoir is cast in the rear engine bed, and in addition two reservoirs are placed under the running board on the left side. This provides a total air-reservoir capacity of 101,600 cubic inches. The Le Chatelier water brake is also applied, in accordance with the road's standards.

Though most of these locomotives are in use in freight service, they all are fitted with air-signal and steam-heat equipment, making them available for passenger-train service.

The tender has a cast-steel water-bottom frame and a tank of riveted construction. The water capacity is 20,000 gallons. The coal capacity is 26 tons.

Six-wheeled swing bolster trucks, with cast-steel frames and top equalizers, built by the General Steel Castings Corporation, are used. The truck wheel base is ten feet. S.K.F. roller bearings are applied. The axles are of annealed hammered steel, with quenched and tempered rolled-steel wheels. A Franklin Friction Type E-2 radial buffer is applied between the locomotive and tender.

It is impossible to do more than skim over the details of a great locomotive like the 4-6-6-4 of the Denver & Rio Grande Western, and we have seen here but a rather fragmentary cross-section of the motive power that hauls freight and passenger trains across the Colorado Rockies.

These haughty-plumed, husky-voiced prima donnas of the rail occupy the center of the railroad stage today, here among the cathedral spires of the Continental Divide, and we cannot help but look on them with awe and solemn wonder, and yet never let it be said that their regal presence will dim the memory of those first little narrow-gauge engines that showed them the way.

CHAPTER XII

Classification Yards

GRANDMA'S CRAZY QUILT offers to the beholder a bewildering assortment of odds and ends of all hues and shapes, which might be compared to the seeming confusion of a big freight terminal. And yet nowhere in the transportation world is there a more perfectly systematized organization for the swift marshaling and make-up of trains—trains like the Merchant Prince and those roaring limiteds of the freight service on the Pennsylvania.

These freight terminals are called classification yards, and they are to the railroad what a sorting rack is to a post office. Incoming trains are broken down, and their cars are speedily built into new trains for various points.

A switch engine pounces on one of these inbound drags and hauls it to the "hump," where a car, or a block of cars, receives a nudge which starts it downgrade. As it trundles away, men with "switch lists" guide it to that track where other cars of like destination are already assembled. So it goes, until all the cars of this train have been absorbed by the network of tracks in this classification yard.

In all the larger freight terminals cars are switched by the hump, or gravity, method. In the old days, a "hump rider" rode each unit. His job was to "club down" the brakes of the car, or cars, and prevent its slamming into the end of this train in the making and damaging the cars or contents. However, the colorful hump rider is fast joining the ranks of the dodo, as cars coming off the hump are now largely controlled by a "car retarder," a device that regulates the movement of this rolling car.

A car retarder is operated by compressed air. It reaches above the rails of the classification tracks, pressing against the sides of the turning wheels, checking or retarding the speed of the car and bringing it to a stop at the proper place.

A car drifting down from the hump is guided by hand-thrown switches, though more and more the big yards are employing power-operated switches, which are moved by electricity or compressed air, and these are controlled from a switch tower on the hump.

Another advanced practice employed is the use of car-inspection pits in these big classification yards. These pits are located under the track leading from the receiving yards and a short distance in advance of the apex of the hump.

The top of this pit is at track level and is for the purpose of permitting close inspection of car underframes, draft gear, trucks, and brake rigging while cars are being classified. The car inspector sits on a swivel seat, protected by a steel hood with windows of shatterproof glass facing in both directions along the track. Floodlights illuminate the underside of the car as it passes over the pit at slow speed.

When a defect is observed, the inspector marks the car truck by a spray of whitewash. These pits have proved very successful in disclosing defects, and two are employed at the Pennsylvania's Enola Yard, and eighteen in eight other yards of the system.

To get a clearer picture of the enormousness of the modern freight terminal, let us look at the Enola Yard of the Pennsylvania. It is situated on the southwest bank of the Susquehanna River, five miles west of Harrisburg, Pennsylvania, and is one of the principal classification yards of the system, and, further, is the keystone of the arch of the Arranged Freight Train Service of the road.

Constructed shortly after the turn of the century, Enola Yard is now the western terminus of electrified freight operation. It contains 145 miles of tracks, with 378 manually controlled switches and 78 remote-controlled. It has a capacity of 9,900 cars and on a big day clears 16,000 cars. Normally, there are over 3,000 employees, with approximately the same number of road trainmen and enginemen operating in and out.

Average operation, excluding extra trains, yard drafts, and extras, involves 32 symbol trains entering the yard from the east and south and 47 symbol trains from the west and north, while 35 trains are dispatched north and west and the same number east and south. This is in addition to the trains re-

Photo by A.A.K.

POTOMAC YARD AT ALEXANDRIA, VIRGINIA, taken from the air, looking towards the south. This great classification yard is used by the Pennsylvania, the Baltimore & Ohio, the Richmond, Fredericksburg and Potomac, the Southern, and the Chesapeake and Ohio.

Photo by Wentz & Hipper.

THE INTERIOR OF ZOO TOWER AT PHILADELPHIA, PENNSYLVANIA.
One of the largest interlocking plants on the Pennsylvania R.R.

INTERIOR OF THE CAB OF UNION PACIFIC'S NO. 825, 4-8-4 TYPE.
The author rode this engine on her first trip in passenger service all the way from Ogden, Utah, to Omaha, Nebraska, hauling No. 28 with eighteen cars out of Ogden and twenty-two out of Green River.

Courtesy of American Locomotive Co.

S-1811
750

ceived and dispatched on the Harrisburg side of the river every twenty-four hours.

Each day the Pennsylvania Railroad System provides direct service for less-than-carload merchandise freight over 2,575 routes without intermediate handling between origin and destination. Service over 2,050 of these routes is by through merchandise cars, and on the remaining 525 by through merchandise containers.

Merchandise containers are steel compartments with a capacity of 10,000 pounds of freight and are made up in batteries of five and eight, which are loaded on specially equipped flatcars. Whenever there is less-than-carload tonnage between specified stations, one or more of these containers may be used. For example, five stations in the East may have freight for Chicago but not enough to justify the use of a boxcar. Each loads a container to Enola. Here, in the Enola container yard, each is transferred to a Chicago car by means of an overhead traveling crane. Thus, ultimately, the original five containers from five widely separated freight stations eventually leave Enola on a fast through freight for Chicago, all grouped together on one flatcar.

This method not only releases many boxcars for full-carload freight but keeps less-than-carload freight away from transfers and expedites the movement of both.

Before World War I most freight moved forward from division to division as cars awaiting forwarding accumulated in division yards. Now the Pennsylvania's entire freight service is so arranged that it moves by schedules like those of passenger trains. These grand trains, notably those carrying merchandise, fresh fruits, vegetables, meats, livestock, and dairy products, hit the ball at 50 miles an hour in the regular daily operation.

We have seen merchandise wheeling better than four hundred miles overnight, and, more and more, in connection with rapid pick-up and delivery service, it is moved not merely from terminal to terminal but literally from door to door. Faster speeds of the rail have been but one factor in quickening the pulse of freight. Equally important, possibly more so, has been the adoption of improved methods by which the time consumed in yards and terminals has been greatly reduced.

By advanced practices in classifying and dispatching and because of more powerful locomotives, freight trains now move unbroken over much longer distances than formerly, eliminating the delays of rehandling at intermediate yards.

Foremost of these modern trends is prior classification. By prior classification we mean that instead of dragging trains of maximum tonnage, terminal to terminal, trains are now made up to arrive and depart at predetermined hours and of such consists that they may move maximum distances without breaking bulk.

On this basis trains are made up to "overhead" as many intermediate terminals as possible. On trains moving from one end of the system to the other, blocks of cars for intermediate set-off are associated together, while such blocks are placed on the rear or head end in order to reduce to a minimum the delay in cutting out such cars.

In other words, prior classification begins at the originating terminal and continues at all intermediate points. It assures the shipper of prompt and efficient service and is a far step from the days when a freight car meandered leisurely down the railroad with no more apparent incentive to get anywhere than the hobo who rode it.

As on the Pennsylvania, the New York Central maintains a scheduled fast freight service. The maintenance of these hot schedules depends not only upon adherence to the allotted running time over the twenty-eight divisions, but also upon the efficient handling in the make-up and break-up yards.

Besides thousands of freight sidings and small yards at towns and factories along its lines, the Central maintains adequate yards at each of the 174 cities it enters. The larger metropolitan centers are served by several yards, varying in size and importance, each located where it may most conveniently accommodate the near-by industrial districts.

There are seven of these yards at Chicago; five at New York, not including the yards at Weehawken; four at Indianapolis; eight at Cleveland; and eight at Buffalo.

Cleveland can serve here as an illustration of the tremendous importance these terminals play in delivering materials to a city's industries, as well as in transporting its outbound products.

Cleveland, with a population of 900,000, is, as you know, located on the south shore of Lake Erie. Four lines of the New York Central System enter the city from the west, east, and south. These lines are linked by a belt line, which swings in a half-circle, east to west, through the outskirts of the city.

The four lines which pierce the city lead from this surrounding loop.

Two of the eight major freight yards in Cleveland are situated in the heart of the city. The Orange Avenue Freight Terminal is a general distribution and receiving point for merchandise freight consigned to or received from the many users of this type of service. The Whiskey Island Yard receives heavy freight from and brings heavy freight to the docks of the city and the large industrial concerns located near by.

In the western sections of Cleveland are the Clark Avenue, Linndale, and Rockport yards. These yards receive freight for Cleveland from the West and the Big Four, serving the industries of their immediate localities. At the Clark Avenue Yard there are emergency facilities for resting, feeding, and watering livestock.

Industries on the south side of Cleveland are served by the Marcy Yard, located directly on the loop line. The Pittsburgh & Lake Erie Railroad enters the city at this yard, hauling coal and basic materials for all industries in the city.

Further east on the loop line is the Buckeye Road Yard, serving the Orange Avenue Freight Terminal. At this yard the merchandise cars from St. Louis and the West are detached from through trains and switched to the Orange Avenue Freight House.

East of Cleveland is the Collinwood Yard, located on the New York Central main line and serving as a junction point with the Big Four. Some consolidation of both eastbound and westbound cars of the Big Four with those of the main line is made here. Westbound classification facilities are primarily for empty cars arriving from the East, which are to be routed over the main line or the Big Four.

The New York Central provides regular freight service for 780 firms in Cleveland. The greatest volume of traffic involving the operations of a single company rolls in and out from the Fisher Body plant. There are twenty-one tracks for freight inside of this company's yards. During the peak season of the plant's operation, the New York Central hauls away a hundred carloads of freight each day.

The vital function of classification for the through freights between Chicago–St. Louis and New York–Boston is performed at DeWitt Yard, east of Syracuse; East Buffalo Yard; Bellefontaine Yard, Bellefontaine, Ohio; Moorefield Yard, Indianapolis; Selkirk Yard, southwest of Albany; and Stanley Yard, Toledo.

DeWitt Yard operates as the hub of a wheel in all freight transportation east and west over the New York Central System. The spokes of this wheel are the lines running east to Boston and New York; north to upper New York State and Canada; west to Detroit on the Michigan Central, to Buffalo, Cleveland, and Chicago on the main line, and to Columbus, Cincinnati, and St. Louis on the Big Four; and south into Pennsylvania.

Practically all trains arriving in this yard must be reclassified for through and local movement. Numerous classifications are made to facilitate the prompt delivery of freight on arrival of trains at destination terminals. In some of these trains up to fifteen different groups are made.

Both the east- and the westbound yards at DeWitt are equipped with a hump and car retarders. Each yard is capable of classifying approximately 3,500 cars a day.

As 99 per cent of the eastbound cars are loaded, compared to 63 per cent unloaded westbound, the hump equipment differs. Thus there are twice as many retarders on the eastbound hump, totaling 32, and the maximum grade is 3½ per cent instead of the 5 per cent on the westbound hump.

To insure "on time" delivery at destinations, the arrival, classification, and departure of eastbound trains at DeWitt Yard fall into four definitely limited periods of time. These are relatively the same each day. The first scheduled period is between 10:45 P.M. and 2:30 A.M. Trains arriving within this period are for classification and dispatchments beginning at 3 A.M. The second period embraces trains arriving between 7:15 A.M. and 11 A.M. for dispatchments beginning at 12:01 noon. The third period includes trains arriving between 12:01 noon and 1:30 P.M., with dispatchments beginning at 3:30 P.M. And the fourth period for trains arriving between 3 P.M. and 4 P.M. for dispatchments beginning about 6 P.M.

The Selkirk Yard, southwest of Albany, is primarily utilized for the consolidation of through westbound trains of empty cars from the Boston & Albany and the River and Hudson divisions. Short destination loads westbound to points east of DeWitt are also classified here. A gravity, car-retarder-operated yard, with a capacity of 3,500 cars a day, is provided.

Eastbound operations at Selkirk consist of flat switching of cars for points on the Hudson and River divisions and west of Springfield, Massachusetts. The icing of perishables is also an important operation here.

The Selkirk Yard is six miles long. It was completed in 1924 as part of a $25,000,000 improvement project, which included the double-track Alfred H. Smith Memorial Bridge. This improvement, called the "Castleton Cut-off," enables through freight traffic to flow swiftly over the main line, avoiding the steep grades at Albany.

The Selkirk Yard's potential efficiency, far in excess of all past demands, has never really been put to the test. For example, in periods of emergency, trains could be routed through DeWitt Yard for classification here.

Little classification work is done in the East Buffalo Yard. The principal service performed here on eastbound movements is the icing of perishables and the feeding and watering of livestock. All livestock en route from the Midwest, destined for packing houses in New York City and Boston, are rested at this point.

Here there are stockyards covering 56 acres, with facilities for the handling of 150 cars of livestock per day. Numerous other smaller stockyards are maintained at cities on the New York Central lines for local service or for use in the event of a single stock car breaking down en route.

Westbound classification work at Buffalo is performed at the Gardenville Yard, located a few miles south of the city. Two yards do the classification at Bellefontaine, Ohio. Here cars are classified for east-west movement, and at the Gest Yard for north-south movement. "Flat" switching is used at both yards.

Through freights from St. Louis to eastern points stop at the Bellefontaine Yard to receive cars from Cincinnati or to drop cars for that city or Toledo. Dropped cars are hauled to the Gest Yard for consolidations in north-south, Detroit, and Toledo-Cincinnati freight trains. The Bellefontaine Yard, further, has extensive facilities for the care of livestock not previously rested at St. Louis or Indianapolis. An icing station is also maintained here.

A triple yard arrangement prevails at Indianapolis, where east-west and north-south movements are co-ordinated through the Moorefield, Brightwood, and Hill yards.

The Moorefield Yard operates as a terminus for the Peoria & Eastern Railway. Cars of hogs, for example, arriving on train PE-10 from Peoria are hauled from the Moorefield Yard to the Brightwood Yard for consolidation in train A/NY-6, eastbound from St. Louis. All east-west through freights use the Brightwood Yard. Tracks from this yard enter the Union Stockyards in Indianapolis.

The Hill Yard handles the north-south, Chicago-Cincinnati traffic, with connections with the other yards for transfer of cars, depending on direction or movement. Flat switching is used in all three yards.

The major portion of the classification work in the Toledo territory is performed in Standley Yard, which is located about five miles south of the city. At this point the New York Central and Big Four cars from the south are received and classified for points both east and west on the New York Central and north on the Michigan Central, as well as to foreign connections in the Toledo area.

In addition, the Standley Yard classifies a large volume of coal cars, which are taken to two coal dumpers located on the Maumee River, four miles north of the yard, for transfer into lake boats bound for the upper Great Lakes region. This, too, is a gravity yard equipped with car retarders and has a capacity of 3,000 cars a day.

The foregoing yards have the important function of keeping all freight traffic flowing smoothly and without delay over the New York Central lines. They are points where fast through freight trains interchange cars with other through freights or with local trains. At each of these yards schedules are maintained similar to those employed at DeWitt.

Terminal yards are vastly important in their relation to speedy freight movement—to the cannonading rush of fast freight across the country—and they have grown and expanded to meet the needs of the times.

We turn again to the Richmond, Fredericksburg and Potomac Railroad, and find its Potomac Yard one of the most important in the country. The yard contains ninety miles of track and handles, in normal times, around a million and a half cars, a maximum of 6,800 cars per day moving through its facilities.

To accommodate the enormous volume of traffic which flows through this yard, it is divided into two separate sections. The northbound facilities consist of twenty tracks for the receipt of trains from the south, and forty-six outbound tracks into which the freight from the south is classified for points north. There are four icing tracks, which re-ice as many as 500 cars a day when the fruit rush is on.

There are, too, a number of tracks for holding fruit cars for reconsigning or diversion purposes, and it is not unusual for as many as 400 to 600 cars of perishables to stand here awaiting consignment to northern markets.

The southbound facilities of the Potomac Yard consist of thirteen receiving tracks and twenty-nine outbound classification tracks. Here trains from the north are broken down and the cars or blocks of cars classified according to routes and destinations, as they are made up into trains for the three lines leading south.

Many modern facilities and methods have been inaugurated at Potomac Yard, including the electro-pneumatic car retarder. As each car starts from the top of the hump, teletypewriters inform the operators in the retarder towers whether the car is loaded or empty, heavy or light, and also designate the outbound track into which it must go.

On this information the car, or cars, is guided into the proper classification track and the retarders applied, with the pressure varying according to the weight of the car and the distance it must roll. Loud-speaker telephones also connect the hump with the car-retarder towers.

Accurate weights of shipments which have not been scaled elsewhere are obtained without delay by weighing the cars as they pass over automatic scales at the top of the northbound hump.

The Potomac Yard is also equipped with the underground inspection pit referred to earlier in this chapter. A modern method of improved lubrication, which also saves time, is the injection by air pressure of hot oil into the journal boxes of cars while moving slowly up the incline to the classification hump.

Still another timesaver is the Recordak machine, previously mentioned in connection with the movement of those fruit trains out of Tucumcari, New Mexico.

In January 1937, when all routes crossing the Ohio River were interrupted by floods, it became necessary to handle through the Potomac Yard a vast movement of freight which ordinarily moves via the Ohio River crossing. It was further necessary to make some record of the waybills for this detoured traffic in order that the route movement through the Potomac Yard be recorded and the freight charges distributed among the lines handling this detoured movement. The Richmond, Fredericksburg and Potomac, therefore, leased a double-camera Recordak machine, with two projectors. The waybills are passed through this machine at the rate of about ninety a minute. The very small film is wound on spools and afterward developed; then placed in the projectors, the waybill photo being flashed on an illuminated glass plate, which shows the full impression of the waybill at one and one-half times its actual size. Thus accurate copies of the bills can be made at any time needed and without in the least delaying the movement of the traffic. First employed to meet an emergency, the Recordak is now regarded as one of the most necessary devices employed in the daily operations of the Potomac Yard.

The operation of a big freight yard is as vital to the unceasing flow of traffic as the heart of the human body is to the blood stream. The same amount of fluid that enters must leave with certainty and precision; any slowing or stoppage would prove disastrous. A choked freight terminal is instantly reflected in the slowing pulse of all main arteries. Trains are blocked, schedules disrupted, and the entire division turns stagnant. Dispatchers start tearing their hair, and the officials rave, and if the poor yardmaster came on a piece of rope he would probably hang himself! But, happily for all concerned, freight yards today are spacious, well equipped, and advantageously located. Further, they are manned by seasoned veterans schooled to the imperative demands of the iron road.

It is a stout forward stride from the days when old "Good Record Pete," of the Pocatello, Idaho, yards, casting his eye in the direction of a boomer switchman, said dryly, "He ought to make a good man; he can throw a ball switch with his foot an' roll a cigarette at the same time."

CHAPTER XIII

Freight Terminals of Manhattan

"Cowboys" once "rode herd" on trains in New York City. This was in the days when the tracks of the old West Side Line ran on the surface. The law required that men on horseback precede all trains to insure their slow movement and to warn pedestrian and vehicle traffic.

Those days are gone beyond recall, and now the most spectacular terminal yard, or series of yards, from the point of view of cost and engineering problems overcome, is the West Side Improvement on the island of Manhattan.

Construction on this project was begun in 1925 and was steadily pursued during the years that followed. It was completed not long ago and stands today as another milestone in railroad achievement. Throughout its thirteen-mile length the West Side Improvement connects, by elevated and subway tracks, the freight yards at Manhattanville, Seventy-second Street, Thirty-third Street, and St. John's Park Freight

Terminal. It is the only all-freight line on Manhattan Island.

The new viaduct between St. John's Park Terminal and the Thirty-third Street yards provides for sidetracks to shipping platforms of industries located along the right-of-way and passes directly through a number of buildings, several of which were designed to take advantage of this project. Thus tenants now receive and ship freight from their own back door, which eliminates the cost of cartage, as well as saving time.

The subway tracks between the Thirty-third Street and Seventy-second Street yards have private sidetracks for such industries as the New York *Times* and the Sheffield Farms Company. Above the Seventy-second Street Yard the tracks pass beneath Riverside Park for a distance of several miles, which adds thirty-two acres of recreational space for the people of New York.

The Seventy-second Street Yard, with a capacity of 3,047 cars, is the main receiving, classification, and departure yard for the West Side Line. It has facilities for the unloading of automobiles and milk and the handling of live poultry.

The 10 tracks that handle milk have a capacity of 87 cars. Through milk trains deliver daily, between the hours of 11:30 P.M. and 3:30 A.M., more than 216,000 quarts of milk, cream, condensed milk, and pot cheese. This represents about 31 per cent of the total rail deliveries in New York City. Other deliveries are made at Westchester Avenue and the 130th Street, or Manhattanville, Yard.

Time was when milk was transported in ten-gallon cans and in bottles in cases, but now about 80 per cent arrives in specially constructed, privately owned milk tank cars. Except for the Sheffield Farms Company operations at West Fifty-seventh Street, where the tank cars are placed directly at their plant siding—the only one of its kind in Manhattan—the tank cars are spotted on unloading tracks and the milk is transferred to tank trucks for distribution to the plants of the consignee, where it is pasteurized and bottled.

Some of this milk arrives from points as far distant as 400 miles, and quick handling is necessary in order that the empty cars may be cleaned and started back to the point of origin. The New York Central owns 313 milk cars, which provide high-speed transportation from contented upstate cows to contented babies on the island of Manhattan.

Before powers of evil kicked over the traditional applecart, an average of 700 carloads of automobiles were handled monthly in the Seventy-second Street Yard. Six team tracks were used for this type of freight alone. One day again there will be automobiles, boxed for export, arriving in this yard to be lightered to steamers at New York City docks.

From 40 to 50 cars of poultry arrive daily. These are consigned to the 14 commission houses located in the West Washington Market. During Jewish holidays in September and preceding Thanksgiving as many as 60 to 80 cars arrive each twenty-four hours. These cars are owned and operated by the Palace Poultry Company, of Chicago. Each car has a capacity of approximately 4,500 fowl and is accompanied by a "poultry porter." In winter months these "cackle cars" come from Texas, Oklahoma, and Nebraska. In the summer they roll in from Indiana, Ohio, and Illinois.

Besides the commodities mentioned, the Seventy-second Street Yard alone handles upward of 50,000 tons of lighterage freight every month.

Since Manhattan is an island, marine freight operations are very important, and they antedate the railroads. All transfers of freight, including delivery from the West Shore, in New Jersey, to markets, piers, and docks in Brooklyn, must of course be handled by water. For these marine operations the New York Central owns one of the largest and finest fleets of craft in the port of New York—268 units of equipment. This includes 25 tugs, 45 car floats, 28 scow barges, 5 lighters, 21 hoist barges, and 103 covered barges. Approximately 500 shifts and tows are made every day by New York Central tugs. In the first six months of 1941 the Marine Department lightered 1,260,387 tons of merchandise and floated 80,320 freight cars.

Within the limits of the Seventy-second Street Yard are four float bridges, three electric and one pontoon, having a capacity of more than 700 cars daily. These bridges are used to handle cars to and from Bush Terminal, Wallabout Union Freight Station, Barclay Street, Weehawken, Pier 34, East River, and the various railroads entering New York City.

South from the Seventy-second Street Yard, the West Side Freight Line runs in an open cut to the Thirtieth Street Yard. Here as many as 25,000 cars are loaded for outbound movement annually. Inbound commodities, unloaded at extensive team tracks, include fruits, vegetables, paper, machinery, furniture, refrigerated products, and manufactured

Courtesy of New York Central System.

THE NEW YORK CENTRAL'S NEW EMPIRE STATE EXPRESS, which was built by the Budd Manufacturing Company, eastbound on the Mohawk Division. The engine is Class J-3, which was specially streamlined for this train.

THE CONVENIENTLY ARRANGED CAB of the world's heaviest locomotive, the new Union Pacific 4000 class, built by the American Locomotive Company, affectionately known as "Big Boy." Note the drifting throttle and four water glasses.

Courtesy of American Locomotive Co.

Photo by R. H. Kindig.

NEW SOUTHERN PACIFIC SAN JOAQUIN DAYLIGHT climbing the grade over the coast range near Saugus, California. The engine is the new GS-4, recently delivered by the Lima Locomotive Company. Note the Mars headlight.

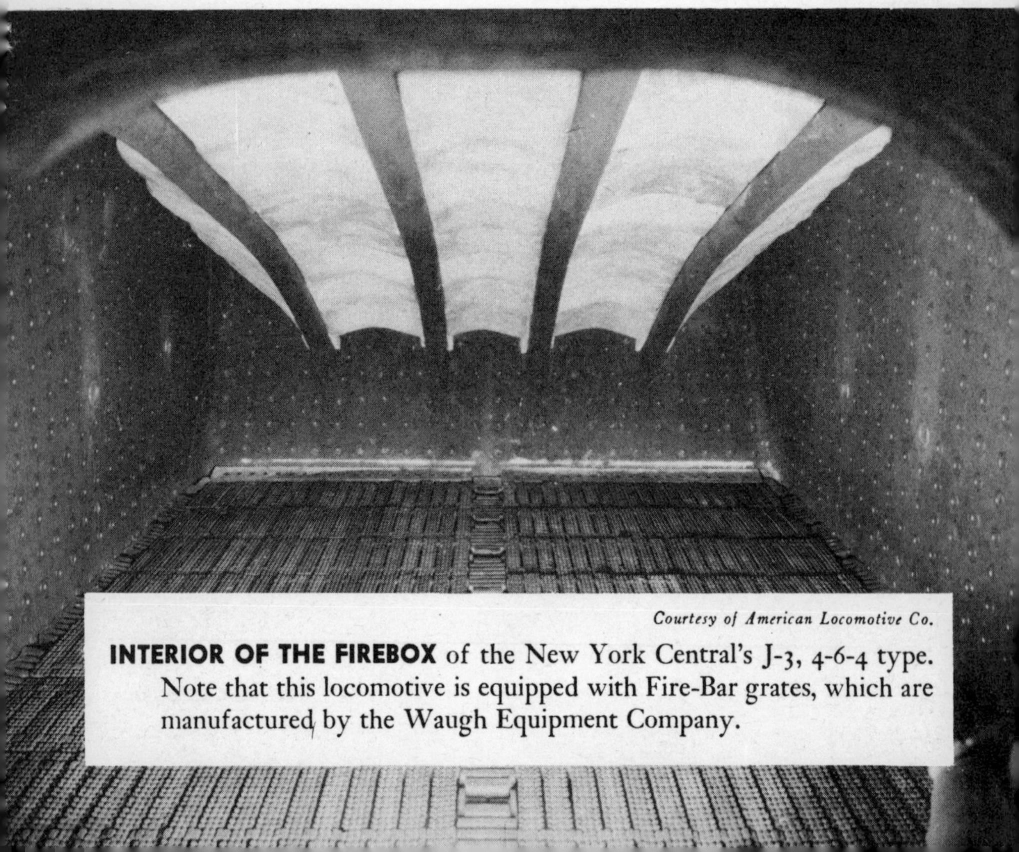

Courtesy of American Locomotive Co.

INTERIOR OF THE FIREBOX of the New York Central's J-3, 4-6-4 type. Note that this locomotive is equipped with Fire-Bar grates, which are manufactured by the Waugh Equipment Company.

steel products. Some 20,000 carloads of such freight arrive in the course of a year.

Shortly after the first of December, Christmas trees come rolling into the Thirtieth Street Yard, harbingers of old Saint Nick. Something like 175 cars deliver their green-laden cargo each season. Quickly gobbled by wholesalers, the trees are distributed and find their way into thousands upon thousands of homes, from the slums to brownstone mansions, carrying their sweet fragrance of the north woods and their symbolism of Christ the King.

North of this yard are the New York Stockyards, where approximately 12,000 carloads of livestock are handled a year. Also adjacent to the Thirtieth Street Yard is the Parcel Post Building. Here are handled 10,000 cars of parcel-post matter, together with 7,000,000 sacks of mail, each swing of the calendar.

The terminus of the West Side Line is the St. John's Park Freight Terminal, two miles farther south. This is reached by trains from the Thirtieth Street Yard by a viaduct, which cuts through several buildings. There are sidings for meat-packing houses and factories in the vicinity. The terminal is 800 feet in length and three stories high. It is served by eight tracks, with a capacity for 150 cars. On the street-level floor back-up space is provided for 127 trucks inside of the building. The second floor is the track floor, while the third is used for storage. The terminal handles both inbound and outbound freight in carload and less-than-carload quantities, including butter, eggs, cheese, and dressed poultry. It was established more than fifty years ago as the principal delivery station for dairy freight in New York City. Many of the cars in the crack New York-to-Buffalo "Merchandiser," the NB-1, carrying l.c.l. shipments, originate here. Other cars in this fast overnight freight are picked up in the Thirtieth and Seventy-second Street yards.

The Weehawken Freight Yard must also be included as a vital part of the terminus for New York Central freight shipments to the New York City port area. Weehawken and the connecting North Bergen Yard have a combined capacity of more than 7,000 cars. Since almost all lightered and floated freight is routed via the West Shore Line, 12 piers are included among the facilities here. There are, too, five slips for passenger ferries. The yard contains the largest grain elevator in the port of New York, with a capacity of 2,000,000 bushels, and it is further equipped with an adequate icing plant.

The Weehawken Yard has long been the origin of heavy westbound banana shipments. These leave every weekday night on the famous "Banana Train," the WB-3, running from Weehawken to Buffalo. Four hundred carloads move out monthly, and special service for these cars includes icing in summer and heating during midwinter months.

Nowhere could we find a better example of the part that the lowly freight car plays in serving the needs of the people than in these great freight yards of the teeming metropolis of the city of New York. Cars of the Pacific Fruit Express, booming through from the Coast; cars from Florida, streaking north; cars from Texas; cars from the Middle West; cars from Aroostook County, the potato kingdom of Maine; cars from the rich agricultural districts of upper New York State —all jostling, swaying, crowding hard behind smokeless Diesel-electrics as they parade endlessly into the yards on the island of Manhattan.

Chicago, the second ranking city in the United States, plays a vastly important part in the freight movement of the country. For operations within the industrial heart of the city, the Chicago Junction Railway and the Indiana Harbor Belt Railroad loom large in the scheme of things. Each of these railways supplements the service of the other, and both render distribution and collection service for the New York Central lines. They further effect connections with other railroads.

The principal freight terminals of the New York Central System in the Chicago area are the Gibson, the Blue Island, and the Englewood yards. The Gibson Yard is principally important in its classification of westbound cars, its consolidation of eastbound cars, and merchandise transfer from industries in the adjacent territory.

The Englewood Yard is located on the New York Central main line, just south of the central Chicago manufacturing district. This is the first collection point for cars destined for eastbound movement and is the final distribution point for incoming cars billed to local industries and markets.

In close proximity to the Chicago Union Stockyards, served by the Chicago Junction Railway, the Englewood Yard receives the majority of livestock cars to be routed over New York Central lines, eastbound from Chicago.

The Blue Island Yard is located nine miles west of Gibson on the Indiana Harbor Belt Railroad. Here is the largest yard in the New York Central System handling interchange traffic. Four eastbound symbol trains are scheduled from the Blue Island Yard daily. These are the NY-4, CDN-4, NY-8, and XN-2, and they operate in from one to four sections each. They have reached a total of as high as nine sections, and that is wheeling preference freight with a vengeance.

The Blue Island Yard is equipped for hump switching, which is further facilitated by car retarders. It has a classifying capacity of 4,000 cars a day. Since approximately 50 per cent of all freight traffic received here is perishable, the yard has extensive facilities for icing. During peak periods as many as 1,500 cars are iced daily.

The territory served by the Chicago Junction Railway and its subsidiary, the Chicago River & Indiana Railroad, extends from Park Avenue on the west to Lake Michigan, and from Forty-ninth Street on the south to Ogden Avenue. This territory may be described as being in five natural groups, which include the stockyards and packing town, the central manufacturing district, which produces a freight tonnage of 100,000 carloads annually, and three other areas which are developing as important industrial centers.

The Chicago Junction Railway, together with its associate line, the C.R.&I.R., operates an inner belt line aggregating approximately 350 miles. The Indiana Harbor Belt Railroad, serving principally as a connecting link between all railroads entering the Chicago area, maintains some 120 miles of trackage.

The amount of motive power involved in the handling of cars in the freight yards of the country reaches an amazingly high figure. As an example, let us look at the number of yard engines employed by the New York Central alone.

This road has 379 six-wheel switchers and 750 eight-wheel switchers. Yard steam locomotives also include 12 Mallet-type engines, with a 0-8-8-0 wheel arrangement. These latter are used in yards equipped with humps for consolidation work. Besides this steam power, the Central also has 127 Diesel-electric and 168 electric locomotives. Of these, 109 of the former and 63 of the latter are used in freight service.

The New York Central was one of the first railroads in the country to use both electric and Diesel-electric power. The first Diesel-electric engine began service in the West Side Yards in New York City in February 1928. By January 1, 1931, 42 engines of this type were in service, and today the Central leads in switchers of this design, and 15 more are on order. Of its fleet of Diesel-electric switchers, the Central assigned 30 to the New York territory, 30 to Detroit, 29 to Buffalo, 12 for use on the Chicago Junction line, 6 to Chicago, 1 to Rochester, and 1 to Auburn, New York. Forty-two of these are three-power locomotives, operating from third rail, from generator and storage battery. When at work within buildings, as often occurs on the West Side in New York, the Diesel engine is shut down and the power is supplied from the storage battery. Of the third-rail or overhead-contact electrics used in freight service, 44 are operated in connection with the handling of road freight and 7 for switching in New York territory. Twelve are used in Detroit for both passenger and freight switching.

The number of freight cars in use in the United States reaches a staggering figure. The New York Central alone owned, on July 1, 1941, 126,665 freight cars, with 5,329 on order. This does not include 6,746 company service cars, or the 313 milk cars mentioned, as the latter are classed as passenger equipment.

We watch a freight drag trundling past, and note with interest that there are cars from every part of the country. We wonder if some of these travel-worn nomads of the rail ever get home; wonder, too, how the various lines represented can ever keep a check on the whereabouts of their rolling stock.

At Buffalo, New York, headquarters of the Central's Car Service Department, several hundred employees are engaged solely in keeping an accurate daily record of the activities of each of the vast armada of hotfooting freight cars, not only on the lines of the New York Central but on all other lines as well. The movements of foreign cars on the Central receive attention at the same time.

Cars never get lost or go astray, except in rare instances, and when they do—well, there is likely to be a story worthy of the attention of the fictioneer.

Whenever a car is spotted at a siding, placed in a yard, or moved along the line, conductors report its location, together with its "consist," when loaded, in their "wheel reports." These wheel reports go forward to the Car Service Department. Interchange reports from agents at junctions with other railroads provide information as to when foreign cars enter the System, or when owned cars take departure for other lines.

The Car Service Department may use these records to inform inquiring consignees as to the location of their shipments. Also, computations are made from the reports which determine demurrage charges and per-diem charges to be collected from or paid other railroads.

The lowly freight car, the tramp of the railroad, has its own share of high adventure. It visits pulsing cities and sleepy hamlets. Its wheels spin across far horizons. It lifts to fury-swept mountains and beats out the miles on plain and desert. It knows blinding blizzard and bake-oven heat; but always there is final triumph as it delivers its burdensome load at the end of the run.

CHAPTER XIV

Pennsylvania Pioneers

THE EARLIEST OF THE LINES now comprising the Pennsylvania Railroad System was originally chartered in 1823 by Colonel John Stevens, who thereby held the oldest charter under which any railroad project was ever undertaken. The proposed line was to extend from Philadelphia to Columbia, Pennsylvania. However, owing to the inability of Colonel Stevens to raise private funds for its construction, the provisions of the charter were changed and construction of the road was subsequently undertaken by the state of Pennsylvania.

The program called for the building of a line connecting the city and port of Philadelphia with the state system of canals on the Susquehanna and Juniata rivers. This road was opened in 1834, and it connected with canal boats operating on these rivers. At the foot of the Allegheny Mountains at Hollidaysburg, Pennsylvania, these boats were converted to land craft by cradling them on unwieldy affairs supported on wheels.

Then, by means of stationary engines and cables, these boats were trundled over inclined planes, to be launched finally in another canal extending to Pittsburgh. Crude though it was, transportation was on the wing, and Philadelphia had a commercial route to and from the new West, and connecting with boats of the Ohio and Mississippi rivers.

This was the Philadelphia and Columbia Railroad, the forerunner of the present vast Pennsylvania Railroad System, terminating at Broad and Vine streets, then the northern limit of the city of Philadelphia.

The line served its purpose after a fashion but was inadequate and cumbersome, and during the winter months the canals were closed by ice. The merchants and other progressive citizens of Philadelphia, therefore, soon started a movement for an all-rail line to Pittsburgh, and it was for this purpose that the Pennsylvania Railroad was financed and organized.

The act incorporating the Pennsylvania Railroad was signed by the governor of the commonwealth of Pennsylvania on April 13, 1846.

In 1852 the Pennsylvania finally wheeled an all-rail route train from Pittsburgh into Philadelphia over the now double-track line of the Philadelphia and Columbia Railroad. This line, together with the canal property between Columbia and Pittsburgh, including the Portage Railroad over the Alleghenies, was acquired by purchase from the commonwealth of Pennsylvania on June 25, 1857. The price was $7,500,000, but the final cost, including interest, reached $15,500,000.

During the years preceding its sale, the Philadelphia and Columbia had not been idle. That incline haul of 2,805 feet over a 15 per cent grade and those frozen canals irked the officials not a little, and they set about the construction of a new double-track right-of-way. This was opened in 1850 and extended from a point just east of Ardmore Station through what is now known as Narberth, Merion, and Overbrook to the Schuylkill River at Market Street. This is the alignment in use today.

From Ardmore west to Dillerville, just west of Lancaster, the main line was originally the Philadelphia and Columbia Railroad, although of the sixty-nine miles of that line acquired between the Schuylkill River and Dillerville only eleven miles of the main line as it now exists occupies that first alignment.

From Dillerville to Harrisburg the main iron was originally the Harrisburg, Portsmouth, Mount Joy and Lancaster Railroad. In its initial operations the Pennsylvania used this line under a trackage agreement, but on January 1, 1861, it was leased for ninety-nine years, and on April 25, 1917, this railroad was absorbed as owned line.

From its connection with the Harrisburg, Portsmouth, Mount Joy and Lancaster Railroad at Harrisburg westward to Altoona, the main line was located and built by the Pennsylvania. Construction was started July 7, 1847, or a little over a year after the incorporation of the Pennsylvania Railroad. This work was completed October 1, 1850, and the line was opened for service in the spring of 1851.

As the line across the Allegheny Mountains had not yet been started, a branch was built from Altoona to the foot of the state-owned Allegheny Portage Railroad at Hollidaysburg. This was completed and united with the tracks of that line on September 16, 1850.

During this period work was progressing on various sections of the Pennsylvania's line between Pittsburgh and Johnstown. By the close of 1851, the Pennsylvania Railroad was able to provide all-rail service between Philadelphia and Pittsburgh, except for a gap of twenty-seven miles between Beatty and Turtle Creek, about ten miles east of Pittsburgh. Here stages and wagons were used. This gap was finally closed, and on December 10, 1852, the chuffing iron horse proudly rode the rail all the way, Philadelphia to Pittsburgh.

The route was as follows:

Philadelphia to Dillerville over the Philadelphia and Columbia Railroad.

Dillerville to Harrisburg over the Harrisburg, Portsmouth, Mount Joy and Lancaster Railroad.

Harrisburg to Hollidaysburg over the Pennsylvania Railroad.

Hollidaysburg to Viaduct Bridge west of South Fork over the Allegheny Portage Railroad.

Viaduct Bridge to Pittsburgh over the Pennsylvania Railroad.

Operation over the Allegheny Portage Railroad involved the use of its inclined planes, but the state eliminated planes Nos. 2 and 3 by the construction of the New Portage Railroad, which used the Pennsy's new line from Viaduct Bridge to Johnstown, eliminating plane No. 1. However, the Pennsylvania Railroad completed its own line over the summit of the Alleghenies from Altoona to connect with its line already built to Viaduct Bridge, opening it for service on February 15, 1854. Service over the Allegheny Portage was then discontinued.

Between Pittsburgh and Chicago the route of the Pennsylvania Railroad was over the Pittsburgh, Fort Wayne and Chicago Railway, a leased line incorporated in Pennsylvania in 1860 and in Indiana and Illinois in 1862. The Pittsburgh, Fort Wayne and Chicago Railway was incorporated under the general laws of Ohio, Indiana, and Illinois and by special act of Pennsylvania, to effect the consolidation of the Ohio and Pennsylvania Railroad Company and the Ohio and Indiana Railroad Company.

On October 6, 1851, trains began running between the initial terminal on the west side of Federal Street, North Side, Pittsburgh, and New Briton. The line to Crestline, Ohio, was completed in the spring of 1853 and opened to service on April 11.

The original bridge spanning the Allegheny River, a wooden structure, was not built until 1857, when service was extended to a temporary station on the west side of Pennsylvania Avenue, Pittsburgh. The tracks finally extended to Pittsburgh's first Union Station, with service inaugurated into that station in March 1858.

Construction work had progressed steadily to the west, and in January 1859 it was possible to make an all-rail journey from Philadelphia to Chicago, although it involved changing cars at Pittsburgh.

The vast new West was opening with a boom. Great wagon trains were slogging across the plains. Pioneers were courageously turning their faces toward the land of the setting sun in ever-increasing numbers. The Mississippi and Missouri rivers were the jumping-off points, and transportation from the East was vital to their needs.

Even as the railhead was pressing on toward Chicago, the Pittsburgh, Cincinnati, Chicago and St. Louis Railroad Company and its various associates were driving for St. Louis. The rails reached Steubenville, and a bridge was built across the Ohio River. Already the Columbus and Xenia Railroad had spiked down rails between these two points. In 1858 the Dayton, Xenia and Belpre completed and put in operation a line to Dayton.

Westward moved the rails. The Indiana Central Railroad was completed in 1854. Meanwhile the Terre Haute and Indianapolis Railroad Company had their finger in the pie. The Vandalia Railroad took a hand, and the steel poked into East St. Louis.

The original Pittsburgh, Cincinnati, Chicago and St. Louis Railroad, generally known as the "Panhandle," was made up of sixty-two predecessor corporations, fifty of which each constructed a part of what was to become the huge Pennsylvania Railroad System, there between Pittsburgh and the West.

Edward Creighton had spun a thin strand of telegraph wire across the western plains. The U.P. Trail was under steam.

Theodore Judah's Central Pacific construction gangs had forged into the Sierra foothills.

On the Pennsylvania Railroad, Philadelphia still stood as the eastern terminus of the line. However, in 1871, by lease of lines in northern New Jersey, it extended its operations to the Jersey shore at the port of New York.

But things had not been entirely idle in New Jersey. In fact the iron horse had been capering thereabouts from as early as 1831. At that time, on November 12, to be exact, an engine named the John Bull gave forth a few tentative snorts and went huffing down the line at Bordentown, New Jersey.

The New Jersey Railroad and Transportation Company, with valuable terminal privileges and ferry rights at Jersey City, together with the right to construct a railroad from New Brunswick to Jersey City under a charter granted March 7, 1832, opened its road from the Hudson River to Elizabeth, New Jersey, in 1834, moving on to New Brunswick late in 1835.

The Camden and Amboy Railroad had been completed between Bordentown and South Amboy in December 1832. At that time it was possible to travel from Philadelphia to New York without too great inconvenience. Of course, there was a small matter that involved taking a boat to Bordentown, changing to a train at South Amboy, then finally boating merrily away to the island of Manhattan. Happily in those days no one ever appeared in too great a hurry to get anywhere.

In 1834 the Delaware and Raritan Canal was completed. The New Jersey Railroad finished its line from Bordentown to New Brunswick in 1838. Meanwhile the Philadelphia and Trenton Railroad had spun its thread of steel, Morrisville, Pennsylvania, to Kensington, in Philadelphia.

The United New Jersey Railroads and Canal Company was organized in 1867. Negotiations between the Pennsylvania Railroad and the United Railroads began in 1869 and continued until June 30, 1871, at which time the Pennsylvania took over. The lease of the United New Jersey Railroads and Canal Company brought to the Pennsylvania Railroad valuable property, including branch railroads, turnpikes, and bridges and ferries over the Delaware and Hudson rivers.

In 1903 the Pennsylvania Railroad began its famous bore under the Hudson. In 1910 it opened the Pennsylvania Station in the heart of the island of Manhattan, with tunnels extending eastward across the city and underneath the East River to connect with the Long Island Railroad.

It was in 1917 that, jointly with the New York, New Haven and Hartford Railroad, the Pennsylvania completed the Hell Gate Bridge route, by which New England is afforded a direct rail outlet to the South and West.

Pennsylvania, the old Quaker State, was the cradle of American railroad transportation, and it is therefore entirely fitting and proper that the Pennsylvania Railroad should stand today as the largest transportation system in the world, when measured by tons of freight and passengers carried, with an investment in facilities and resources of more than 3 billions of dollars.

In 1860 there were 30,635 miles of railroads in the United States. Following the close of the Civil War came a period of rapid expansion, and the turn of the century found the country with nearly 200,000 miles of railroad line. The present mileage is 233,670, with 405,975 miles of track. Thus we find the United States, with 6 per cent of the world's population and 5 per cent of its area, owning nearly *one third* of the world's railroad mileage.

The present figures give the Pennsylvania 11,727 miles of line and 28,408 miles of track, and it performs nearly one eighth of the freight service and one fifth of the passenger service of the country. A further measuring stick is the fact that the Pennsylvania has performed public service equivalent to carrying one ton of freight 39,757,786,116 miles and one passenger 3,443,503,871 miles.

The Pennsylvania Railroad was the first to use steel rails; the first to use the air brake; the first to install track tanks, enabling a locomotive to take water on the run; the first to use the telephone for train dispatching; the first to protect its trains with block signals.

It was the first with all-steel passenger equipment and all-steel freight cars. The first of the former was built in 1908; the first of the latter in 1898.

It was the first to co-ordinate motor, airplane, and rail transportation.

The road operates more than one third of America's electrified standard railroad trackage.

It was the first in the country to use the principle of gravity, or the "hump yard," for classification. This was at the Honey Pot Yard, near Wilkes-Barre, Pennsylvania.

The Pennsy owns 4,533 locomotives, with a tractive power

of 258,408,190 pounds. It has 5,126 passenger cars, with a carrying capacity of 207,315 persons, and 233,765 freight cars capable of hauling 12,856,105 tons. These figures are as of December 31, 1940.

In September 1941 it was operating 2,249 daily passenger trains and 2,589 freight trains.

The System serves that densely populated region east of the Mississippi containing 51 per cent of the country's population, linking together nine of the ten largest cities in the country.

To provide for added comfort and safety, the Pennsylvania Railroad has adopted the use of the 152-pound rail on its high-speed lines, and at the close of 1941 some 570 miles of track carried this heavy-duty steel, the heaviest in use in the world; 1,659 miles of track are laid with 131-pound rail.

The 152-pound rail is 8 inches high, with a 6¾-inch base and a 3-inch head. It was designed for 100,000-pound axle loads, moving at speeds of 100 miles an hour.

The first 70-ton hopper car was built for the Pennsy in 1941. Recent additions to the equipment were covered hopper cars with roof hatches for loading bulk cement and other material. These had an inside height of 10 feet 8 inches to provide larger cubical-capacity loading space. Further, there were gondola cars 52 feet 6 inches long, weighing 70 tons; 65-foot and 46-foot gondolas for long mill products, and 250,000-pound-capacity depressed flatcars for handling large castings and heavy machinery.

In the twelve-year period from January 1, 1930, to the end of 1941, installations of new equipment on the Pennsylvania totaled over 35,000 freight cars and 336 locomotives, all of the most advanced and efficient design. In the same period the railroad spent an aggregate of $667,500,000 on improvements and additions to its general facilities for rendering service.

At present the road has 310 units of floating equipment, which include 2 steamboats, 12 ferryboats, 34 tugs, 134 barges, 95 car floats, and 33 miscellaneous.

The Pennsylvania has what might be termed a four-track right-of-way between New York and Chicago, though not all tracks are on the same alignment. However, in many cases six and eight tracks are in service over a portion of the route.

Just east of Harrisburg, for instance, there are eight tracks, with four on each side of the Susquehanna River. At Rahway, New Jersey, there are six tracks on the same alignment. The same is true of the Long Island Railroad just outside of New York.

Frequently, where a four-track line exists, there is an independent double-track right-of-way on a different alignment. In many cases low-grade lines have been built to carry freight trains around ruling grades, and here we find the symbol trains of the freight service booming through.

Looking backward, we find that the traveler setting out on the journey from Philadelphia to New York was faced by an undertaking of considerable magnitude. It involved a long, tedious, and often adventuresome trip. Today traveling between these two cities is but a brief and pleasant interlude and no more tiring than two hours spent in a comfortable chair in a hotel lobby.

Thus, here on the Pennsylvania, we have seen the growth and development of a great transportation system. And yet this is only one of the many railroads that spin their steel webs across the domain of Uncle Sam.

Large or small, every road in the country has performed its own valiant deeds down the years. Many of yesterday's lines are gone, but never let it be said that they will be forgotten or will fail to find a place in the annals of American railroads. Like those little narrow-gauge pikes, riding the ghostly rails of yesterday, they are as deserving of honored memory as the pioneers of the frontier that was our new America. More than ever since December 7, 1941, the American railroads have come through with the greatest transportation job successfully accomplished in world history.

CHAPTER XV

Maintenance—Track Pans

TRACK MAINTENANCE spells the difference between the safe flight of the thundering trains and disaster. Here is the fundamental factor underlying the whole structure of the iron road, with its continued assault on the ramparts of time and distance.

As a chain is no stronger than its weakest link, the main iron of any railroad is no stronger than the last seemingly insignificant spike or bolt that enters into the make-up of the railroad track itself.

The marvel is that so small a thing as even the largest 152-pound rail—viewed in comparison with the size of engines and trains—can safely carry an explosive iron thunderbolt, weighing two hundred tons or more, at the smashing speeds demanded.

Steel fists are incessantly hammering at the rail—the thing called dynamic augment—with all the fury of a maddened

Photo by H. W. Pontin.

PENNSYLVANIA'S EASTBOUND GOTHAM LIMITED NO. 54 double-headed with two K-4s drifting around the famous Horseshoe Curve, descending the east slope of the Allegheny Mountains on the Pittsburgh Division.

Photo by R. H. Kindig.

UNION PACIFIC'S OWN TYPE EXTRA 9011, hauled by a 4-12-2, leaving Denver for Laramie, Wyoming.

READY TO ATTACK SHERMAN HILL. Union Pacific's No. 5, the California fast mail, westbound, leaving Cheyenne, Wyoming. The helper is Engine 809, one of the original U.P. 4-8-4s with 77-inch wheels, and the road engine is 823, latest 4-8-4 built for the road with 80-inch drivers and 23,000-gallon tank.

Photo by R. H. Kindig.

demon. There is the savage thrust of screaming flanges against the railhead on curves; the lunge and sway of engines and heavy trains; perhaps, too, the murderous impact of some spinning wheel that has developed a flat spot. All of this, and more, in the never-ceasing war of destructive wear and tear of the track.

And yet, over the millions of car-miles traveled, accidents caused by track failure are comparatively few.

Give the locomotives and the fast-wheeling trains all the glamour-gloss and romance due them, crown the engineer with glory, sing paeans of praise for the train dispatcher; search all up and down the line for heroes of the rail; chant hosannas for the officials who turn your stock-dollars into dividends, but don't forget the "king snipe" and his hard-weathered crew.

A king snipe, in the parlance of the railroad, is a section foreman. He has charge of the maintenance of track over some four to seven miles along the right-of-way, with a varying number of men under him.

The section foreman and his track laborers perform many duties, but of primary importance is a constant, eagle-eyed inspection of every foot of rails and roadbed, particularly when weather is in the making. Rain, snow, and frost are their eternal enemies. Neither storm nor cold can keep them home-bound, and they bend against the fury of the elements to safeguard the going of the trains of the iron road.

Not long ago a section foreman and his crew, beating into a blinding snowstorm at night on the Mojave Desert, were struck by a backing helper engine. Every man on the little motor section car was killed. There have been many instances when men of the section have sacrificed their lives in the line of duty. From the Irish bucko to the *paisano* of old Mexico, they are faithful soldiers in the legion of the railroad.

The labors of the section gang consist of "dressing" the right-of-way, of keeping the track and roadbed spick-and-span. They cut and burn grass and weeds, straighten signposts, mend fences, clean out culverts, replace stringers, align track, tighten flange bolts, renew rails, oil side plates and switches, see that frogs and switch points are free of obstructions, and perform countless other tasks necessary to the policing and maintenance of the line.

All lines have well-ballasted roadbeds today to begin with, but when you ride the limited and your train seems to fairly float over those silver ribbons of steel, think of the section foreman and his little corporal's squad of men in overalls, for it is their fine touch in maintaining the track that gives the rails their velvet smoothness.

The old handcar with its pump handles has, mostly, joined the ranks of the buggy whip, and a motorcar has replaced it, but little else has changed on the section. The tools of these hornyhanded sons of the iron road are, in the main, the same as they always have been; namely, the pick and shovel, claw bar, tamping bar, spanner, spike maul, and many others necessary to the upkeep of the track.

It is hard work, keeping the railroad in shape, yet it calls for artful skill as well, and no small detail may be overlooked, for fast freight is rolling and speed queens of the rail are thundering through: the Merchant Prince; the Century; the Broadway Limited; the Daylights.

The next time you are in a diner, notice your water glass when the train is streaking down a tangent at eighty or ninety miles an hour, and judge the smoothness of the track by the undisturbed calm of the liquid in that filled glass. And then, as next you flash past a little group of bronze-faced men beside the rail, remember that here are the sons of toil who are watching always over the shimmering path of steel on which you travel. Common as an old shoe, they may seem, but they are a vital part of American railroading, and your safety is as much in their hands as it is in those of the engineer in the cab ahead.

Major track repair, of course, falls to regular construction gangs, and here today we find every conceivable modern labor-saving device. Constant studies have been carried on in recent years to develop tools and mechanical appliances for use in the Maintenance of Way Department, tools to produce quicker and more efficient results than the old methods.

These studies include field and time observations, laboratory research, as well as extensive co-operation with the makers of such equipment. Nearly 25 per cent of the total man-hours in the Maintenance of Way Department are represented in mechanized work, and additional man-hours will result from new equipment now in the process of development. There is a broad field of hand operations yet remaining, and in order to make it possible further to do away with tedious hand labor, constant efforts to improve equipment now in service are being made.

An important requirement in connection with the economical use of machinery is its full use during the working season, thus avoiding the purchase of surplus or unnecessary equipment. This is accomplished by carefully planned programs, strictly observed.

One of the major problems in connection with the maintenance of track is that of keeping water away from the rails. Improved ditches, both at track and berm, the top of the slope of cuts, are being constructed in many places. This work is done largely by machinery for the purpose.

In order to drain quickly water actually falling on the track in time of storm, the ballast must be kept clean of all foreign matter. This is done by mechanical ballast cleaners, the most modern of which is the "Brownhoist" or "Big Liz." This machine is equipped with continuous diggers, and when operated on a day of light traffic has established a record day of nearly 6 miles of inter-track space cleaned in 16 hours.

The following list includes labor-saving equipment employed by the major railroads in the country:

Tie Adzes	Switch Heaters	Concrete Mixers
Ballast Cleaners	Power Jacks	Concrete Vibrators
Power Ballasters	Spike Drivers	Crawler Cranes
Ballast Levelers	Spike Pullers	Locomotive Cranes
Power Brooms	Jordan Spreaders	Truck Cranes
Earth Drills	Dirt Suckers	Ditchers
Gauging Machines	Track Sweepers	Rail Drills
Rail Grinders	Concrete Breakers	Timber Drills

On-Track Mowers	Rail Saws	Rail-Highway Trucks
Off-Track Mowers	Timber Saws	Weed Burners
Track Oilers	Scarifiers	Weed Diskers
Paint Sprayers	Tie Borers	Electric Welders
Pile Drivers	Tie Tampers	Acetylene Welders
Snowplows	Tractor Bulldozers	Power Wrenches
Pumps	Trucks, Auto	

Thus we find employed almost every conceivable labor-saving device, calling for an army of skilled operators, which means that the "gandy dancers" of yesterday, the sweating track laborers, are turning their hands to machines and doing it with the natural aptitude that your Yankee son has for anything mechanical.

And yet, for all this forward surge of labor-saving machinery on the railroad, no smartly turned device or combination of devices can ever supplant the section foreman and his alert and faithful crew down the path of singing rails.

Many installations along the right-of-way have crept into the railroad picture since the days when the iron horse was young—the silent semaphore that is the sentinel beside the rail; cab signals; color-searchlight signals; position light signals; train control, the electric brakeman that stops the train if, at any time, anything goes wrong in the cab; and many other devices for speeding and yet further safeguarding the flight of roaring limiteds.

Time, relentless in its march as stalking death, is, above all else, the first enemy of the railroad, and to defeat its ominous count of seconds, high-speed lines have spent vast sums and waged ceaseless warfare in their efforts to slow the clock. Every minute saved is a battle won.

This is why the New York Central, Pennsylvania, and other roads installed track pans, which enable their rushing iron monsters to satisfy their endless thirst without the loss of precious minutes. And now many hurrying engines take their ration of water in one prodigious gulp, only slowing to a moderate lope, before hitting their furious stride again, whistle wetted and content.

A track pan is merely a long trough between the rails, and the matter of taking aboard the water which fills it is childishly simple. And yet many factors are involved which require precision, careful planning, and constant supervision, as we shall see.

A track pan varies in length from 1,400 to 2,500 feet. It must of necessity be located on level track; preferably on non-curving sections, though there are track pans in service on slight curves.

The pans are situated midway between the rails. They are built of rolled-steel plates, the inside cross-section dimensions being eight inches deep and nineteen inches wide, with the top of the pan one inch below the top of the rail.

Markers are provided which indicate to the engine crews the exact place to drop and raise the scoops through which the water is transferred from track pan to the tank on the locomotive tender.

At each pan location there is a roadside tank of sufficient capacity to fulfill the requirements of the pan as to the volume of water used at that particular location. These tanks are kept full at all times. Water flows from the tank to pan by gravity, passing through automatic valves, controlled by floats. Thus, when the water in the track pan falls below a certain level, the opening valve replenishes the supply. In a like manner the valves close when the water in the pan has reached a predetermined point.

In the winter months, in northern climates, it is necessary to provide heat to keep the water in the track pan from freezing. This is accomplished by means of steam furnished by adjacent stationary plants and is regulated manually by the employee in charge. This steam line releases live steam directly into the water contained in the pan.

The process of scooping up the water is attended by a naturally high percentage of waste, and, so far as possible, this water is caught in traps and returned to the initial supply. At all track-pan locations it is extremely important, from the standpoint of maintaining satisfactory roadway conditions, to provide perfect drainage.

The equipment on the locomotive for lifting water consists of a scoop, telescopic in construction, which has two moving parts, actuated through a cylinder by means of air pressure. Attached to the scoop is a pipe which extends up through the cistern in the tender at approximately its middle. Laterally and longitudinally located, the top of this pipe is equipped with a U bend, the outlet of which is above the water level when the tender cistern is full. This U bend is directed toward either the forward or the rear of the cistern, depending upon the necessities of the particular design.

When the scoop is lowered to take water, it is 6¼ inches

below the top of the rail, or 5¼ inches below the top of the track pan. Therefore, it is immersed into the water approximately 4½ inches. During the period when the engine is not taking water, the scoop is 4 inches above the top of the rail. The air-actuated cylinder moves the mouth of the scoop through a total distance of 10¼ inches.

Tests have indicated that approximately 2½ to 2¾ gallons of water are transferred from the track pan to the tender's cistern per lineal foot of scooping distance.

Approaching a track pan, the engineer and fireman announce the fact as they might call and repeat a signal. When the locomotive is opposite the "entering" marker, the engineman calls again to the fireman, who immediately operates the valve which supplies air to the scoop-actuating cylinder.

The scoop is left down until the tank is full, or until the "leaving" marker is reached, at which time the scoop is raised. The speed, in the meantime, has been reduced somewhat—perhaps to forty or fifty miles an hour.

Then comes again that full-throated roar, and the train quickly swings back into its high-wheeling stride. The operation of slamming some 5,000 gallons of water aboard the thirsty giant has taken not much longer than it would for you to say Jack Robinson. Just a *swoosh!* and a spatter, and it's done.

The saving in time on a high-speed road like that of the New York Central or Pennsylvania between New York and Chicago is enormous. The further cost of starting and stopping is eliminated and more than offsets the maintenance cost of the pans themselves.

Courtesy of R.F.&P.R.R.

RICHMOND, FREDERICKSBURG AND POTOMAC'S NORTHBOUND POTOMAC MERCHANDISE hauled by Engine 553, the General J. E. B. Stuart, descending Franconia Hill, Virginia.

Photo by W. H. Thrall, Jr.

UNION PACIFIC'S CHALLENGER NO. 7 nearing San Bernardino, California. In this territory the Union Pacific runs over the Santa Fe's Los Angeles Division, hence the number of the engine instead of the train number, as is standard Union Pacific practice. This is President William M. Jeffers' train that first popularized low-cost coach travel all over the United States.

The following table indicates the location of track pans on the Central's New York–Chicago main line:

Hudson Division	Clinton Point	Tracks 1–2–3–4
	Tivoli	" 1–2
Mohawk Division	Schenectady	" 1–2
	Yost's	" 1–2
	Rome	" 1–2–3–4
Syracuse Division	Seneca River	" 1–2
	East Palmyra	" 1–2
Buffalo Division	Churchville	" 1–2
	Wenda	" 1–2
Erie Division	Silver Creek, N.Y.	" 1–2–3–4
	Westfield, N.Y.	" 1–2–3–4
	Springfield, Pa.	" 1–2–3–4
	Painesville, Ohio	" 1–2–3–4
Cleveland Division	Huron, Ohio	" 1–2
Toledo Division	Stryker	" 1–2–3
	Corunna, Indiana	" 1–2
	Grismore "	" 1–2
Western Division	Lydick "	" 1–2
	Chesterton "	" 1–2

CHAPTER XVI

Signals—Safety Devices—Telephones

THE LEAST USED of all railroad equipment today is the "Big Hook"—the wrecker. It stands ready, as always, there on its lonely spur in the railroad yards, like a brooding giant, but seldom is it called on to rush to a scene of disaster. This in spite of heavier engines, faster schedules, and a larger number of trains in operation, as a whole.

Fifty years ago it seemed that the railroads might be getting too big for their boots. Profits went into the pockets of rail tycoons and stockholders instead of into equipment and maintenance, and the Big Hook spent almost as much time hotfooting it to the scene of the latest wreck as it did on spot in the terminal yard.

Railroading in those days was a slapdash, haphazard affair. Passenger trains on many roads were apt to be slow and uncertain; shippers were never sure where or when a bill of goods would show its shameful face. People referred to timetables as joke books, and the whiskered yarn about putting the cowcatcher on the last car to keep cows from boarding trains and biting folks was prevalent.

Passenger trainmen barked at the customers, and the customers barked right back at them. Train crews and telegraphers and dispatchers worked brutally long hours.

All in all, the railroads were a mess. Came a day, however, when the officials realized that something would have to be done, and they buckled down to the job. Tired of being prodded by various agencies, along with the heckling of old John Q. Public, the big moguls began to apply a little hard-headed horse sense to railroad transportation, and there was a perceptible brightening along the horizon, with conditions vastly improved.

After a time, though, the iron horse drifted away to a shady corner of the pasture for another siesta. It woke up with a distressful snort, to discover that the automobile and the truck were cutting frightful swaths across its grazing preserves.

It was then that things really began to happen in the vicinity of the old homestead. Streamliners waltzed down the rail, and bald-faced road engines began to prance around in petticoats. Because the railroads were increasingly concerned with keeping the Big Hook out of the picture, there was a growing development and use of safety devices. The "Safety First" slogan had been coined; and as far back as 1906 the first upper-quadrant semaphore signal appeared on the Pennsylvania.

It is interesting to note in this connection that, in 1870, the old Camden and Amboy Railroad put in operation at Trenton, New Jersey, the first mechanical interlocking system and the original semaphore signal of the lower-quadrant type.

Down the years block signals did much to eliminate railroad hazard, and they were followed by various types of improved signal systems, including cab signals and automatic train control. Experimental work on the latter dates back to 1880, when tests were made near Altoona, Pennsylvania, with a device consisting of an air pipe extending downward to a few inches below the tender truck, the end having a glass tube which made contact with a lever arm reaching upward from the track when signals were at danger. However, these experiments were discontinued in 1883.

In 1910 the Pennsylvania Railroad installed a pneumatic trip-stop device in the New York terminal area and the Hudson and East River tunnels.

In January 1922 the Interstate Commerce Commission ordered the Pennsylvania to install automatic train stops on five engine divisions, and immediately the road offered to install as an experiment the three-speed continuous-control device, developed by the Union Switch & Signal Company, on its Lewistown Branch and a portion of the Williamsport Division between Lewistown and Sunbury, Pennsylvania. This installation was placed in service on July 11, 1923, and all trains operated continuously under it until January 1926, when it was removed from service, having served its purpose.

To comply with the order of the Interstate Commerce

Commission, a "continuous induction" system was devised and placed in service on the Columbus and the Baltimore divisions and on the West Jersey and Seashore Railroad. This system provided not only automatic train stop, but also a signal which reproduced the indications of the wayside signals in the locomotive cab itself.

The operation of the cab signal proved so effective that later the Interstate Commerce Commission permitted the removal of the automatic train control. The cab-signal system is now in service on 1,276 miles of road and 3,502 miles of track on the Pennsylvania.

In 1940 an automatic block system employing cab signals without wayside signals, except home signals at two interlocking and one block station, was placed in operation on fifty miles of double track of the Conemaugh Division between Kiskiminetas Junction and Conpit Junction, Pennsylvania. This installation has proven satisfactory and has resulted in increased efficiency and safety compared with the former manual block system in this territory.

Automatic signaling came into being on the Pennsylvania Railroad in 1890, when automatic block signals were put in service between Pittsburgh and East Liberty. Their use was extended rapidly, and by 1921, 1,390 miles of road and 3,917 miles of track were so equipped.

In 1941 the mileage of road protected by automatic signals was 3,153, with a track mileage of 7,041. Of this track mileage, 6,400 miles are equipped with "position light" signals.

In 1937 there began the respacing of automatic signals. This was done to provide adequate braking distance for

RULE	INDICATION	NAME	A	B	
280	PROCEED; MANUAL BLOCK CLEAR.	CLEAR-BLOCK			
281	PROCEED.	CLEAR			
282	PROCEED APPROACHING NEXT SIGNAL AT MEDIUM SPEED.	APPROACH-MEDIUM			
283	PROCEED; MEDIUM SPEED WITHIN INTERLOCKING LIMITS.	MEDIUM-CLEAR			
285	PROCEED PREPARED TO STOP AT NEXT SIGNAL. TRAIN EXCEEDING MEDIUM SPEED MUST AT ONCE REDUCE TO THAT SPEED.	APPROACH			
285-A	TRAIN EXCEEDING MEDIUM SPEED MUST AT ONCE REDUCE TO THAT SPEED. WHERE A FACING SWITCH IS CONNECTED WITH THE SIGNAL, APPROACH THAT SWITCH PREPARED TO STOP. APPROACH NEXT SIGNAL PREPARED TO STOP.	CAUTION			
287	PROCEED; SLOW SPEED WITHIN INTERLOCKING LIMITS.	SLOW-CLEAR			
288	PROCEED PREPARED TO STOP AT NEXT SIGNAL. SLOW SPEED WITHIN INTERLOCKING LIMITS.	SLOW-APPROACH			
289	BLOCK OCCUPIED; FOR PASSENGER TRAINS STOP; FOR TRAINS OTHER THAN PASSENGER TRAINS, PROCEED PREPARED TO STOP SHORT OF TRAIN AHEAD.	PERMISSIVE-BLOCK			
290	PROCEED AT RESTRICTED SPEED.	RESTRICTING			
291	STOP; THEN PROCEED AT RESTRICTED SPEED. NOTE-FREIGHT TRAINS OF 90 OR MORE CARS OR HAVING TONNAGE OF 80% OR MORE OF THE PRESCRIBED ENGINE RATING MAY PROCEED AT RESTRICTED SPEED WITHOUT STOPPING AT SIGNALS DISPLAYING A YELLOW DISK ON WHICH IS SHOWN THE LETTER "G" IN BLACK.	STOP-AND-PROCEED			
292	STOP.	STOP-SIGNAL			
293	LIMIT OF THE BLOCK. NOTE-FIG. A- YELLOW LIGHT TO BE PLACED NEXT TO TRACK GOVERNED.	BLOCK-LIMIT	STATION NAME		
294	ORDERS. NOTE-FIG. A - BY DAY THE YELLOW LAMP IS NOT DISPLAYED. NOTE-FIG. B - TO APPLY TO TRAINS GOVERNED BY FIXED SIGNAL UNDER WHICH LOCATED.	TRAIN-ORDER	Y	MAST OF FIXED SIGNAL FLASHING	

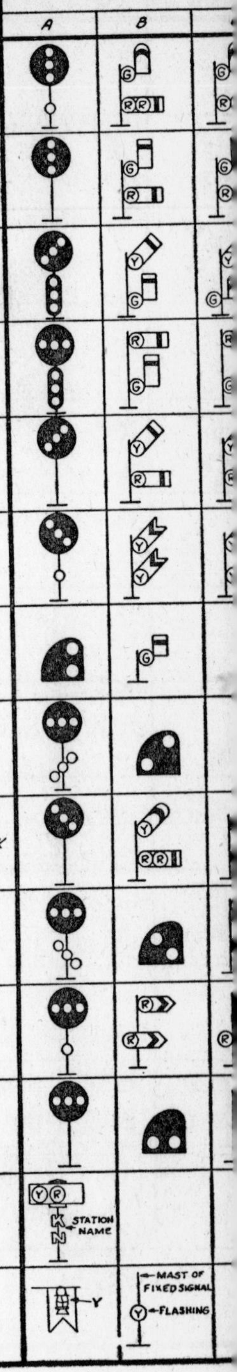

FIGURE			
D	E	F	G
G R	G R	G Y	G Y
Y G			
Y R	Y R		
R Y	Y		
R RR	R R	R RR	P

NOTE:-

IN THE ILLUSTRATION OF TYPICAL ASPECTS, RULES 280 TO 294, INCLUSIVE:

R – RED
P – PURPLE
Y – YELLOW
G – GREEN

SPEEDS

MEDIUM SPEED - NOT EXCEEDING ONE-HALF THE SPEED AUTHORIZED FOR PASSENGER TRAINS BUT NOT EXCEEDING 30 MILES PER HOUR.

REDUCED SPEED – PREPARED TO STOP SHORT OF TRAIN OR OBSTRUCTION.

SLOW SPEED - NOT EXCEEDING 15 MILES PER HOUR.

RESTRICTED SPEED - NOT EXCEEDING 15 MILES PER HOUR PREPARED TO STOP SHORT OF TRAIN, OBSTRUCTION OR SWITCH NOT PROPERLY LINED AND TO LOOK OUT FOR BROKEN RAIL.

REVISIONS
REDRAWN FROM APPROVED PLAN S-602-F, DATED JANUARY 5, 1938 AND REVISED.

1 SHEET

S-602-G

THE PENNSYLVANIA RAILROAD

STANDARD

SIGNAL ASPECTS

OFFICE OF CHIEF ENGINEER, PHILA., PA., JULY 12, 1941.

Approved N. L. Stanton
Assistant Chief Engineer-Signals

Approved
Chief Engineer

higher-speed trains, and it has further reduced the cost of signal operation and maintenance.

The first position-light signals on the Pennsylvania were installed between Overbrook and Paoli in 1915. These signals were the joint invention of employees of the Corning Glass Works and the Pennsylvania Railroad. During the succeeding years they have been greatly simplified and improved.

Position-light signals are superior to the semaphore type because colors are eliminated, and the position of the signal is indicated by a row of lights, the indications being the same day and night. Their advantage over the semaphore is particularly noticeable at dawn and dusk, when the lights are not as sharp as in the dark and the arm is not as clearly visible against the half-light as in the daytime.

Position lights have no exposed moving parts, and no motors are required in their operation, as is the case with the semaphore signal. The hue of the position light is one that best penetrates fog and mist. Four positions can be given with this newer-type signal, whereas only three positions are feasible with the semaphore.

The basic principle of the position light is speed signaling. In other words, its purpose is to inform the engineman as far in advance as possible by signal indications how fast he can safely operate his train. In my opinion these position light signals are the finest in America.

The consolidation and remote control of interlocking plants has progressed rapidly in recent years. For example, there were 834 interlockings on the Pennsylvania in 1916;

today there are 514, of which 146 are remotely controlled from other interlocking stations.

In Philadelphia terminal switches and signals formerly operated by thirteen interlocking plants are now operated by three. At other places the more modern interlocking system has eliminated three or more existing plants.

In single-track territory, centralized traffic control is extensively used. This concentrates under one-man operation the control of switches and signals over an extended territory, instead of having attendants at frequent intervals to operate interlocking and block stations, and saves valuable time at meeting points.

Long ago railroads discovered that the control of trains was child's play beside attempting to regulate the motorist who came projecting down the turnpike all in a lather and with but one idea in mind, which was to beat the approaching engine to the railroad crossing.

In those dim and distant yesterdays when Father and Maggie went courting in a Concord buggy and folks believed in signs with quaint simplicity, the railroad's black-worded admonition to STOP, LOOK, LISTEN was sufficient unto the needs thereof. And anyway Dobbin's very soul rebelled at the mere sight of that hateful, huffing locomotive, which made it advisable to draw rein at least a quarter of a mile from the grade crossing.

Came then the gasoline buggy and the birth of an era when people no longer believed in signs, as they started romping gaily back and forth in front of rushing boiler front decks, aging distressed enginemen before their time.

Thus it fell to the lot of the railroad's signal department to provide something that it was hoped would discourage the rambunctious motorist from flirting with the front end of the line's best trains. In consequence, wigwags and automatic flashing signal lights came into general use. They did not entirely discourage the driver bent on hunting a short cut to the mortuary, but they helped.

Crossing gates have long been installed in the more populous areas, but many times they seem to arouse in the motorist a thirst for assault rather than to serve the purpose for which they were intended. Crossing watchmen have even been pursued to their lairs by automobile drivers.

We await with interest the inventive mind that will develop something to check the headlong flight of automobile drivers who not only dash onto grade crossings in the path of oncoming trains but not infrequently crash into them broadside midway of their length.

It is a problem. On the Pennsylvania Railroad alone there are 13,042 highway crossings at grade, with 1,700 flashing signals in service, while 215 are protected by bells, 592 by gates, and 492 by watchmen.

Further safety devices on various railroads include dragging-equipment detectors. These are for the purpose of preventing train derailments caused by failure of running gear, brake rigging, or other dragging parts. The detectors have proved their worth many times. They consist of four breakable cast-iron "fingers," which are placed between and outside of the main track rails where they will be struck and broken by dragging parts of equipment or lading. The fingers are so connected with the signal circuits that when one of them is broken a stop indication is given the train involved. Of these detectors 434 have been placed at the approaches to important interlockings and bridges on the Pennsylvania, and all such locations will eventually be so equipped. The first installation was at "Midway" tower, on the New York Division, in 1936. Between that time and December 31, 1940, there were 3,132 actuations of these devices, many of which were the means of preventing derailment of equipment, with consequential damage to property and interference with traffic.

A source of possible hazard on a railroad is that of rock and earth slides, and we find this peril being met by "slide-protection fences." The fences are attached to circuit controllers so that when earth or rock strikes it the signal circuits are opened and the signals for that section of track give a "stop" indication, as in the case of the broken finger of the dragging-equipment detector.

Thus we find applied science everywhere on the modern railroad, and the great transportation systems of the country are forever striving to contribute further to the safety of those who ride the rails.

In connection with the development of electrical devices on the railroad, a word here concerning the Sperry Detector Car—the Sherlock Holmes of the rail, the detective that sleuths out insidious flaws and defects in those gleaming silver bands down which speed the trains.

Perhaps there was a hidden fissure in the new rail, or pounding wheels may have started a hair-fine break deep in the steel. Danger lurks here, for one day the rail may break under the weight and thrust of a fast-moving freight or passenger train. The main-line tracks of a railroad are regularly checked by this detector car, which, creeping slowly along, sends an electric current through each rail, and any interior defect is indicated by a recording device. When this instrument gives such indication, the car is stopped and the rail marked for removal.

The processing of steel has improved with the years, and fewer flaws creep into its make-up. The early railroads used strap rails, which were simply flat metal strips spiked to stringpieces laid on the ties. This type of rail was in use for a number of years and was the cause of the deadly "snake-head." Often one end of a strap rail would come loose and stab up through the floor of a car like a furiously striking reptile, hence the name snakehead.

"Edge" rails were in use on some roads for a time. Came then the first iron T rails, which were in use generally until after the Civil War. Meanwhile, Sir Henry Bessemer, an English inventor, had been experimenting with a method of producing steel cheaply. In this he was successful, and the first steel rails were used in the United States around the close of 1865.

The iron rails weighed between 40 and 50 pounds to the yard; the early steel rails about 56 pounds; then 67 to 75 pounds, always growing heavier to meet the needs of larger engines and equipment, until now we find rails on some lines weighing 152 pounds, which is in itself a powerful safety factor.

Electricity and electric circuits have always played an important part in the development of the railroads. The telegraph allied itself with train movement as far back as 1850 and for a great many years marched shoulder to shoulder with the iron horse. Wherever you saw the rails reaching away to the far horizons, there too were telegraph poles and wires. Every old red depot echoed to the chatter of telegraph instruments–the whispering relay, the racketing sounder. Every country station agent was a telegraph operator, the mysteries of the Morse code alive in his fingertips, the fast-spattering dots and dashes a language that he knew.

The "brass-pounder"* in his little depot bay was a definite and important cog in the railroad scene, and it is impossible to look into those yesterdays of the iron road and not know a pang of regret at the passing of the old-time telegrapher.

The telephone and the teletype have taken over, but never can they erase the memory of the telegraph operator who has written his own proud page in the annals of American railroading. But he is signing off, and soon, down at the end of the page, there will be his last "30." No more.

The telephone and telegraph system on the modern railroad is an intricate and complex affair that reaches out to every mile of track, and beyond. As we point to the highest mountain, the tallest skyscraper, to impress the stranger in our midst, so we now give you the telephone and telegraph lines of the Pennsylvania as the largest private plant on any railroad in the world.

This system consists of 8,748 miles of pole line, 363 miles

*Telegrapher.

of underground-conduit system, 87,444 miles of aerial wire, 56,279 miles of aerial cable conductors, and 77,267 miles of underground cable conductors. Of the total of 220,998 miles, more than 178,000 miles are now in use to handle the enormous volume of telegraph and telephone traffic required to operate the railroad.

Train dispatchers alone use 19,339 miles of wire.

Local telephone message circuits use 17,600 miles, enabling supervisory forces to reach all passenger and freight stations anywhere on the entire railroad.

Train operation uses 10,250 telephones exclusively for dispatchers, block operators, yard employees, signalmen, and others who are involved in the movement of trains and maintenance of track, bridges, and signals.

To handle train "consist" reports, reservations, diversion messages, and other communications, the Pennsylvania owns and operates 275 teletype machines. These handle 860,710 or more messages a month. The telephones handle 163,838 messages. Morse circuits still in use carry 69,263.

The railroad operates its teletypewriters through a switching unit, whereby each machine of the system can send and receive from any other teletype, the same as with a telephone system, except, of course, that the message is printed instead of spoken. These teletype exchanges are located in Philadelphia, New York, and Pittsburgh.

The railroads up and down the country have gone a long way since the first brass-pounder copied a train order, just as the safeguarding of trains has reached a high state of perfection.

CHAPTER XVII

Passenger Power Development

We have seen the general development of freight motive power and have, from time to time, examined briefly the types of locomotives that haul some of our crack limiteds, and we come now to the progressive design of certain engines built for steam passenger service.

In 1904, when the Consolidation, the Ten-wheeler, the Atlantic, and the Prairie types were still the conventional freight and passenger locomotives in common use for heavy duty on the New York Central System, the first of a series of Pacific-type engines, the Class K-80, was introduced on the Michigan Central.

During the following year similar locomotives were placed in service on the Boston & Albany and on the Cleveland, Cincinnati, Chicago & St. Louis Railway. In 1907 the Central and the Lake Shore & Michigan Southern, now New York

Central Lines West, received modifications of this type in the form of somewhat larger locomotives, designated as Class K-2.

These engines successfully performed the work assigned to them, and succeeding locomotives of the same type were installed until 1911. At this time a somewhat heavier and more powerful Pacific type was produced. This was the Class K-3, a considerable number of which are still in service.

Shortly after the introduction of the last of the K-3s, it became evident that a further substantial increase in power was required. An attempt was made to meet this demand by a yet larger Pacific, having 25 × 28 inch cylinders instead of 23½ × 26 inch, and with firebox and boiler capacity increased proportionately.

With 79-inch drivers and a working boiler pressure of 200 pounds, these locomotives developed a rated main-engine tractive force of 37,650 pounds, which, through the use of a booster, was increased to 47,350. This design was designated as Class K-4, and, in view of its increased size, hand firing was no longer practicable for capacity operation; hence mechanical stokers were installed.

Came the Class K-5, built in 1925 and 1926. This engine was supplied with a tender carrying 15,000 gallons of water, which marked the introduction of the large-capacity tender for system passenger operation, the progressive elimination of service stops, and the extension of locomotive runs.

A survey undertaken in 1926, uncovering facts and conditions relating to the necessity for a further increase in the power of main-line passenger locomotives, together with

TABLE I

THE PROGRESSIVE DEVELOPMENT OF THE PACIFIC-TYPE LOCOMOTIVE ON THE NEW YORK CENTRAL

Type of locomotive	4-6-2	4-6-2	4-6-2	4-6-2	4-6-2
Road class	K-80	K-2a	K-3q	K-3r	K-5b
Date built	1904	1907	1923	1925	1926
Maximum tractive force:					
Engine (lbs.)	28,500	29,160	30,900	32,200	37,650
Booster (lbs.)			9,700	9,700	9,700
Weight:					
On drivers	142,500	173,000	194,500	169,000	185,000
Total engine	224,000	268,000	295,500	278,000	302,000
Driving wheels. Diameter (ins.)	75	79	79	79	79
Cylinders (ins.)	22 × 26	22 × 28	23½ × 26	24 × 26	25 × 28
Boiler:					
Steam pressure (lbs.)	200	200	200	200	200
Diameter first ring. Inside (ins.)	70⅝	70⅝	70⅝	70⅝	79½
Grate area (sq. ft.)	50.2	56.5	56.5	56.7	67.8
Heating surface (sq. ft.):					
Evaporative (total)	3,283	3,789	3,424	3,421	3,952
Superheater	672	724	832	839	1,150
Tender:					
Water capacity (gals.)	6,000	7,500	8,000	10,900	15,000
Fuel capacity (tons)	14	12	12	16½	16
Trucks. Wheels	4	4	4	4	6
Maximum increased hp.	1,700	2,000	2,100	2,140	3,200
At m.p.h.	39	45	45	45	54
Maximum drawbar hp.	1,430	1,655	1,720	1,750	2,530
At m.p.h.	35	40	40	40	45

consideration of probable future needs, quickly led to the definite conclusion that a unit of an entirely new design and type must be developed.

The basic problem presented was the creation of a locomotive having the following characteristics, as compared with the Pacific types in use up to that time:

1. Greater starting tractive force, with increased horsepower capacity and maximum output at much higher speed.
2. Boiler of ample sustained capacity to satisfy the cylinder requirements for maximum power development under severe weather and running conditions.
3. Weight distribution, wheel loads, and counterbalance to be such that impact forces and rail stresses should be confined to lower limits than previously observed, thus contributing to higher standards of track maintenance and obtaining better train-riding characteristics.
4. Increased thermal efficiency.
5. Clearance to permit operation without restriction on various parts of the system.
6. Symmetrical appearance, with smooth lines, free from the effects of miscellaneous appliances.
7. A high degree of reliability for uninterrupted service under dense traffic conditions, especially on the western section of the system, requiring relatively simple but adequate machinery, combined with the use of well-proved auxiliary equipment, such as feed-water heaters and mechanical stokers.

After the preparation of several preliminary designs in which the American Locomotive Company, the Superheater Company, and others co-operated, the conclusion was reached that the objectives desired could be most efficiently attained by using a 4-6-4 wheel arrangement, which would satisfy the requirements for capacity and weight and avoid the addition of a fourth pair of driving wheels, with a resultant increase in size, weight, and first cost, as well as higher maintenance costs.

This arrangement represented the first six-driver locomotive ever built with four-wheel leading and trailing trucks for service in America.

To meet the demand for exceptional steaming capacity at sustained high speed with heavy load, the size and proportions of the boiler of this new 4-6-4 in the making were given first consideration, ample heating surfaces being essential, with extra-large superheater and a grate area sufficient to insure an economical rate of firing under maximum conditions of steam generation.

To carry the added weight this imposed on the rear of the locomotive, without excessive loads on trailing or coupled axles, the four-wheel trailing truck was used, thus securing the advantage of providing for large firebox capacity with comparatively light individual axle loads and consequent low rail loads.

In developing the boiler design, the provision of a combustion chamber was carefully considered, but because of serious difficulties then being experienced with riveted-seam construction, it was finally omitted.

To reduce the pressure drop and other losses and to provide for more efficient use of the steam in the cylinders, the steam and exhaust passages were enlarged, as compared with the K-5 Pacific, and a front-end throttle was installed. A large-volume steam chest with valves 14 inches in diameter, similar to those of the K-5, was retained.

Other special features included air compressors mounted on the front deck for improved weight distribution and, for the first time, a specially designed cast-steel pilot and drop coupler and pocket for clearing effectively possible obstructions on the right-of-way. The centrifugal-type boiler feed pump was first introduced on this design, with the heater located in a recessed portion of the smokebox top and a large portion of the piping concealed under the jacket. Careful attention was given to the arrangement of controls and gauges in the cab for convenience and clear vision.

We are watching the creation of a new locomotive, destined to become famous the world over—from drafting table to shop, from blueprint to the railroad, step by step, until there emerges from its embryo of fabrication a mighty engine, an explosive giant high-wheeling down the rails. The first Hudson-type locomotive.

In Table II are shown the principal dimensions of the last of the J-1 class as received in 1931, with engine dimensions and proportions of the design as finally determined for that first sample J-1a, No. 5200, built in 1927, except that the weight on drivers of the latter was 182,000 pounds, with a total engine weight of 343,000 pounds. A tender with four-wheel trucks was used with this first engine, which had a capacity of 10,000 gallons of water and 18 tons of coal.

From 1927 to 1931, a total of 205 of these locomotives was received and placed in service. And the Hudson type was on its way to making railroad history.

Photo by W. H. Thrall, Jr.

THIRD SECTION OF THE SOUTHERN PACIFIC'S ARIZONA OVERNIGHT running as extra 4202 west, hauling the pride of the S.P.'s arranged less-than-carload freight service from Los Angeles to Tucson over the divisions of those names. The engine is a Class AC-8, of the Southern Pacific's 4-8-8-2 type.

Courtesy of R.F.&P.R.R.

RICHMOND, FREDERICKSBURG AND POTOMAC'S NO. 602, the Governor Thomas Jefferson, hauling the Atlantic Coast Line's Florida Special, west coast section, crossing the Rappahannock River Bridge at Fredericksburg, Va.

TABLE II

FURTHER DEVELOPMENT OF SIX-COUPLED LOCOMOTIVES ON THE NEW YORK CENTRAL

Type of locomotive	4-6-4	4-6-4
Road class	J-1e	J-3a
Date built	1931	1937
Maximum tractive force:		
Engine (lbs.)	42,360	43,440
Booster (lbs.)	10,900	12,100
Weight in working order (lbs.):		
On drivers	190,700	201,500
Total engine	358,600	360,000
Driving wheels. Diameter (ins.)	79	79
Cylinders (ins.)	25 × 28	22½ × 29
Boiler:		
Steam pressure (lbs.)	225	275
Diameter first ring. Inside (ins.)	82 7/16	80⅝
Combustion chamber. Length (ins.)	None	43
Firebox volume (cu. ft.)	428	519
Gas area through tubes & flues (sq. ft.)	9.67	8.91
Grate area (sq. ft.)	81.5	82
Heating surface (sq. ft.):		
Evaporative (total)	4,484	4,187
Superheater (type)	1951-E	1745-E
Tender:		
Water capacity (gals.)	15,000	14,000
Fuel capacity (tons)	24	30
Trucks	6-Wheel	6-Wheel
Maximum increased hp.	3,900	4,725
At m.p.h.	67	75
Maximum drawbar hp.	3,240	3,880
At m.p.h.	58	65

Subsequently, all the J-1 class were dynamically counterbalanced to provide smoother operation and to permit the use of shorter running cut-off, as well as to improve the track effects. Roller bearings were installed on all engine and tender trucks, likewise on drivers of eight locomotives. All engines were fitted with speed recorders. Later cut-off-selection equipment was added.

Cast-steel beds with integral cylinders are applied, the engines already being equipped with one-piece cast-steel tender frames, engine-truck, trail-truck, and tender-truck frames. The substitution of integral construction for the multiple-bolted parts of earlier locomotives eliminated a large number of bolts and contributed to increased availability and continuity of operation with substantial reduction in maintenance costs.

At the end of 1940, a total of 437 locomotives of this 4-6-4 type had been placed in service in the United States and Canada, including 275 on the New York Central. The total weight in working order for each of these locomotives ranged from 310,000 to 415,000 pounds, with corresponding variations in maximum tractive force.

Performance and Capacity Tests, J-1 Hudson Versus K-5 Pacific

Class J-1a, No. 5200, was subjected to complete performance and capacity tests shortly after delivery in 1927. Because of the total engine weight, 343,000 pounds, and the smaller and lighter tender being used, the locomotive delivered a maximum drawbar horsepower of 3,300 at 58 miles per hour. However, subsequent improvements already referred to increased the weight of the Hudson-type locomotives and, consequently, the principal test results here given are for the last-built and heavier Class J-1e tested in 1937.

The complete performance and capacity test of classes J-1e (No. 5339) and K-5b (No. 8363) were conducted under spring and summer weather conditions over the Mohawk Division of the New York Central between Albany and Syracuse, New York, a distance of 140 miles. This division is generally representative in profile and operating characteristics of the main line between New York and Chicago, with the exception of the severe though comparatively short grade westbound between Albany and West Albany, a distance of about three miles. Here the maximum grade is 1.63 per cent on a curvature of 3½ degrees. With a total rise westbound of 384 feet in the 140-mile division over a rolling profile, the average grade is 0.05 per cent, with a maximum of about 0.5 per cent for approximately 1.5 miles westbound and about 0.75 per cent for slightly over two miles eastbound.

All tests were made under regular road-service conditions of operation. The trains consisted of empty standard steel passenger coaches, varying in number from 10 to 20, which, with a dynamometer car, provided train weights of 780 to 1,465 tons.

These trains were selected as representative of normal daily operation expected of the locomotive. Average test results demonstrated that the Class J-1 Hudson type surpassed all previous New York Central locomotives in maximum horsepower, coal and water consumption per horsepower, weight per horsepower, and over-all efficiency.

A comparison of the principal results obtained for a single division run with representative trains is given in Table III. It should be especially noted that, except for the maximum power characteristics which may be duplicated at will with full boiler pressure and locomotive in first-class condition, the results shown are on the basis of over-all averages for the complete division runs and indicate regular daily service performance rather than maximum values for short periods, or under controlled conditions for the separate items.

With a starting effort approximately 12 per cent greater than the K-5, increasing to 37 per cent more at a speed of 70 m.p.h., and with an increase of 28 per cent in maximum drawbar horsepower at a speed 29 per cent higher, the weight per horsepower of the J-1 Hudson type has been decreased.

As early as 1931, when the last of the J-1 class was built, consideration was already being given to the future development of this type in anticipation of greater power demand, necessitated by the constantly increasing weight of trains and faster schedules. In order to reduce the weight and also to gain experience in the use of alloy steel of high tensile strength, with a view toward increasing the steam pressure, three of these locomotives were equipped with nickel-steel boilers. Two of the three also had roller bearings on all wheels except on the trailing truck, and all had roller bearings on the engine truck and tender wheels.

Subsequently, one of the three, No. 5344, received lightweight roller-bearing rotating and reciprocating parts and

TABLE III

Comparison of Test Run for K-5 and J-1 Locomotives

	Maximum Power *K-5*	*J-1*	*Improvement in J-1. Per Cent*
Tractive effort with booster (lbs.)	48,750	55,100	13.0
Main-engine tractive effort (lbs.)	40,000	45,400	13.5
Main-engine drawbar pull (lbs.)	37,000	41,300	11.6
Cylinder horsepower	3,200 at	3,900 at	22.0
	54 m.p.h.	67 m.p.h.	24.1
Drawbar horsepower	2,530 at	3,240 at	28.1
	45 m.p.h.	58 m.p.h.	28.9

Average Performance Data

Number of cars and weight in tons	15-1053	18-1244	
Average working speed, m.p.h.	51.2	55	
Average firing rate, dry coal per hour (lbs.)	5,867	6,940	
Water delivered to boiler (lbs. per hr.)	40,636	57,200	
Evaporation per pound dry coal (lbs.)	6.94	8.24	18.7
Combined efficiency: boiler, feed-water heater & superheater (per cent)	67.8	74.6	10.0
Steam per increased hp. hr. (lbs.):			
Cylinders only	15.42	15.44	
Including auxiliaries	17.00	17.28	
Dry coal per increased hp. hr. (lbs.):			
Cylinders only	2.22	1.94	12.6
Including auxiliaries	2.46	2.10	14.6
Coal as fired per car-mile (lbs.)	7.22	7.03	2.6
Weight per increased hp. (lbs.)	94	90	4.3
Total working-order weight of engine	302,000	352,000	

the counterbalance was reduced proportionately, providing lower rail stresses and improved riding qualities. At this time, the boiler pressure was raised from 225 to 250 pounds per square inch, and the cylinders were bushed to preserve the same starting tractive force and adhesion factor as on the others of the same class.

Successive lots of the J-1 class, as has been pointed out, received various improvements when built, and subsequently with gradual increase in the weight of engine and tender. The comparative weights of the original Class J-1a and the latest class J-1e are shown in the following table:

TABLE IV

Final Effect of Improvements in the J-1 Class on Increase in Weight

	Original J-1a	*Latest J-1e*
Engine truck	63,500 lbs.	63,700 lbs.
Drivers	182,000 "	190,700 "
Four-wheel trailing truck	97,500 "	102,200 "
Total engine, working order	343,000 "	358,600 "
Tender, fully loaded	212,200 "	305,600 "

On the basis of the J-1 test results, the experience accumulated with the altered locomotives of this class, and other considerations, the general objectives for the new design were set as follows:

1. Maximum cylinder horsepower approximately 20 per cent greater at a much higher speed.
2. Boiler pressure 275 pounds per square inch compared to 225 pounds.
3. Equal main-engine starting tractive force, with some additional help from booster because of increased pressure.
4. Boiler and superheater proportioned for higher capacity de-

mand and to insure ample supply of steam under all conditions.

5. Approximately same over-all length and clearance limitations.
6. Highest capacity tender possible within the then total length limitation.
7. Least possible increase in weight and weight distribution no less favorable from track standpoint.

Careful study, with the utmost attention to all details of design, indicated that these objectives could be attained while still adhering to the 4-6-4 wheel arrangement, rather than using another pair of driving wheels.

Fifty of these locomotives were built in the fall of 1937 and the spring of 1938. Ten were streamlined. Five had roller bearings on main and side rods.

The improved J-3, with a boiler pressure of 275 pounds per square inch, cylinder sizes of 22½ × 29 inches, were fixed to produce a main-engine starting tractive force of 43,440 pounds, or slightly more than the 42,360 pounds of the J-1 class. The booster provided an additional 12,100 pounds of starting effort. A large-volume steam chest, with 14-inch valves, similar to that of the J-1, was retained, but the steam passages from dome to exhaust were enlarged in proportion to the cylinder area to provide free passage of the steam and reduce losses in transmission.

The improvement in locomotive design these past years is clearly indicated in the comparison tables shown, and they are, indeed, worthy of close study.

True, speed records were made a great many years ago that were amazing, but for smooth race-horse speed over

TABLE V

Performance of J-3 Class Locomotive Compared with J-1 Class

	Maximum Power *J-1*	*J-3*	*Improvement in J-3. Per cent*
Tractive force with booster (lbs.)	55,100	55,000	
Main-engine tractive effort (lbs.)	45,400	45,000	
Main-engine drawbar pull (lbs.)	41,300	41,500	
Cylinder hp.	3,900	4,725	21.1
At m.p.h.	67	75	11.9
Cylinder hp. per pair of driving wheels	1,300	1,575	21.1
Drawbar hp.	3,240	3,880	19.75
At m.p.h.	58	65	12.1

Average Performance. Division Run of 140 miles

	J-1	J-3	Improvement in J-3. Per cent
Number of cars & weight (tons)	18-1,244	18-1,253	
Working speed, m.p.h.	55	59	
Firing rate, dry coal per hour (lbs.)	6,940	6,419	
Water delivered to boiler per hour (lbs.)	52,200	54,900	
Evaporation per pound of dry coal (lbs.)	8.24	8.32	1.0
Combined efficiency: boiler, feed-water heater, and superheater (per cent)	74.6	76.3	2.3
Steam per increased hp. hr. (lbs.):			
Cylinders only	15.44	14.76	4.4
Including auxiliaries	17.28	16.89	2.3
Dry coal per increased hp. hr. (lbs.):			
Cylinders only	1.94	1.84	5.15
Including auxiliaries	2.10	2.03	3.3
Coal fired per car-mile (lbs.)	7.03	6.21	11.7
Weight per increased hp. (lbs.)	90	76	15.5
Total weight of engine in working order, as tested (lbs.)	352,000	360,000	

long distances as well as slugging, work-horse power and stamina, there is nothing better equipped to stand up and take it on the chin, week in and week out, than a modern steam locomotive.

Let us look at the special design and equipment that is a part of this super J-3, the Hudson of the Central.

Roller bearings applied to all wheels.
Reciprocating parts of special lightweight design.
Revolving parts reduced in weight.
Dynamic counterbalancing.
Reverse-gear cylinder located on center line of engine to assist in reducing irregularities or inequalities in valve travel due to deflection or other causes.
Speed-recorder and cut-off-selection equipment.
Waughmat rubber, twin-cushion, double-acting draft gear movement substituting controlled resiliency to obtain smooth and efficient operation of trains. (The ten streamlined engines received tight-lock couplers.)

The requirements for increased cylinder power and consequent greater boiler capacity and higher working steam pressure, together with roller-bearing equipment, improved brakes, additional sandbox capacity, and certain minor items, indicated a weight increase of about 14,750 pounds over that of the latest Class J-1, but, as previously stated, one of the major objectives was to hold the weight as closely as possible to that of the J-1 class, and to accomplish this the following features were incorporated in the design:

Nickel-steel boiler-shell sheets.
Cast-steel unit-bar grates.

High-tensile-steel drop coupler.

Cor-Ten steel main air reservoirs.

Aluminum cab, running boards, casings, and gauge board.

Magnesia-block lagging of light weight.

Tubes and flues to close tolerance.

Booster exhaust piped to tender instead of to stack.

Integral cast-steel frames and cylinder, cradle, engine-truck and trailing-truck frames of lightened design.

Lightweight new-design valve gear.

Lightweight reciprocating parts and alloy-steel rods also contributed to the saving in weight.

The resulting weight reduction amounted to 13,350 pounds, making the net addition only 1,400 pounds, with a total weight of engine in working order of 360,000 pounds, of which 201,500 pounds were placed on the drivers.

With the total weight and the distribution thus obtained, together with the use of reduced-weight rotating and reciprocating parts and dynamic counterbalancing, the calculated stresses on the track structure were satisfactory and well within permissible limits.

The tests of the J-3 were conducted with engine No. 5408 during the latter part of 1937 over the Mohawk Division, and under regular service conditions of operation. The trains consisted of 22, 17, and 10 cars each, which, with the dynamometer car, furnished weights back of the tender of 1,609, 1,244, and 766 tons, or trains of heavy, medium, and light weight.

The principal results of representative performance are given in Table V, the figures for the Class J-1 being repeated for ready comparison.

While the same main-engine starting tractive force has been obtained in the new design, as desired, the drawbar pull at 70 m.p.h. has increased nearly 25 per cent, and the maximum drawbar horsepower is 20 per cent greater at a speed 12 per cent higher than the J-1.

Coal and steam consumption per horsepower have been decreased with a reduction of 15 per cent in weight per horsepower. An average thermal efficiency of 6.06 per cent at the drawbar was obtained for a complete division run, corresponding to 9.6 per cent at the cylinder.

This is modern design as it goes into the make-up of the present-day locomotive, and nothing could better illustrate the trend along the railroads than the refinements of those Pacifics and the subsequent thought and preparation that went into the building of the Hudsons.

From the first the 4-6-4 type engine was destined to find ready acceptance on many railroads, and we find these engines hauling a lot of the crack trains of the country.

CHAPTER XVIII

Locomotive Performance

THE INCREASING DAILY MILEAGE of steam passenger locomotives, some of which now operate as much as 20,000 miles a month, is the result of greater reliability and range.

Many developments now under way indicate that groups of locomotives are capable, and will be increasingly capable, of maintaining a still higher average of working time per month. There is no present indication that the limit of utilization of steam power has been reached.

The measuring stick of the movement of trains is the on-time performance, the success or failure of which is shown in daily reports of trains and of delays due to mechanical difficulties, resulting in lost time that could not be made up.

One of the major contributions to the improvement of locomotive design has been the application of roller bearings. This equipment made its appearance on the New York Central in about 1929, and by 1934 practically all high-speed passenger engines were so equipped.

At that time more than 14,000,000 miles per year were made, with no delays chargeable to roller-bearing equipment. During 1940, in better than 19,000,000 miles there were no engines out of service owing to failure of these roller bearings.

Over an eight-year period there were 3,376 delays caused by friction-bearing driving boxes. In this period it was found that on tender trucks the roller bearings made 60 times the mileage of the friction bearings per delay.

As this is written, there are on the Central 350 locomotives equipped with engine-truck roller bearings, 309 with tender-truck roller bearings, and a total of 84 engines, including all the newer locomotives, with roller bearings on driving boxes.

To demonstrate the improvements due to this form of equipment, the record is given in Table VI for nine years, starting in 1927, when all engine trucks were friction-bearing equipped.

An improvement that has a direct bearing on utilization of power is water treatment. Frequently it was necessary to wash the boiler on arrival at the terminal, but with the present full water treatment the number of days between washouts has been extended so that the majority of engines can be promptly made ready for service.

With the one-piece cast-steel bed many separate parts and several hundred bolts have been eliminated, which further contributes to the reliability of the locomotive, as it reduces enginehouse maintenance.

TABLE VI

AVERAGE MILEAGE PER CUT-OUT OF NEW YORK CENTRAL MAIN-LINE PASSENGER LOCOMOTIVES DUE TO HOT ENGINE-TRUCK JOURNALS

Before Application of Roller Bearings on Engine Trucks

(Principal Type of Passenger Locomotives in Use Being the K-2 and K-3)

Year	*Miles per delay*
1927	373,295
1928	814,469

All Important Passenger Locomotives Equipped with Roller Bearings

(Most of the mileage made by Hudson-type locomotives)

1934	14,486,923	(No delays)
1935	15,480,723	
1936	15,754,913	
1937	17,624,429	(No delays)
1938	19,261,201	(No delays)
1939	19,379,594	
1940	19,780,391	(No delays)

Sometimes it is asked if in former years locomotives working on one division did not, because of being turned back on a regular train, make a higher monthly mileage that engines are making now when they run through on many divisions. In 1920 the highest monthly mileage was less than 10,000. At that time a considerable number of the new Class K-3 locomotives came into service, and the average miles of this type became approximately 14,000. Around 1929 the Class J-1 was introduced and immediately began to pile up mileage in the 18,000-mile range. Then in 1938 a fourth class, the J-3, or latest group of Hudsons, began making close to 20,000 miles.

When improved power came strutting down the road, it

not only started to hang up records but suggested ways of improving engines already in service. The most striking example is the third and fourth classes of power. That is, with the appearance of the fourth class, the mileage of the third class was materially increased, until both were fairly close.

Mileage between classified repairs for all classes and types of motive power on the Central increased from 75,573 in 1931 and 80,363 in 1937 to 110,213 in 1939, and largely because high mileage was being obtained from the Hudsons. For 37 locomotives of this type shopped for classified repairs in 1937, the average mileage was 221,000. Thirty-one engines exceeded 200,000 miles, while one reached a maximum of 276,761 hard-traveled miles.

To insure full utilization of locomotives certain systems have been developed. These appear under the following four headings:

(1) Checking Passenger Stations for Surplus Locomotives

At each passenger terminal station, whether large or small, a study is made periodically covering a period of two weeks, and all arriving and departing trains are charted. As passenger trains run on regular schedule, this system is found to be practical. The result is the dispatching, if possible, of the arriving engine on a departing train regardless of direction.

(2) Checking Enginehouses for Surplus Locomotives

The arrival and departure of each locomotive at an enginehouse is charted, and, considering the performance of the necessary work at the house, the expected average turning time is established.

The enginehouse can be considered as a store, where profits can be made only if there is a high percentage of turnover of stock on the shelves. Stock beyond a certain amount is a dead loss. Surplus power, likewise, represents a loss, not only of the approximately $250 per month it costs to maintain a locomotive ready for service, but on the overhead in more locomotives than are necessary.

The average turning time at each enginehouse, of course, varies from day to day during the week. The peak traffic occurs between Friday and Sunday. On these days there will be a short turning time, but the normal figure can readily be established. When the turning time is above the established fair figure, the storing of power begins, with resulting loss.

(3) Obtaining Capacity Performance from the Locomotive

There have been radical changes in locomotives in recent years. Counterbalancing has been improved, and where an engine used to ride hard when the engineer was "working her down in the corner," it now rides far better. Exhaust tips have been enlarged, and in consequence the "bark" in the stack is much softer; so we find it difficult to estimate the capacity at which the engine is being used just by listening to the exhaust.

When it is necessary to get every pound of available tractive force from a locomotive, experience has demonstrated the necessity of providing the engineman with some means

Courtesy of Santa Fe Ry.

IN THE HOLE FOR NO. 24. The eastbound Santa Fe Grand Canyon Limited running around a freight train in Cajon Pass. The freight's engine is one of the old Santa Fe 1600 class, a 2-10-2 type. Note the head brakeman of the freight train about to give the passenger train a running inspection from the ground.

Photo by W. H. Thrall, Jr.

TAKING ORDERS ON THE FLY. No. 69, the Southern Pacific's Coaster, takes a 19 order at Burbank Junction. The hoop in the tower man's right hand contains the copies for the train crew. The engine is the 4356, one of the famous Southern Pacific 4-8-2s, Class MT-3.

Photo by W. H. Thrall, Jr.

EXCHANGING MESSAGE AND ORDER ON THE FLY. The conductor of Southern Pacific's first No. 813 west is shown dropping a message (note hoop in mid-air) as he aims to grab the order hoop from the operator at Burbank Junction, California, on the Los Angeles Division. This train was making between 45 and 50 miles per hour when this picture was snapped.

by which he will know whether or not he is working the engine to the best advantage.

Let us take a look at the recording tapes used on three trains. The trains were made of ten, twelve, and fourteen cars each, and the recording tapes show that the distance before each train attained a full speed of 70 m.p.h. was 8¼, 12, and 17 miles respectively. The increase in distance might be expected with the increasing weight of trains, yet when specific studies were made in the territory covered by the tapes it was found that the heavier trains could be accelerated to full speed in 6.1, 7.6, and 8.2 miles. The possibility of getting over the road in the minimum amount of time is affected also by the rate of deceleration, although, in general, more time is lost in accelerating than in decelerating. An actual test showed the time that can be saved by proper braking and accelerating after a slowdown to 30 m.p.h. It was found that decelerating time had been reduced by one half and that accelerating time could be reduced by almost the same amount with the locomotive worked at maximum capacity. Locomotives can be operated with the minimum loss of time where there is a definite indication for the engineman as to how to operate with the greatest degree of efficiency.

It may seem that accelerating at maximum capacity is a minor item, but with long runs the pick-up necessary because of stops and slowdowns may, upon analysis, be found of such frequency as to make this an important item. On the New York Central, daily checks are made of tapes or charts from locomotives handling some seven hundred train divisions, for it is essential to obtain the full power effort from as expensive a piece of machinery as one of those steam giants.

The particular value of such charts is that, instead of having later to answer the implicit complaint, "Couldn't you have gotten the old girl rolling a little quicker?" the engineman can know for a certainty that if, five miles out of town, she is rolling at 70, he has saved two minutes of running time.

It takes about a ton of coal to make up a minute of lost time, and coal costs money, and money makes the mare go; so it can readily be seen what we are driving at.

With the ever-increasing efficiency of the railroad locomotive, a recording tape has been found to be a necessary part of the equipment, for by this means the economical cut-off under various running conditions can be determined. Thus it is written in the "Officials' Bible" that "after a train has reached full running speed, the engineman should be encouraged to shorten the cut-off as much as is practicable in maintaining the schedule."

However, your veteran at the throttle is pretty well versed in the art of "hooking her up until she is talking right back at you," exactly as he knows how, when the occasion demands, to "drop her into the corner and rap her stack off."

(4) Supplying Coal and Water for Long High-speed Runs

Experience has shown that adequate tender capacity is about 16,000 gallons. To save time, track pans have been installed on some roads. Engines usually take water at regular stops, with a standpipe of sufficient capacity to fill a tender in about three minutes, and, further, pick it up on the fly.

A study made over a period of eleven years on the New York Central indicates the increasing amount of coal required to steam its fast trains through on time. This because of constant schedule reductions and heavier trains, pounding out the hard-won miles. Comparisons are drawn in Table VII, p. 244.

For instance, in 1932 two hours were cut from the schedule of the Century between New York and Chicago, with a sharp reduction of time for other important trains. In succeeding years there were additional reductions. This was possible because of the ample reserve power in the locomotives.

By 1938 the Century was down to sixteen hours, and the average schedule reduction between 1926 and 1940 for fifteen main-line trains was nearly three hours, representing an increase in average over-all speed of about 8 m.p.h., although in that time the maximum permitted speed had been increased only from 70 to 80 m.p.h.

With the introduction of the Class J-3 engines, the increased power had a beneficial effect in reducing train-miles through the handling of more cars per train, and we find a saving of more than 900,000 train-miles in 1939, as compared with 1930.

With heavier trains and faster schedules constantly pressing to the fore, it was indicated that, to obtain higher utilization, ways and means must be provided in the way of obtaining longer runs between coal stops.

The tendency in tender design is to materially increase

the coal-carrying capacity. This trend in tender design has resulted from the installation of sufficient track pans with which to maintain service with a tender capacity of about 16,000 gallons.

TABLE VII

AVERAGE PASSENGER LOCOMOTIVE MILEAGE PER TON OF COAL DISBURSED
NEW YORK CENTRAL MAIN LINE, HARMON–CHICAGO
(*All classes of passenger locomotives*)

Year	*Average Locomotive-miles per ton of coal*
1930	19.26
1931	18.85
1932	17.95
1933	18.30
1934	17.73
1935	17.43
1936	16.26
1937	16.12
1938	16.01
1939	15.55
1940	15.14

It will be noted from the foregoing table that the fuel consumption for passenger locomotives is nearly a ton every fifteen miles. This covers all weights of trains.

In summarizing the last eleven years it is found that the possibility of passenger locomotives making high mileage has been increased 27 per cent. Reliability, coal capacity of tender, and track pans have played an important part in the performance of these road engines.

At present plans are being made to provide more than three times the coal capacity of the locomotives in use in 1928.

Thus, to obtain greater utilization of passenger engines,

it is necessary not only to increase the number of hours per day the locomotive is in service, but also to decrease the out-of-service time required for daily inspection or for reconditioning. The ultimate goal is, naturally, to have a minimum number of locomotives producing the maximum amount of service.

We have seen this increase in utilization as a direct result of the improvements in locomotive construction through progressive design down the years. And the end is not in sight. The iron horse is yet destined to range far and fast, like the magnificent thoroughbred that it is.

CHAPTER XIX

Record Run on the Santa Fe

During the years 1937 and 1938, the Atchison, Topeka & Santa Fe placed in service 27 Baldwin locomotives, representing three wheel arrangements. They were the 4-6-4 or Hudson, the 4-8-4 or Northern, and the 2-10-4 or Texas types.

In another chapter we watched the creation of the Hudson 4-6-4 passenger hauler, there on the Central. In turning now to the Santa Fe, we find that this road has been using the 4-6-4 type locomotive since 1927. This early type of Hudson had cylinders 25 × 28 inches and 73-inch drivers and carried a steam pressure of 220 pounds. They were known as the 3450 class. They have now been modernized and boast 79-inch wheels, and blow off at 230 pounds.

The later 4-6-4 type, designated as the 3460 class, carried 300 pounds of steam pressure and had 84-inch drivers. One of these engines, the 3461, was destined to write railroad history, thereby carving for itself a niche in the Railroad Hall of Fame.

However, before we give you the story, let us first turn our attention to this new motive power of the Santa Fe in general.

The 4-6-4 and 4-8-4 engines were intended for fast passenger service, and the 2-10-4 for fast freight. Special interest in their design centers in the high capacity of the locomotives and certain details of their construction, which, following Santa Fe practice, include interchangeable parts, where practicable, and high boiler capacity, together with the large driving wheels essential in modern motive power.

The earlier 4-8-4 type engines, the 3751 class, had 73-inch drivers, cylinders 30 × 30 inches, and carried a steam pressure of 210 pounds. They were later modernized and given 80-inch wheels and the steam pressure was raised to 230 pounds.

The new locomotives differ considerably from their predecessors, the 3450 and 3751 classes, and this is largely accounted for by the fact that present-day speed requirements are far more exacting than they were when the 3450 and 3751 were designed.

The later 4-6-4 and 4-8-4 engines are known as the 3460 and 3765 classes respectively. There are six of the former, one of which, the 3460, is streamlined, and, without doubt, high-hats her less fortunate sisters, quite after the manner of snooty humans. But it is conceivable that the other ladies bounce back with the retort that they at least still look like steam engines and not like overdressed city girls on a fishing or duck-shooting trip.

The 3460, with all her regalia and pomp, has further to contend with the disdain of the 3461, who promptly, when she made her debut on the Santa Fe, stole the show by waltzing off to Chicago on a record run.

The 3460 is, nevertheless, as sweet to look at as a pretty girl in her first party dress. Her contour blends into that of the train and is adorned in two shades of blue, with under-portions, including the running gear, in blue-gray. The striping is in silver leaf, the handrails are stainless steel, and the handrail columns, cab handles, and certain other fittings are chromium-plated.

There is stainless-steel trim 18 inches in depth on the sides of the running-board skirt and pilot; also on the tank. The outer faces of the driving-wheel tires and hubs are painted with aluminum paint, as are the rims of all engine and tender truck wheels. Small wonder that the builders made a snob out of the 3460! In my opinion she is the best-looking streamlined 4-6-4 so far turned out.

The boiler shells of both classes are nickel steel, with inside fireboxes of carbon steel, except in the streamlined engine, which has a firebox of nickel steel. In both classes the safety valves are set at 300 pounds, but the boilers are designed for a working pressure of 310 pounds. They were tested with a steam pressure of 330 pounds and a hot-water pressure of 414 pounds.

In the 4-8-4 type a 64-inch combustion chamber is used and three siphons are installed, two in the firebox proper and one in the combustion chamber. The 4-6-4 also has two firebox siphons, but the combustion chamber is omitted. The steam domes of both classes are steel castings, without removable dome caps. The opening under the auxiliary dome is sufficiently large to enable a man to enter the boiler for inspection purposes.

Both locomotive types are equipped for the use of oil as fuel, but are so designed that they can be changed subsequently to burn coal if necessary.

A one-piece bed is used in each class. The back cylinder heads, together with brackets for the air pumps, feed-water-heater pumps, waist sheets, guides, valve-gear and driver-brake cylinders, are cast in one piece with the bed. To provide for possible future application, supports for the stoker-conveyor and grate-shaker cylinders are also cast integral with the bed.

The driving wheels of the 4-8-4 and 4-6-4 types are 80 and 84 inches in diameter respectively, with Baldwin Disc type centers. These centers, furnished by the Standard Steel Works, are Double Anchor brand, high-tensile steel castings, normalized and tempered. The main wheels of the 4-6-4 and the main and intermediate wheels of the 4-8-4 are cross-balanced; and 40 per cent of the reciprocating weight is balanced. S.K.F. roller bearings are used on all engine and tender axles of the 4-6-4, with Timken bearings on the 4-8-4.

Special materials are largely used for the machinery details. The piston rods and crankpins are Standard steel forgings, except that chrome-nickel steel is used for the crankpins on the main and intermediate wheels of the 4-8-4 type. The Laird guide, which is standard on the Santa Fe System, is used in both classes. The main and side rods are chrome-nickel molybdenum-steel forgings. Tandem main rods, connected to the second and third pairs of driving wheels, are used on the 4-8-4s.

Walschaerts valve gear, controlled by a Baldwin Type C power reverse having a stroke of 24 inches, is used on both classes.

The 4-8-4 type locomotives are also fitted with a design of by-pass valve which is a modification of the Wagner valve as introduced some years ago in Germany. Placed above the steam chest is a cylindrical bushing, 9¼ inches in diameter, with a piston fitted in each end. Openings through the bushing communicate with the steam passages leading to the cylinder. The pistons have suitable ports cut in them and are separated by a coiled spring, and they can be moved closer together by steam pressure acting on their outer ends. When the throttle valve is open, steam acts against the pistons, moving them closer together and holding them in such a position that there is no communication through the bushing between the two ends of the cylinder. When the throttle is closed and the steam pressure relieved, the spring forces the pistons apart, so that the ports in them register with the steam passages leading to the cylinder, and there is free communication from one end of the cylinder to the other through the bushing.

Both types of engines have leading trucks of the Batz design, as developed by the railway company. This is an equalized truck with a cast-steel one-piece frame. The equalizer on each side serves as a seat for eight vertical coil springs;

on top of these springs is placed a steel casting on which the frame has a single support at mid-length. The General Steel Castings Corporation's constant-resistance device is applied, and the principal parts of the trucks interchange on the 4-6-4 and 4-8-4 types. The rear trucks are of the Delta type, and here again the principal parts interchange on the two types of locomotives.

The equipment of these engines includes Worthington Type 6-SA feed-water heaters, located in a depression at the top of the front end of the smokebox.

Three mechanical lubricators are applied to each engine and are driven, through suitable connections, from link trunnions. The streamlined locomotive has three Nathan lubricators of 36-pints capacity, and each of the others has one similar lubricator and two Chicago lubricators of 40-pints capacity. These feed oil to all driving and engine truck box pedestal faces, to the two main guides, the cylinders and piston valves, and to the hot-water pump.

Both engine types are fitted with the Electro-Chemical Engineering Corporation's Signal Foam-meter and Electro-magnetic Blowoff Cock equipment. The Union Switch & Signal Company's three-speed continuous-train-control movement, with all-electric governor, is applied to the 4-6-4 locomotives. Speed recorders are on all of them.

The tenders of both classes are similar in construction, with capacity for 20,000 gallons of water and 7,000 gallons of oil. The tenders are carried on six-wheeled trucks of the passenger-car type and have one-piece cast-steel frames.

The oil tank is built as an integral part of the water tank.

The 4-6-4 type locomotives and their tenders are designed so that they can be turned on a 90-foot table; the 4-8-4 on a 100-foot turntable.

The 4-6-4 type locomotives are used for service on the eastern lines, between Chicago and La Junta, Colorado, where the grades are moderate. The 4-8-4s operate through mountainous country west of La Junta, where the steepest grades are 3½ per cent. Ten more of these 4-8-4 locomotives were built by Baldwin in 1941. These included certain improvements, and all have tenders with 25,000-gallons capacity of water and 7,000 gallons of oil. They are carried on eight-wheeled trucks.

The 2-10-4 type locomotives, known as the 5001 class, are a direct development of Santa Fe's Engine 5000, which was built by Baldwin in 1930.

The latter locomotive, it should be noted, was not the first of the 2-10-4 type to be built for the road, as in 1919 Engine 3829, one of a group of big ten-coupled engines then under construction, was fitted with a four-wheeled rear truck instead of a two-wheeled truck, as used on the other locomotives of the group.

Engine 3829 was undoubtedly the first 2-10-4 type built in the country, and yet it had little in common with the real 2-10-4, or Texas type, built by Lima for the Texas and Pacific in 1925.

Engine 5000 has driving wheels 69 inches in diameter and develops a maximum tractive force of 93,000 pounds. At the time it was built it attracted considerable attention because of its high horsepower and speed capacity.

In the 5001 class, ten of which have been built at this writing, the wheel diameter is 74 inches, and, by raising the steam pressure from 300 to 310 pounds, the same starting tractive force can be developed without increasing the cylinder dimensions. The boiler at the front end has been increased from 92 inches to 94 inches. The grate area remains the same, but the heating surface is slightly less, due to a reduction in the number of 2¼-inch tubes. The diameter of the rear boiler course in both classes is 104 inches.

Originally, five of the locomotives, Nos. 5001–5005, burned coal, with Nos. 5006–5010 burning oil. However, in 1940 the five coal-burning engines were converted to oil burners. All these big freight engines have been doing yeoman work in the freight service, up there at the storming front of the fast freights. They were built to take it, and they have the largest and heaviest one-piece beds yet produced, the over-all length being 61 feet 8½ inches, with a shipping weight of 87,128 pounds with pedestal binders in place.

Like the 4-8-4 type, they are fitted with tandem main rods, limited cut-off and by-pass valves. The main valves have a steam lap of 2 inches and cut-off at 60 per cent of the stroke in full gear. Walschaerts valve motion is applied and is controlled by a Baldwin Type C power reverse.

The transverse tire spacing on the first, third, and fifth pair of drivers is 53 inches, and on the second and fourth pairs, and also on the front and rear trucks, the spacing is 53¼ inches. The driving axles are carbon-steel forgings, hollow-bored, with holes 5 inches in diameter. Chrome-nickel steel is used for the crankpins on the third and fourth pairs of drivers, and the remaining pins are of carbon steel, quenched and tempered. Plain bearings are used on all engine and tender axles.

The tenders of these freight locomotives are similar in design to those of the 4-6-4 and the 4-8-4 types.

And now we come to the story of the 3461, that famous Hudson.

The Santa Fe was not long in discovering that a 4-6-4 Hudson had what it takes, and on December 12, 1937, highballed the 3461 on a cross-country trek that made history. Up to this time four locomotives were required to take a train through on the Los Angeles / Chicago run. Later this was reduced by two.

Shortly after Baldwin delivered the 3461, along with the rest of that new passenger power, the officials in Los Angeles, the City of the Angels, coupled her onto the head end of a conventional train of big steel cars and said, in effect, "All right, my friend, you've got the railroad. Let's see what you can do."

The result was what is believed to be the longest continuous run ever made by a steam locomotive in regular scheduled passenger-train service, for her royal highness, Locomotive 3461, made it all the way to the Dearborn Street Station in Chicago with mail and express train No. 8—without change.

And she did a pretty job of it, laying 2,227.3 steel miles behind her, just like rolling off a log. The train was made up of 10 to 12 cars and a dynamometer car, with a total trailing load of 757 to 939 tons.

No attempt was made at a speed record, and the elapsed time was 53 hours and 40 minutes, of which about 4 hours and 35 minutes were spent at stations en route. This time was consumed in loading and unloading mail and express and cutting cars in and out of the train, etc. This left a running time of 49 hours and 5 minutes, with an average speed of about 45 m.p.h. The maximum speed was 90 miles an hour. The only time Engine 3461 was uncoupled from the train was while picking up or dropping cars.

Locomotive and train, of course, received careful inspection at all regular inspection points.

Helper service was provided on the 2.2 per cent grade between Los Angeles and Upland, California; on the 2.2 per cent grade over El Cajon, out of San Bernardino, California, and on the 1.8 per cent grade, Ash Fork to Williams, Arizona. Then, too, there was a helper for the 3.3 hump, Raton to Lynn, New Mexico, and also from Lamy to Glorieta.

Fuel was taken at five points: Hackberry, Arizona, Albuquerque, New Mexico, Dodge City, Kansas, and Newton; also at Shopton, Iowa. The total consumpton was 20,450 gallons of fuel oil. Water was taken at 18 stations, the total being 208,400 gallons. In this connection it should be noted that tests indicated that the feed-water heater, with which the locomotive was equipped, had a condensate return of about 14 per cent.

The fuel oil was supplied from regular wayside tanks, which are equipped with heater lines to keep the oil in free-flowing condition. Indirect heating pipes in the tender fuel tanks keep the oil at a temperature of about 160 degrees, with a small amount of heat being supplied by the injection of live steam when necessary to agitate the oil.

Treated boiler water was used for the most part, being supplied from the usual station standpipes. An important feature in connection with the maintenance of suitable boiler-water conditions is the provision of intermittent, automatic, blow-down equipment, which keeps the concentration of accumulating solids in the boiler within desired limits, thus preventing trouble from foaming. Manual blow-down is used to supplement the automatic feature when necessary.

Of primary importance on this long run was the provision for adequate lubrication of all working parts.

On this 4-6-4 type engine we find force-feed lubrication to valves and cylinders through a four-feed mechanical lubricator, while an eight-feed lubricator supplies oil to the guides, driving-box shoes, and hub faces. Air-compressor cylinders are lubricated by means of a mechanical lubricator, and a driving-tire lubricator is also used.

All driving axles, engine-truck axles, and tender-truck axles are roller-bearing-equipped.

During the run, full dynamometer-car records were kept and steam-indicator cards taken during daylight operation. The back pressure varied from 7 to 16 pounds, and the maximum superheat temperature observed was 750 to 800 degrees Fahrenheit.

With a boiler pressure of 300 pounds and 7-foot driving wheels, this Hudson proved to be just so much concentrated dynamite, with a tractive force of 49,300 pounds, or 6,000 pounds more than those J-3s of the Central.

Thus these 4-6-4s of the Santa Fe combine high speed and hauling capacity to a degree that is unusual in a six-coupled engine.

On this Chicago run, the 3461 never hesitated or faltered, but did everything she was called on to do, and did it with amazing ease. Fresh as a daisy, she braked to a stop in the Dearborn Street Station in Chicago, and was ready, after receiving nominal lubrication attention and standard adjustments, to turn and highball it back to Los Angeles.

And so, to those who had declared that the steam locomotive was not adapted to making long runs, this Hudson, the 3461, gave answer, there on the old Santa Fe Trail.

If the writer was asked to name his favorite locomotive of all that he has ridden on American railroads, he would instantly answer, "The engine of the Santa Fe 3765 class, because for speed, tractive effort, horsepower, hauling capacity, and riding qualities they are hard to equal." These engines make the longest run in the United States and do all that they are asked to do and more—westbound with trains like the Santa Fe Chief, Fast Mail, and California Limited—they get a helper over Raton, over Glorieta—they will make it alone with twelve old-type cars or fourteen lightweight. On the 157 miles from Albuquerque to Gallup uphill almost all the way, most of it over one half of one per cent, they beat the pants off them, but 70 or 75 miles per hour is nothing. They take the Arizona Divide in stride and race up the east side of Cajon from Barstow to Victorville and Summit like the frightened jack rabbits that run away from them on the way. It takes a mighty heavy train for them to need assistance on these grades. You should ride one out of the new Los Angeles Union Station and see them take fourteen cars up the 2.2 per cent grade to Highland Park and Pasadena from a standing start in the station. With twelve cars or less, many times they go up Cajon alone, then over the hard pull from Needles to Yampai and Seligman and never slow up except for the water and fuel stop at Hackberry. The Arizona Divide is again taken in stride, and they get a helper for Glorieta and Raton. I have made that entire trip on three of them without getting off and wasn't very tired when I arrived at La Junta. These engines are asked to do more than any others in the United States and are now running through from Wellington, Kansas, to Los Angeles, 1,765 miles, via Amarillo and Belen.

Give me an oil-burning locomotive every time if possible. I have never ridden but two that would not steam, and no time was lost on either occasion, and on one trip the engine was blowing off again within sixty miles. Easy to fire and clean and, of course, economical in the parts of the country where they are used, an oil-burning locomotive is tops with me.

The Santa Fe's 4-6-4s are great power, but the Milwaukee's F-7 and Northwestern's E-4s are, of course, more powerful with the same size wheel, 84-inch. The Lackawanna also has a wonder with an 80-inch wheel. The Santa Fe's 2-10-4s of the 5001 class are the most remarkable and one of the finest types of freight engine in this country. Think of it—a ten-coupled locomotive with a 74-inch driving wheel! They really can highball a tonnage train. The Chesapeake and Ohio's T-1s are close behind. The Santa Fe's 2-10-2s are also the leading Santa Fe type in the country for speed and power, with the Baltimore & Ohio's, Reading's, and Great Northern's close behind.

My favorite 4-6-6-4 type is the Rio Grande's L-105 class, and I also like the Northern Pacific's Z-6 extremely well. All locomotives of this design are marvelous and are a great addition to the various motive-power rosters of the roads that employ them.

Of the larger articulateds, the Union Pacific's Big Boy is, of course, outstanding, owing to its high wheel, but I am extremely partial to the Southern Pacific's AC engine, not only for its magnificent performance but for its head-end cab, which, to my mind, is a master stroke in locomotive design in cleanliness, vision, and comfort for the crew when operating over mountain grades, sharp curves, and through tunnels. The service these engines perform is simply incomparable, and a whole book could be written about them alone. The Northern Pacific's Z-5 2-8-8-4s are also great engines, as are the Western Pacific's, Great Northern's R-2, and Rio Grande's L-131 2-8-8-2s.

The Boston and Maine's R-16 mountain type power is the author's favorite of that wheel arrangement, with the Pennsylvania's M-1A and Missouri Pacific's 5335-5339 class following.

The author's choice of Pacific-type locomotives would be the Baltimore & Ohio's P-7 President-class engines, the Pennsylvania's famous K-4s, the Chesapeake and Ohio's F-19 class, the RFP 321-325 class and the Santa Fe's converted 3400 class. However, there are plenty of Pacific-type locomotives giving marvelous service in the United States, just as there are so many wonderful 4-8-4s. The Southern Pacific's GS 3-4 engines, the Union Pacific's 820s, the Atlantic Coast Line's 1800s, and the Great Northern's S-2s, which all have 80-inch wheels, are the last word. So are many others in this group with 77-inch wheels, 75-inch wheels, 74-inch wheels, and so on right down to those with 70-inch wheels. To really judge them you have to take them in groups according to the size of their driving wheels and the conditions under which they are operated on the roads that own them.

My favorite of the Decapod type are the Pennsylvania's I-1s and the Western Maryland's I-2s.

My favorite 2-8-4s are the new M-1s of the Louisville & Nashville, the Erie's S-4s, and the Nickel Plate's.

My choice of 2-8-2s would be the K-3 engines of the Chesapeake & Ohio, the Baltimore & Ohio's Q-4s, the New York Central's H-10s, the Southern's, Rock Island's, the Delaware, Lackawanna and Western's 2100 class, and Great Northern's.

Of the 2-6-6-4 type I like the Norfolk and Western's Class A and the Seaboard's R-2, and for the old Atlantic type give me the Pennsylvania's E-6 all the way. The same goes for the Pennsylvania's G-5, for the 4-6-0 wheel arrangement, and that road's C-1 for the 0-8-0 switcher.

Of the 2-8-0s, the Reading Company's and Western Maryland's have made the biggest hit.

I prefer the Southern Pacific's SP-1-2-3 over the Union Pacific's 5000 for a 4-10-2, and of course there is only one

UP type, 4-12-2, but I do not care for a 3-cylinder locomotive.

The Pennsylvania's GG-1 tops all the electric engines I have ridden, and as for the Diesels of new design, one is as good as the other of the same horsepower.

I could write several books on why I prefer some locomotives to others, but unfortunately space does not permit me to dwell on that subject in this volume.

Now that I have listed a few of my motive-power favorites, perhaps the readers of this book would like me to express my opinion of my favorite train. There are too many wonderful trains in the United States to try to compare them or even try to list them, but if I were asked to pick one train that is hauled by a steam locomotive I should pick the Santa Fe Chief for speed, service, the best food, and the most luxurious and commodious accommodations, not to mention its fine year-round, everyday on-time performance.

If I were asked to name my choice of a train that was hauled by a Diesel locomotive or possibly one that did not run daily, my pick would again go to the Santa Fe, and the train would be the Super Chief, trains No. 17 and No. 18, and I would also give the Santa Fe the nod for operating the finest mail train in the country—their Fast Mail, trains No. 7 and No. 8.

For an overnight coach train I would pick the Atlantic Coast Line's Champion or the Pennsylvania's Trail Blazer, and for one that makes only a day run, the Southern Pacific's Daylights are probably the most beautiful trains in the United States, and the Milwaukee's Hiawatha would win the prize if I were presenting one.

CHAPTER XX

Preference Freight

THINGS WERE PRETTY TOUGH. Some folks called it the "recession," which was sort of sugar-coating the fact that Old Man Hard Times of the depression era was with us again. We thought he had "put out to go," but he was back again, like poor relations.

Business had a hitch in its git-along. Over in Europe bad boys were playing with matches again. That was in the fall of 1938. At about this time the Louisville & Nashville Railroad, faced with a declining less-than-carload freight traffic, occasioned in part by the hard times and in part by ever-increasing truck competition, discarded precedent and took the bull by the horns.

Something had to be done, and Old Reliable was just the coon to try anything once. No. 71, the Silver Bullet, had long been a fixture on the L.&N.'s main-line freight service between Cincinnati and New Orleans, operating by way of

Louisville, Nashville, Birmingham, Montgomery, and Mobile, and its performance had been outstanding. However, now, with the recession and all, the management chucked over all practices of the past and hopped No. 71 up with a 39-hour schedule and then stood back a little dubiously, perhaps to see how the medicine was going to react on the patient.

Under the old schedule between Cincinnati and New Orleans, No. 71 had made the trip in about 50 hours, which had been considered a right smart piece of going, but, as it developed, those 11 hours saved were much more important than their trade-in value would indicate.

Before the hopping-up mentioned, No. 71 arrived at the Gulf coast late in the afternoon of its second day out of Cincinnati—too late for its cargo of less-than-carload freight to be delivered to merchants and others that day. To be exact, 6:45 P.M. was the arriving time.

But this new schedule, now. Ah, that was something else again. It placed our preference freight, the Silver Bullet, at the depots along the Gulf coast in the early hours of its second morning out, permitting delivery of its merchandise to consignee in ample time for the day's business. And everybody was happy. The merchants had a quicker turnover, there were more contented customers, and 71's tonnage increased by leaps and bounds. The officials went around looking very pleased.

Hacking eleven hours off a schedule previously considered hot stuff was not as simple as it may sound. When you start grabbing minutes from the clock, you are in there slugging it out with a champion. But down on the L.&N. the boys have been shooting the works ever since Hector was a pup. You remember they built a railroad in the 1850s, with the cards all stacked against them.

No. 71's new schedule meant that everybody had to get together and heave ho. It meant close co-operation between all departments and the adoption of such innovations as the employment of night warehouse forces to receive, classify, load and unload freight, and a reduction in the number of stops for coal and water—among other things.

Now let's see how the Louisville & Nashville set about speeding up its magic transportation rug. No. 71 is one of those railroad aristocrats which hauls only the cream of the crop. No empty boxcars for the Silver Bullet; no grimy, groaning whale-bellies filled with coal; no iron ore, or rocks or bricks. No indeed. Generally speaking, 71 goes in more for store merchandise and the like, including such items as canned goods, perishables, paints, mops, dried fruits, machinery, furniture—mostly that less-than-carload "consist" already referred to. Not fancy stuff, perhaps, but as needful as rain.

The Silver Bullet is made up in the yards at Covington, Kentucky, just across the Ohio River from Cincinnati, where much of its freight originates. Too, Covington itself, as well as the cities of Louisville & Nashville, contributes to the train's "consist."

The L.&N. has two freight depots in the Queen City, the East and West End stations. Here Old Reliable accepts freight for the Bullet as late as 4:00 P.M., both from wholesalers and connecting lines. The lists then are closed and the loaded cars are quickly shoved across the C.&O. and N.&C. bridges to the Covington yards.

Here they are classified and placed in the train in the order of their detraining, which is to say that those which will be the last to be dropped off are coupled in behind the engine, with cars for Louisville, the next stop, placed, of course, on the rear end.

First No. 71 highballs out at 11:35 A.M. with the freight then on hand, arriving at Louisville at 5:15 P.M. Second No. 71 arrives with a bang at 9:00 P.M., with cars assembled later. Here at the Louisville's Strawberry Yard the "consists" of First and Second 71 are correlated and made up into one train.

Here things take place in a hurry, with switch engines carrying out a fast mechanized attack as they shuffle the cars. The dispatcher's office is shaping up a fast railroad south. Clerical forces are busy with waybills. Freight-station employees have been wrestling goods around with warehouse tractors and trailers.

At last the new Silver Bullet is ready. A big new Berkshire M-1 backs on and at 9:45 P.M. is snaking out onto the main track with some 1,500 tons of preference freight.

The 71 cracks off the 187 miles, Louisville to Nashville, stopping only to take coal and water at Bowling Green, Kentucky. The latter point is reached at 1:35 A.M., and at 6:00 the Bullet is whistling for the Radnor Yard outside of Nashville. Here the Bullet drops certain cars but garners others, some of which have breezed down from St. Louis, Evansville, and other points.

At Radnor, 71 gets a new crew, a fresh engine, and another caboose. Its perishables are re-iced, and a close inspection is given all rolling stock. Because of this work and the considerable classification and consolidation necessary, the train is at Radnor until 8:00 A.M., but every minute is crowded with activity.

Already the pick-up and delivery service has pounced on "consist" billed to Nashville and is hustling it away to various points in the city and waiting merchants and factories.

No. 71 highballs with two whistles and a spread of swishing wings from cylinder cocks and continues to bore into the South to the tune of iron thunder. Its singing wheels kiss the soil of Tennessee good-by and salute then the state of Alabama. Past the roaring steel mills of Birmingham, into the sweet piny woods of southern Alabama, along the sunny shores of America's Riviera—the Gulf Coast—and on into the one and only Crescent City—old New Orleans.

The Bullet reaches Birmingham at 2:00 P.M.; Montgomery at 5:45; Mobile at 12:15 A.M. All along the line cars have been picked up and set off. At 8:15 A.M. that engine pokes into New Orleans and spreads the tidings of her coming with a triumphant whistle blast.

The long miles behind the Bullet's old red hack total 917. The time—38 hours and 45 minutes. Meanwhile 71 has picked up and delivered several thousand tons of less-than-carload freight, done it with a speed and precision sweet to behold. Day in and day out this preference job rolls, thanks to the fighting spirit of Old Reliable, the rail kingdom that never says die.

One of the crack arranged freight runs in the United States

is No. 39 on the Santa Fe, running between the Corwith Yards in Chicago and the Argentine Yards in Kansas City. The distance is approximately 450 miles. The total elapsed time is 13 hours and 30 minutes, representing an average speed of 33.3 m.p.h., with the remarkable record of an on-time operation of 97 per cent.

Baldwin Mikado 2-8-2 type locomotives, Santa Fe classes 3160 and 4000, are used on this train and are assigned a maximum of 1,600 tons. In ordinary freight-hauling service, these engines handle 4,000 tons between Chicago and Fort Madison, and 3,600 tons between Fort Madison and Kansas City. One engine handles the train from Chicago to Shopton, Iowa, a distance of 228.6 miles, and a second then picks up the drag and rolls it into Kansas City. Engine and train crews change at Chillicothe, Illinois, 124 miles from Chicago, while another crew change is made at Shopton.

In connection with this sort of fast overnight freight service, there are not a few problems presented. Among these is the handling of the necessary paper work. According to ordinary procedure, the shipper supplies a bill of lading, and from this the railroad makes a waybill to accompany the shipment. Before the goods can be delivered to the consignee, a freight bill must be made out. With these overnight trains on the railroad, this presented something of a problem—a fly in the ointment, so to speak—for, in order to make the service meet the needs of the shipper, freight must be accepted late in the afternoon. This makes it impossible to complete the mass of clerical work necessary and have the documents ready before the train leaves. The Santa Fe overcame this obstacle very neatly. This was done by transmitting the waybills, Chicago to Kansas City, by teletype. Here a night shift makes out the freight bills, and when No. 39 arrives at 7:30 A.M. the goods can be cleared immediately and the city delivery started without delay.

Travel where you may in the United States today and you will find great freight engines highballing through at speeds up to 75 miles an hour. On many roads these big steam locomotives are even shading the time of passenger trains over the same lines, and always with the percentage against them.

Freight, unlike the human cargo of a passenger train, is inanimate and has continually to be shifted and shoved about. Passengers show up at certain stations and climb aboard, and that, except for delivering them pronto at their destination, is all there is to it.

Freight cars are something else again. They have to be rounded up and close-herded and branded like a bunch of white-faced cattle. En route certain of them are continually spooking off to all points of the compass, and every last straggler has to be tabbed and accounted for and finally corralled at its ultimate destination with neatness and dispatch.

Let us look at No. 91, Rock Island time freight, westbound out of Chicago, and follow its fast schedule down that fine road.

No. 91 is dispatched from Chicago at 10:00 A.M. for faraway California. This train is due at Kansas City at 7:00 A.M. the second day; Tucumcari, New Mexico, at 1:00 P.M. the third day; El Paso, Texas, at 3:30 A.M. the fourth day; and Los Angeles at 7:00 P.M. the fifth day.

No. 91 also carries freight for the Colorado area, which is dispatched from Silvis Yard, 158 miles west of Chicago. Here the greater part of all westbound classification is carried on. Colorado-California 91 makes connection with the Denver & Rio Grande Western in Denver, where it becomes the "Ute," and this freight goes booming over the Rockies behind one of those mountain locomotives of the 4-6-6-4 type, and into Salt Lake; thence by Western Pacific to Pacific Coast terminals in the Bay District of San Francisco.

Another section of No. 91 operating out of Silvis Yard, and which is made up from the 91 out of Chicago, becomes Train 903, which serves Cedar Rapids, Iowa, and destinations between Cedar Rapids and the Twin Cities.

To save time, once the wheels are rolling, 91 is made up in three parts at Burr Oak. Hence when it rolls into the Silvis Yard these blocks of cars quickly find their way onto the tracks in which traffic for the various destinations already has been classified, and soon this train is out on the main and away again.

The handling of the waybills and records covering 91 is of the utmost importance. There is the "Red Ball" symboling of the cars, the lining up of waybills, and the typing of the entire record of the train on the teletype machine. This before the waybills can be released to the conductor.

This system of symboling each car of commercial freight comes under the classification of "Red Ball," or Symbol Freight. It provides an advance record for receivers at car destinations, as was explained in the chapter dealing with the California fruit trains.

The cross-country wires are red hot with "manifest" reports. Trainmasters make out their car cards and get ready to handle the train upon arrival. Transportation superintendents notify traffic representatives that shipments are kicking up dust just over the hill, and everywhere the goose hangs high.

There is merely the small matter of wheeling some hundreds of tons of freight a couple of thousand miles. The thing is in the bag before 91 has much more than started.

To insure a fast schedule for this 91, an advance section leaves Chicago about 6:00 A.M. every morning. This train picks up freight at stations between Chicago and Silvis; getting traffic from connecting lines at Joliet and Depue, which includes cars from the Michigan Central and the New York Central.

The California section of 91 not only serves the Pacific coast and the Texas-Arizona territory, but also carries important "consist" for Oklahoma, Arkansas, and Louisiana.

No. 91 is reclassified at Kansas City, and that jolly shuffling of cars starts all over again. In the meantime a No. 915 has popped her nose around the bend from St. Louis way, and there are more shipments to be absorbed by 91.

This Coast manifest highballs out at 11:45 A.M., with all her troubles behind her—a long train of them—and lifts the stubby pilot of her big Rock Island 5000-class to the western slopes of the Continental Divide.

At one P.M. Wednesday, Time Freight 91 is dumped into the lap of the Southern Pacific at Tucumcari, New Mexico. The S.P. then bats her through. It sounds simple, but it is a he-man job to roll a train out of Chicago on Monday and lay this bill of goods on the doorstep in Los Angeles Friday afternoon for sixth-day delivery. Nevertheless it is done, day in and day out, around the calendar, come fair weather or foul.

The volume of manifest freight moving in the United States through every cycle of the clock is tremendous. The system of arranged or scheduled freight-train service on the Pennsylvania Railroad alone reaches the startling total of over 400 trains operating daily, or daily except Sunday or Monday.

These preference trains run on regular schedules, with fixed arrival and departure time. This schedule confers no timetable rights, but the movement has preference over all non-schedule trains.

The arranged freight schedules are based primarily on leaving as late as possible at the initial terminal and arriving as early as practical at the final destination. Some of these wonderful cargo trains are listed herewith.

(*Lists of P.R.R. symbol freight trains on pages immediately following.*)

WESTBOUND

Train Symbol	Name	Origin	Point of Destination	Character of Freight	Basis of Arrival
NE1	The Speed Witch	Boston	Philadelphia Baltimore	Carload merchandise	1st morning
BEC1	The Excelsior	Buffalo	Crestline	All freight	3rd morning (Chicago)
CO3	The Challenger	Cincinnati	Chicago	Perishable merchandise	1st morning
FC1	The Queen City	Cleveland	Cincinnati	All freight	2nd morning
LM1	The Rocket	Columbus	Cincinnati	All freight	3rd morning
NW85	The Big Smoke	Columbus	Chicago	All freight	1st morning
NW99	Lightfoot	Columbus	Logansport	Perishable	1st morning
DC9	Dynamic	Detroit	Cincinnati	All freight	2nd morning
BF3	The Purple Emperor	Enola	Buffalo	All freight	2nd morning from Baltimore. 3rd morning from Norfolk
BF5	The Blue Goose	Enola	Buffalo	All freight	2nd morning from seaboard and Potomac Yard
VC1	The Meteor	Enola	Cleveland	All freight	2nd morning from seaboard
ED1	The Arrow	Enola	Detroit	All freight	2nd morning Toledo and Detroit from seaboard
PF1	Star Union Line	Enola	Chicago	All freight	3rd morning from seaboard
VL7	The Comet	Enola	Indianapolis	All freight	2nd afternoon from seaboard
PG11	The Ace	Harsimus Cove	Enola	All freight	2nd morning Pittsburgh
CO5	The Renown	Indianapolis	Chicago	All freight	1st morning
P5-NL1	The Yankee	New York	Chicago	All freight	3rd morning from seaboard and New England
BF1	The North Star	Pittsburgh	Buffalo	All freight	2nd morning
PF3	The Peerless	Pittsburgh	Chicago	All freight	2nd morning
PG13	The Dividend	Wilkes-Barre	Altoona	All freight	2nd morning at Pittsburgh

("Seaboard" refers to New York, Philadelphia, and Baltimore.)

East and North

Train Symbol	Name	Origin	Point of Destination	Character of Freight	Basis of Arrival
NE2	The Speed Witch	Baltimore	Boston	Carload merchandise	1st morning
BF2	Flying Cloud	Buffalo	Pittsburgh	All freight	2nd morning
BF4	The Bison	Buffalo	Enola	All freight	2nd morning seaboard
BNY14	The Cornucopia	Buffalo	Harsimus Cove	All freight	2nd morning
BNY16	Guts	Buffalo	Harsimus Cove	All freight	2nd morning
FW8	Man of War	Chicago	Seaboard	Stock	3rd morning
CMB	The Packer	Chicago	Enola	Perishable	3rd morning
PF2	The Mercury	Chicago	Enola	Merchandise	3rd morning seaboard
BEC2	The Salesman	Canton	Buffalo	All freight	3rd morning from Chicago. 2nd morning from Canton
NW84	The Virginian	Chicago	Columbus	Perishable merchandise	1st afternoon
NW86	The Reliable	Chicago	Columbus	Perishable merchandise	Same evening. Western connection traffic
IL2	The Derby	Chicago	Louisville	Perishable merchandise	1st morning
CO8	The Invincible	Logansport	Cincinnati	Perishable merchandise	1st morning from Chicago. Western connection traffic
LM4	The Spark Plug	Cincinnati	Pittsburgh	Perishable merchandise	1st morning to Phila-Columbus
LM8	The Captivator	Cincinnati	Columbus	Perishable merchandise	2nd morning Greenville. 2nd afternoon other seaboard points
DC8	Cock of the Walk	Cincinnati	Cleveland	All freight	1st morning
FC2	The Forest City	Cincinnati	Cleveland	All freight	1st morning

East and North—*Continued*

Train Symbol	Name	Origin	Point of Destination	Character of Freight	Basis of Arrival
CE2	The Eagle	Cleveland	Harsimus Cove	All freight	2nd morning seaboard
ED2	The Gas Wagon	Detroit	Enola	All freight	3rd morning seaboard
PH10	The Greyhound	East St. Louis	Seaboard	Stock	3rd morning
VL8	The Ranchman	East St. Louis	Enola	All freight	2nd morning Greenville. 2nd afternoon other seaboard points
D2	The Catbird	Norfolk	Harsimus Cove	Perishable	2nd morning New York
MD12	The Oriole	Potomac Yard	New York	Perishable	1st evening
TC12	The Dixie	Detroit	Cincinnati	All freight	1st evening
CSB2	New Englander	Altoona	Wilkes-Barre	All freight	2nd night. Connections Chicago and St. Louis

We could go on, but this will give you an idea of the heights to which fast freight is soaring. North, south, east, and west the wheels are rolling. In peace or war thundering engines and speeding trains answer the needs of the nation.

Engine No. 231, a giant 4-8-4, or Northern type, is standing on the outgoing engine track at Bensenville, Illinois, Chicago freight terminal of the Milwaukee road. It couples onto Coast Time Freight No. 263. Let's see what happens now.

No. 263 is due to leave at 11:15 A.M. The train is made up of important time freight consisting of merchandise and machinery, together with several cars of very urgently needed armament material for the Bremerton Navy Yard on faraway Puget Sound. The Indiana Harbor Belt Line has just tacked on 20 cars of steel for Milwaukee, along with some cars for Fort Lewis, Washington—army stuff.

The fireman brings the pressure of the 4-8-4 up to 285 pounds. The engineer is out having a look around. A switch engine couples on the old red hack—the caboose. The runner—our engineman—climbs into the cab. The train line has been hooked up, and now the air pumps start whaling away, building up pressure, but there is a leak somewhere. A car inspector finds a broken air hose. This is replaced.

Now there is 70 pounds in the brake pipe, and the regulation tests are completed. The train conductor hands the engineer a clearance slip and reveals that there are 118 cars in the drag, 4,750 tons. Comes the highball, and that first deep-throated bark from the exhaust. The slack runs out, and the heavy train begins to move.

The fireman watches the smoke pounding into the sky and

turns on the smoke-abatement device. He then adjusts the stoker jets to insure proper distribution of the coal being sprayed into the firebox, which now is a roaring, white-hot inferno.

The whistle screams for the board, or signal, at the Dubuque & Illinois main-line crossing. As the speed increases, the cut-off is shortened. The needle of the steam gauge holds on the pin—full pressure. The pyrometer shows a temperature of 750 degrees. The water glass indicates half a gauge of water.

The speed now is 45 miles an hour. No. 263 slows for Sturtevant, where it will take the siding for No. 101, the afternoon Hiawatha. Later the speed queen of the Milwaukee lunges past at 100 miles an hour.

The 263 rolls out onto the main and starts hotfooting for Milwaukee, arriving there at 2:45 P.M. The engine is uncoupled and trundles away to the coal shed. The tender is heaped with black diamonds. Then the ashpan is cleaned and water gushes aboard.

A new engine crew takes over. There are 89 cars in the train now, 3,750 tons. The engineer receives a clearance, a "31" train order and a "19." He and the conductor compare watches. The fireman and head brakeman check the orders. The whistle cracks twice as a semaphore shows "clear."

The 11 miles to Brookfield are tough going, and the reverse is at about half-stroke; the throttle is all the way back. The exhaust is cannonading like a battery of field guns, and sparks and cinders are pelting the heavens. Twenty-one miles an hour now, and the 263 is working her passage. Approaching

Brookfield, the grade eases and the speed increases to 26 miles per hour.

At Brookfield the 4-8-4 gulps 5,000 gallons of water. The 263 slams past Pewaukee at 50 miles an hour, and holds this speed until the slowdown for the North Western crossing at Watertown. Fifty again. The 263 breezes down the grade from Rio at 60 in a cloud of dust, running like a scared rabbit. On the curves beyond, engineer and fireman look back to see if there is anything getting hot, but everything is right as rain. Not a smoking journal in sight.

The whistle screams for Portage, and the time freight slows, snakes into the yard. The engine is serviced, which includes taking on coal and water. Another crew climbs aboard, fresh and saucy.

The 263 remains at Portage fifteen minutes. Other cars have been added to the train—merchandise for the Northwest, including several carloads of Diesel engines from the Fairbanks, Morse & Company plant at Beloit, Wisconsin. These are consigned to one of the shipyards on the Coast and are wanted in a hurry.

Ready to go, but suddenly the stoker stops, and the fireman comes up with a little staple and assorted cussing. However, he is a resourceful soul and soon locates a piece of scrap iron that had been mixed in with the coal. He gets it out of the crusher and builds up his fire. He mops his perspiring face and says, "Let's go!"

As soon as the 263 is rolling in good shape, the engineer opens the sludge remover and blows some water out of the boiler, getting rid of accumulated solids and other harmful agents that have settled in the boiler. Then water glasses and gauge cocks are checked.

The speedometer says 55 miles an hour. Comes then the slowing for New Lisbon, where coal and water are taken again. At La Crosse there is another change of engine crews. The ashpan is cleaned; there is another drink for the engine, and the sandbox is filled.

In the meantime a yard crew has built the train up to 120 cars—5,175 tons. The conductor appears with an order to run extra to St. Paul. The fireman places white flags on the boiler front and lights the white marker lights.

After the engineer has received a "bridge card" from the operator at "BK" tower, giving him authority for the train to cross the Mississippi River, the 263, now Extra 231, rolls on.

Down the main past River Junction tower. The engineer has that big iron-whiskered freight hauler really talking. Soon she is picking them up and laying them down at fifty miles an hour. Coal and water again at Wabasha.

This is a constant water-level grade, and the big parade is hitting it off—120 cars trailing that Northern locomotive, with St. Paul coming at them. And then, back on the rear end, the ominous glow of a red flare. The engineman shuts off and starts talking to himself, like a sheepherder too long in the sagebrush.

The head brakeman picks up his lantern and trots back. He comes on the conductor half way down the length of the train, and the hotbox burning there merely adds heat to what the "brains" is saying, brains meaning the conductor. The two of them repack the journal and soup it up.

Twenty minutes has been lost when the engineer finally whistles in the flag. The train rolls on past Red Wing. All eyes are cocked in case that hotbox has a relapse. On the curve at Hastings the conductor swings a highball, signifying that the goose hangs high, and the engineman cracks two whistle blasts.

Things are looking up, and the man at the throttle is giving her a pasting, with a view to making up a little time, but on the railroad you never can tell. Sometimes if it isn't one thing it's another. Suddenly a caution signal winks into view, and then a pinprick of red appears in the blackness.

The heavy train grinds to a stop, and it is discovered that the Inland Waterways is giving the railroad the merry go-by. A tugboat is herding a long string of barges through the draw bridge.

Finally the signals clear, and the Milwaukee's time freight really gets down to business. At 2:45 A.M., extra 231 is nosing into the yards at St. Paul. Late? Not on your tintype! The train is forty-five minutes ahead of time, which is, possibly, the reason the dispatcher issued that order instructing 263 to run extra, La Crosse to St. Paul.

They say you have to have hair on your ears to railroad on the Milwaukee. Anyway, the boys up there certainly put them over the road.

The 231's job is done. She has covered 400 miles, giving a fine performance. Another big road engine glides down out of the steamy blackness and settles snugly against the train. This engine will haul the train to Harlowton, Montana, a distance of close to one thousand thumping miles. This is one of the longest, if not *the* longest, runs without change for a coal-burning locomotive in the world.

Out at Bremerton, Washington, they are waiting for that important ship material, and there is that army stuff for Fort Lewis, and those marine engines, but they won't be waiting long, for this is preference freight.

CHAPTER XXI

Pullman

THE AVERAGE AMERICAN is an inveterate traveler. He will ride anything on hoofs, wheels, or wings to get somewhere else. Always he is nursing a desire to see what is over the hill, and in the United States he has, fortunately, been blessed with ways and means of satisfying his wanderlust.

Possibly no one in the country has done more to encourage these foot-loose inclinations than a man named George M. Pullman, who in 1858 built the first modern sleeping car, a reconstructed Chicago & Alton day coach, and introduced the sleeping section with its folding upper berth.

Before this there had been sleeping cars with built-in bunks, but they had the disadvantage of being available only at night. The trick Pullman berths changed all that, and the seat the tourist occupied in the day became his bed at night.

Sleeping-car construction grew by leaps and bounds, and in 1880 the Pullman Car Works were built, occupying a site near Chicago. At the outset only sleeping and parlor cars were constructed, but later production was extended to include all types of passenger and street cars.

The early cars were of wooden construction, and they served their purpose very well over a period of twenty-five years. Came then the advent of the steel car, and the Pullman Car Works passed through its first major transition period.

The plant was reconstructed, new shops were added, and the most modern steel-working machinery was introduced. Craftsmen who for years had worked in wood quickly adapted themselves to meet the new conditions, as they set about turning out heavy, riveted structural steel cars for the Pullman Company.

The steel Pullmans were a lot better than the old wooden cars, but they too passed on to the railroad graveyard, being replaced by cars as strong, but of much lighter weight.

With the construction of the first streamliner in 1934, the Pullman-Standard Car Manufacturing Company began the development of railway passenger cars employing the use of new alloys, as well as newer methods of fabrication and assembly.

Cars built by Pullman in this new era have been of four types of construction, listed as follows:

1. High-tensile low-alloy steel—welded girder frames and sheathing.
2. High-tensile low-alloy steel—riveted girder frames and sheathing.
3. High-tensile low-alloy steel—welded truss frame and stainless-steel sheathing.
4. Aluminum alloy—riveted girder frame and sheathing.

The type of structure used involves certain economics. The welded type is a natural, both from an engineering and a fabrication standpoint. It is therefore the cheapest to build. The truss type, with stainless-steel sheathing, is slightly more expensive and somewhat lighter and is furnished to those who like the bright, shiny exterior, though it is sometimes painted. Aluminum is slightly more expensive than either of the other two, but supplies the means of building the lightest cars, and without any sacrifice in strength.

With the advent of streamlining, the passenger-car manufacturer more and more operated on a special custom-building basis. This was partially the result of change in car construction and also because of conditions existing down the years when various individual ideas took deep root under the hats of different railroad officials. These concepts are the result of diversified traffic conditions which each railroad has to meet.

The building of a passenger car embraces a wide variety of manufacturing and engineering problems, with the result that such organizations are arranged into divisions having the following classifications: truck engineering; body structure; equipment engineering; art and color; interior-finish engineering; electric engineering; and air conditioning. There is also the department of bill and estimate making.

Some idea of the volume of the work produced through the construction of one passenger car, which is called a Pullman bill of material, can be gained from the fact that the average material list makes a book of over 1,500 pages. Requisitions are made out and go to the stores department.

These are in quintuplicate. One copy remains in the stores department, one goes to the purchasing department, one to the accounting department, and two to the stock room.

The material is assembled and set down as needed, and to the casual observer the first evidence of progress on a particular car comes as the sub-assemblies are started in the steel shop. Here one underframe, two side frames, two end frames, and one roof are completely assembled on jigs. In the case of steel cars the parts are joined by spot or arc welding. Aluminum structures are joined by steel or aluminum rivets.

As the four major sub-assemblies get under way in the steel-erection shop, work on the main assembly is started and the car is said to be "laid down."

Now various items of equipment are installed. Conduit pipe is applied. This, for the layman, is the interesting stage, for he becomes acquainted with all the vast and intricate network of hidden parts that will soon be concealed forever, like the contents of a cornerstone.

The traveler who will one day be riding the streamliner little realizes the vast extent of air ducts, conduit pipes, wires, and fittings that lurk behind the walls, ceiling, and floor of his Pullman. From two to five miles of electric wiring are required to meet the needs of one car.

Behind the apparent ease with which the car is fabricated are years of accumulating experience, development, and study. The Pullman Company has contributed, and is contributing, its years of skill and knowledge to the comfort and convenience of those who ride the trains.

In an age of rapid progress, the continued development and

perfection of facilities for safe, convenient, and dependable travel are vitally important. And it is only when the present is compared with the past that the radical growth and change become apparent.

The Pullman car covers a vast field of operations. Some cars spend their lives shuttling back and forth over the same line, never escaping that monotony, except when they are "shopped" and reconditioned, which might be compared to devoting one's vacation to a major operation. Other cars roam the continent, taking in the most interesting sights and associating with the "nicest people."

Let us consider the "traveling life" of a Pullman car, a "winter" job, assigned to service between New York and Miami, Florida. It is standing in the Sunnyside Yards, in Long Island City, being made ready for its trip south.

Upon its arrival, a specially trained supervisor gave it a beady-eyed inspection, determining just what special cleaning attention was required. This person arranges for all necessary work to be done, such as the thorough blowing of various parts, including ventilators, with compressed air; the vacuuming of all bedding, washing or waxing of interior painted surfaces, removal of carpet for vibrating and vacuuming, the exchange of pillow covers and blankets.

Then all upholstered parts, carpets and floor coverings come in for further cleaning, right down to the last remote nook and corner. Two of the cleaning crew dust down all metal parts, clean and deodorize hoppers, polish all metal parts, wash mirrors and windows throughout the car. The tiling is scrubbed.

Meanwhile, the car is aired out. Then, to be sure that nothing has been overlooked, another Pullman employee, a "touch-up" cleaner, goes over the entire interior, picking up any loose ends that may not have been detected and attended to by the others. The entire job is then passed upon by a qualified supervisor and pronounced ready.

The exterior of the car is kept free from road dirt by washing with a light oxalic acid, the frequency of such washing depending upon the length of the run. In such applications the finish is thoroughly gone over by a fountain-head bristle brush through which water passes.

The windows receive the same treatment with water and light oxalic acid, following which any remaining streaks are removed by tools specially prepared for this purpose.

And now that our Pullman has been freshened and scoured in preparation for its trip to Miami, it falls to the lot of the local storekeeper, here at the Sunnyside Yards, to supply the car with its necessary suit of linen.

In this case it is a 12-section sleeper, with one drawing room. Among other supplies, it carries the following:

200 towels
120 pillow slips
160 sheets
54 blankets
26 headrest covers
6 car bags
5 porters' coats

This is the regular complement of linen required for an overnight run to Florida. Multiply this by more than 5,300 cars in daily operation and it can be readily understood why a catalogue of all articles, ready for immediate issue, assumes the proportions of a mail-order-house catalogue and weighs 8¾ pounds.

While all this housekeeping has been going on, electricians, mechanics, and other skilled employees have checked the car to make sure that each mechanical part is in perfect operating order.

Several hours before the car is ready to make its appearance at the station in New York, the Pullman porter arrives on the scene. He is the human element attached to some ninety tons of traveling steel. Tactful, attentive, cheerful, and worldly wise, he is part of a tradition to which the Pullman Company points with pride. Carefully he checks over the linen, seeing that every piece is accounted for. He goes over the sections, drawing room, men's and women's dressing rooms—a last look to see that everything is right.

Ice is placed in the cooler but does not come in contact with the water, for care must be exercised against any possible contamination.

And now the Pullman car is ready to roll. The yard engineer has his orders, and the big sleeper becomes part of the train that shortly will be Florida bound. Other Pullman cars, with a wide variety of accommodations, are part of the train.

Intricate as all this may seem to the layman, the Pullman Company regards it as part of a simple routine, a routine that is applied daily throughout the nation, wherever Pullman cars are readied for the road. It explains why 10 Pullman laundries and 23 commercial laundries handle over 150,000,-

000 pieces of laundry annually, with a yearly laundry bill of 1½ million dollars. Some 80 storerooms, 113 sub-storerooms, and 6 shop storerooms are required to keep the cars serviced. These "special stations" are strategically located throughout the United States, Canada, and Mexico.

There are other Pullman cars on the train, and each car may run to a different destination. The Pullman Company refers to the points between which a car operates as a "line." Then, too, a "line" may operate over long distances, requiring many cars distributed among a number of trains, as between Chicago and the Pacific coast. Or a car may cover a short run only.

In regular lines there are about 5,300 cars. Over 1,600 are used for shifts and reserves. Of course, not all are in operation on a given date; they must take turns in the shops.

The requirements of the railroads vary. One road, for instance, served its Florida travel in October with an average of 24 cars, but required 105 in February. A New England road got along nicely with 46 cars in March, but in August used 104.

Every day Pullman-car service headquarters at Chicago receives reports showing where every car is. From these, and from reports on trend and volumes of traffic, it is known what shifts are needed.

Thus, long in advance, the Pullman Company receives information relative to, say, an international convention which will open on a certain day in a certain city. To meet its needs, extra cars will be required on lines all over the country. For weeks in advance Pullmans are gradually drawn in to the areas where they will be required. At the same time, directing authorities must always keep in mind and plan for full provision on regular lines. It is a real job to be sure that exactly the right number of cars will always be on location where and when they are needed.

These special movements make demands for equipment that could not possibly be met except through such an organization as the Pullman-car pool.

Operating its own cars over all railroads, the Pullman Company can meet peak demands of seasonal and regional traffic by simply shifting cars from one area to another, quite as a general might use his reserves. Thus fewer cars perform the service.

Pullman standards are high always, and the additional cost for this service is far exceeded by the comforts and convenience afforded.

The Pullman Company is confronted by another nationwide problem that requires detailed attention. Buffet, lounge, and club cars are operated on many trains. These are for the convenience of those who desire a snack or a drink. On other trains there are restaurant cars which offer complete menus.

This is where the Pullman commissary goes into action. Some 39 commissary depots are required to supply these services. The layman can better picture the extent of this service by considering the fact that over seven million services are handled annually, ranging from smokes and beverages to complete meals.

The train passenger, walking down the ramp at the New York station, has small realization of the preparations that have been painstakingly performed pending his arrival aboard. Little more could have been done if he were a potentate.

His luggage is stowed away; the Pullman conductor checks his ticket against the diagram of the car to establish definite proof of his claim to occupancy; the train conductor thumbs his watch, and soon the traveler is on his way.

His traveling home de luxe is air-conditioned; he has plenty of hot and cold water, towels and soap—everything, in fact, that the most fastidious could ask for. There is an absolute freedom from the mechanics of his trip. The engineer at the throttle, the Pullman and train conductors, the porter in charge of his car—they are ambassadors of travel, assigned to the task of making his journey a period of complete relaxation and comfort. From "All aboard" to "Miami, next stop" he enjoys a friendly and hospitable service.

This is part of the Pullman system—the warp and woof of unification running through the country's transportation establishment. Only such an organization, maintaining a certain autonomy, yet working at all times in all areas in perfect harmony with the country's railroads, could have brought about the ease, comfort, and appeal which are characteristic of present-day travel.

The Pullman family represents over eighty years of experience in the field of transportation. The building of equipment, both passenger and freight, has been developed to a fine art, an exact science. Your Pullman cars are manned by crews skillfully trained in the technique of the hospitality of the iron road.

The name of Pullman itself has become a common noun in

a score of languages. It headlines the story of modern comfort as associated with the speed queens of the rails, of streamlined service, luxurious and efficient equipment, resulting from many minds and many hands devoted to an important industry in the field of American railroad transportation.

CHAPTER XXII

The Generals and the Governors

PULLMAN TRAIN OR FREIGHT—it makes little difference to the 4-8-4 or Northern type of locomotive. All through these pages we have seen this dual-service engine in action. From the Atlantic to the Pacific, it is booming down the American railroads from Canada to the Rio Grande.

It can highball the limiteds on a schedule that will take your breath away, and it will just as readily knuckle onto a tonnage freight and knock hell out of her.

In the early pages we mentioned the fact that the Richmond, Fredericksburg and Potomac purchased five 4-8-4 type locomotives in 1937. These were named after famous Confederate generals. Later the road acquired six more 4-8-4s, which were named after former governors of the state of Virginia.

The Generals were assigned to freight service, while the Governors hauled passenger trains. And that is what you might call railroad aristocracy. What is more, the reviving of the old practice of naming locomotives after famous people was a fine gesture on the part of the Richmond, Fredericksburg and Potomac.

We shall return to the Generals and the Governors in a minute, but in the meantime let us go back and review briefly our acquaintance with a few of those 4-8-4 type locomotives.

The glamorous Daylights of the Southern Pacific are pulled by the 4-8-4 type engine. It is a 4-8-4 that wheels the Scenic Limited across the Rockies on the Denver & Rio Grande Western. We saw Engine No. 231, a 4-8-4, hauling time freight on the Milwaukee, where they also do heavy passenger work.

We saw these big 4-8-4s, equipped with 80-inch drivers, rolling down the Santa Fe in passenger service. On the Soo Line, with 75-inch drivers, they wheel freight. The Great Northern uses them on cracking fast passenger runs.

In 1929 the Rock Island bought a 4-8-4 and labeled it the 5000 class. After severe tests the road ordered 24 more. This in 1930. Later 40 others were acquired, making a total of 65. The 4-8-4s were now operating on the Chicago, Rock Island & Pacific's Panhandle, Missouri-Kansas, and Des Moines divisions. After a survey by the operating, mechanical, and engineering departments, it was found that by strengthening bridges and re-laying some rail the 4-8-4 type could take in much more territory.

In 1937 ten of these engines were modernized, and roller bearings were applied to the driving wheels. The capacity of the tenders was increased. Still later more of the 4-8-4s were brought up to date, and their territory was extended to take in the Rock Island, the Cedar Rapids, the Western, the Oklahoma, and the Southern divisions.

The bruising, iron-fisted 4-8-4 Northerns more than proved their mettle in the handling of time freight. They covered tough, mauling runs of around 800 miles and averaged better than 10,000 miles per month.

We see a big 4-8-4 roaring past on the smoky front of the North Western's crack flier, the Corn King; another wheeling the U.P.'s Pony Express; and on the Burlington, the Northern Pacific, the Lehigh Valley, the Lackawanna, the Chesapeake and Ohio, the Missouri Pacific, Atlantic Coast Line, Norfolk and Western, St. Louis Southwestern, Nashville, Chattanooga & St. Louis, Canadian National, Canadian Pacific, Grand Trunk, Wabash, St. Louis-San Francisco, Spokane, Portland and Seattle, Toledo, Peoria & Western, Temiskaming & Northern Ontario, and as this is written some are being built for the Western Pacific.

But to get back to the Generals. These 4-8-4 type locomotives have 77-inch drivers, cylinders 27 × 30 inches, 275 pounds of pressure, and weigh 466,040 pounds without tender. They exert a tractive force of 66,500 pounds. Particular attention was given to their appearance, including polished machinery parts and certain attractive coloring, as befitted engines of their rank. They were numbered and named as follows:

No. 551..........General Robert E. Lee
No. 552..........General T. J. Jackson

No. 553..........General J. E. B. Stuart
No. 554..........General A. P. Hill
No. 555..........General J. E. Johnston

These locomotives, you understand, are in freight service, and the Richmond, Fredericksburg and Potomac reports that during peak traffic periods the Generals average 52 one-way trips per month.

During the months of February to May 1936, inclusive, 657 double-header freight trains were operated, while during the same months of 1938, with the Generals storming down the railroad, only 199 double-headers were run. This in spite of the fact that the freight-car-miles increased from 11,615,924 during the 1936 period to 14,729,910 in 1938. On the basis of eliminating this number of double-headers, the direct saving from this source alone amounted to $55,926 per annum.

The later 4-8-4s were built by Baldwin, and they were specially designed to operate in heavy passenger service between Richmond and the Washington Union Station. These locomotives are named after former governors, as we have told you—famous governors, patriots. Watch for them, if you ride that way. The road numbers and the names are as follows:

No. 601........Governor Patrick Henry
No. 602........Governor Thomas Jefferson
No. 603........Governor Thomas Nelson
No. 604........Governor Benjamin Harrison
No. 605........Governor James Monroe
No. 606........Governor John Tyler

Late in 1942 six more were delivered by the Baldwin Locomotive Works. The only difference from the first six was a change in the design of the fender:

No. 607........Governor Edmund Randolph
No. 608........Governor Henry A. Wise
No. 609........Governor John Letcher
No. 610........Governor Fitzhugh Lee
No. 611........Governor William Smith
No. 612........Governor Claude A. Swanson

These engines, like the Generals, have 77-inch drivers, exerting a tractive force of 62,800 pounds. Provision has been made for the future application of a trailing truck booster, if and when this should be desirable.

The Governors have eye-compelling beauty, for they are handsomely painted and finished right down to the last rivet. Polished brass handrails stand out like golden service bars. Proudly they wear on their tenders the monogram of the line. Personality here. Majesty. Power.

A great engine, the mighty 4-8-4; built to do a job, as were the Hudson, the 4-8-2 Mountain type, of the Merchant Prince, and all the others. In peace or war, in passenger service or fast freight—all-purpose, all-American. The writer is pleased to say he has ridden most of them.

A great road, too, the Richmond, Fredericksburg and Potomac. The biggest little road in the country.

And here we leave you, at the "Gateway to the South," just across the Potomac from our nation's capital—in proud Virginia, with the Generals and the Governors.